Coinage and Finances in the Reign of Domitian

A.D. 81 – 96

Ian Carradice

BAR International Series 178
1983

B.A.R.

122 Banbury Road, Oxford OX2 7BP, England

B.A.R.-S178, 1983 'Coinage and Finances in the Reign of Domitian'

ISBN 9780860542285 paperback
ISBN 9781407332819 e-book
DOI https://doi.org/10.30861/9780860542285
A catalogue record for this book is available from the British Library
This book is available at www.barpublishing.com

CONTENTS

PREFACE

The principal aim of this work is to investigate the surviving coinage of Domitian for the information it may yield on the monetary and financial history of his reign. This project began as a study of the denarius coinage alone, and it will be observed that the denarii have been given the most comprehensive treatment, especially in the quantitative surveys. However, in order to achieve a satisfactory overall picture of the coinage, the other major denominations from the mint of Rome have also been investigated. The coins minted in Domitian's reign in the Provinces (the "Greek Imperial" issues) are also mentioned, though only briefly, in Chapter 1.

The Roman coinage of Domitian is listed in all the standard catalogues of Roman imperial coinage (eg. Cohen, BMCRE and RIC). Although the volumes of these catalogues which deal with Domitian are now all out of date and in need of revision, it is not the intention here to offer a new catalogue to replace these, but instead to present a revised chronological arrangement of all the issues of coinage. This involves a deliberate shift of emphasis away from the detailed discussion of individual coins. Instead, prominence will be given to the mass-produced issues of the reign. This should ensure that the most important developments in the monetary history of the period will be revealed, whereas the overall pattern of a coinage can sometimes be obscured when too much attention is focused on rare and variant individual pieces. Also, as it is intended that the coinage should be investigated as a source of evidence for financial history, the large-scale issues of new currency are obviously the most important in this context and are therefore the most worthy of special attention. However, an effort has been made to correct errors in detail which have appeared in the standard catalogues and also to fill gaps in these catalogues by including newly discovered or researched material. Most important are the quantitative surveys of Domitian's surviving coinage, based on the evidence of hoards and loose finds, and the interpretation of the data provided for estimating rates of coinage emission during the reign. The Roman coins of Domitian are on the whole very well ordered and closely dated; they are therefore most suitable for statistical analysis. The resulting information, when allied to our knowledge on other aspects of the coinage, such as metrology, should enhance our understanding of both the monetary and financial history of the period. The surveys should also serve to test the usefulness of the methodology involved in such studies for ancient coinage and finances in general.

I first began this project as a research student and the work published here represents an adapted version of a thesis which was admitted for the degree of Ph.D. by the University of St. Andrews in 1980. It was accepted for publication by B.A.R. soon afterwards, and I must thank the Editors for their patience in waiting a further three years before receiving the final copy.

There are also many individuals whom I should like to thank for all their help over the years. I am indebted to the staff of the numerous museums (listed in Appendix 3) who have kindly provided photographs, casts or information on coins in their collections. In the British Museum I owe a particular debt to Mr. M. Cowell of the Research Laboratory, who undertook coin analyses and harnessed the Museum's computer for mathematical calculations that were far beyond my competence to understand. To my colleagues, past and present, in the Department of Coins and Medals, who have spared their time to discuss Domitian's coinage with me, I shall always be grateful. I also wish to record my gratitude to Mr. Michael Crawford, whose advice and encouragement helped the project to develop in the first place, and to all the other scholars (many of whom attended the "Domitian" seminar in the British Museum in 1981) with whom I have had discussions. Finally, I wish to express my thanks to Professor Geoffrey Rickman for his patience and consideration as my supervisor at St. Andrews.

The British Museum

October 1983

LIST OF TABLES AND FIGURES

ABBREVIATIONS

The following abbreviations are used, particularly in the Catalogues of coinage issues, but also elsewhere in this work. For abbreviations of published works, including _BMC_, _RIC_ and _Cohen_, see Bibliography (3).

AU	Aureus
AUQ	Gold quinarius
AR	Denarius
ARQ	Silver denarius
S	Sestertius
Dp	Dupondius
Quad	Quadrans
AE	_Aes_, bronze coinage
obv	obverse
rev	reverse
in	inwardly (for legend direction)
out	outwardly (for legend direction)
r.	right
l.	left
laur	laureate
rad	radiate
adv	advancing
std	seated
stg	standing

CHAPTER 1

INTRODUCTION

The coinage of Domitian's reign

The coinage minted in the Roman Empire during the reign of Domitian can be divided broadly into the two major categories under which all the coinage of the first three hundred years of the Empire is usually classified. These two categories : "Roman Imperial" and "Greek Imperial" (or "Roman Provincial") have been devised to differentiate between the product of the principal mint or mints (in Rome or elsewhere in the West), and the product of the numerous smaller mints located at various times throughout the Empire, but predominantly in the eastern (Greek speaking) provinces. Apart from mint location, the factors to consider in assessing the relative importance of these coinages are the authority and control over production, the volume and regularity of issue, and the extent of circulation.

A) Roman Imperial coinage and the mint of Rome

In the reign of Domitian the principal mint was situated in the city of Rome. Another "Imperial" mint, usually identified as Lugdunum, has traditionally been put forward as the source of a small group of bronze coinage issues dated to the reign of Titus and the earliest years of Domitian's reign[1]. The existence of this separate mint is, however, questionable, and it will be discussed in more detail below (Chapter 5). The "Roman Imperial" issues of Domitian are defined, for the purposes of this work, as all the issues of the mint of Rome and the so-called "Lugdunum" mint. They include all the gold, silver and bronze coins with Latin inscriptions produced during this period for circulation either throughout the Empire or for all the western provinces. The only precious metal coins with Latin legends that do not qualify under this definition are the "cistophoric" tetradrachms of the province of Asia[2]. There were also, under Domitian, a small number of bronze issues with Latin legends which were produced for circulation in certain specific areas or cities in the East, and these are similarly excluded.

The mint of Rome issued the following denominations in the period AD 81-96:-

metal	denomination	value
gold	aureus	25 denarii
gold	quinarius aureus	12½ denarii

silver	denarius	4 sestertii
silver	quinarius	2 sestertii
orichalcum	sestertius	4 asses
orichalcum	dupondius	2 asses
copper	as	
orichalcum	semis	$\frac{1}{2}$ as
copper	quadrans	$\frac{1}{4}$ as

The frequency and volume of issue of Domitian's Roman Imperial coins will be analysed in detail later in this work, but here it can be noted that most of these coins were, in comparison with contemporary "non-Roman" issues, much the commonest. The coinage of the mint of Rome also enjoyed the widest circulation. The standard gold coin in the time of Domitian, the aureus, circulated throughout the Empire, unchallenged by any local issues in gold save those of the distant client-kingdom of Bosporus. The half-piece of the aureus, the gold quinarius, was a much less significant coin. In Domitian's reign it only appeared on a single isolated occasion[3]. Domitian's Roman denarii circulated throughout, and indeed travelled far beyond, the Empire, although in the eastern provinces they were often supplemented by locally produced silver coins. The silver quinarius (half denarius) of the mint of Rome was issued in much smaller quantities than the denarius; it therefore had a much less significant position in the currency of the Empire at this time. Domitian's Roman Imperial bronze coins were not so universally dominant as the principal denominations of precious metal coinage from the mint of Rome. The largest bronze coins, the sestertius, dupondius and as, circulated throughout the central and western provinces of the Empire, where they were the only available official <u>aes</u>. These coins are also found in the eastern provinces, but there they were outnumbered by locally produced "Greek Imperial" bronzes. The smallest denomination coins from Rome, the semis and quadrans, seem to have had a more restricted circulation. They are found much more frequently in, for instance, civic sites in Italy, than in military camps on the frontiers[4]. It seems these were the smallest-change coins of the market place; their distribution was therefore concentrated in the main urban centres, especially in Italy, but they are also found in certain parts of the urbanised East[5].

B)The Provinces

i. <u>Gold</u> The only official gold coinage from the "Roman world" produced outside the city of Rome in the reign of Domitian was issued by the client kingdom of Bosporus. From AD 80 the aurei of Bosporus have on one side the head of the king, and on the other side a portrait of the ruling Roman emperor. The coins are dated according to the era of the kingdom, and examples have been recorded with dates corresponding to most of the years of Domitian's reign, but it seems the individual issues were not very large[6]. This coinage was apparently struck under license from the Roman emperor, and the denominations, in gold and bronze, were related to those of the Roman system[7]. There were obviously special circumstances which caused the exceptional existence of a separate and entirely internal gold coinage in this particular area. Finds suggest that only local currency circulated there[8]. Presumably it must have been to the Roman emperor's advantage to permit the striking of gold coinage in the Bosporus, but because it was such an isolated and localised phenomenon its significance should not be overplayed.

ii. Silver. Production of provincial silver coinage in the reign of Domitian was quite widespread in the eastern regions of the Empire. Issues of silver coins with Greek legends were minted for the provinces of Egypt and Syria and for certain other localities, namely Tarsus, Lycia and Caesarea in Cappadocia; and the province of Asia was provided with silver "cistophoric" tetradrachms with Latin legends. However, the issues of all these coins were only intermittent:-

Province/Mint	Denomination	Years recorded[9]
Asia	tetradrachm	82, undated (early issues), 95, undated (one issue, after 83).
Egypt (Alexandria)	tetradrachm	82/3, 86/7, 88/9.
Syria (Antioch)	tetradrachm	81/2, 86/7, 87/8, 88/9, 90/1, 92/3.
Tarsus	tetradrachm	undated (one issue, after 83).
Caesarea	didrachm	93/4, undated (late issue).
Lycia	drachm	95.

These eastern silver coins had values corresponding to the Roman money system. In the time of Domitian they were related as follows:-

1 denarius	=	1 Lycian drachm; 1 Alexandrian tetradrachm.
2 denarii	=	1 Caesarean didrachm.
3 denarii	=	1 "cistophoric" Asian tetradrachm; 1 Syrian tetradrachm[10].
4 denarii	=	1 tetradrachm of Tarsus[11].

To some extent these coinages represent the continuation of old established silver coinages dating back to the pre-Roman period, but of course now they had to be authorised by the emperor. It has been argued that in the time of Domitian similarities of style and typology between eastern and Roman issues, and a recognition of changing metrological standards in the separate mints confirms the exercising of central control[12]. In some cases the output of eastern mints has been related directly to the activities of Roman forces in the region, again illustrating the influence of central government in these issues[13]. It seems the emperors or their officials were also not ignorant of the publicity value of these coins. For example, the earliest issues of "cistophoric" tetradrachms produced for Asia under Domitian include types portraying the new Emperor and Empress and the newly restored Temple of Capitoline Jupiter in Rome[14].

The circulation of all these eastern silver coinages was much more restricted than that of the Roman Imperial gold and silver. In general Domitian's eastern silver coins are only found in the environs of the provinces for which they were issued. The only exception is the Lycian drachma which appears in small numbers in many second century coin hoards in Europe. This is because its dimensions and weight were sufficiently close to the contemporary denarius for it to circulate on an equal footing with the Roman piece.

iii. Bronze. Bronze "Greek Imperial" coinage was produced by numerous mints in the eastern regions of the Empire. The issues can be divided into the following categories, all of which are represented by examples from the reign of Domitian:-

a) "Official" : being of eastern mintage, but with wider than usual circulation, and with types and legends indicating direct official sanction - eg. the bronzes of Antioch (Syria) with Latin legends and S C reverse type[15].

b) "Provincial" : struck in a provincial centre under the authority of the Roman governor (directly or via the provincial "council") and for circulation throughout the province.

c) "City" : having an imperial portrait on the obverse, but with reverse types (and usually legend) relating directly to the issuing city.

d) "Autonomous city" : as c) above, but with both obverse and reverse displaying local types; confined to smallest denominations.

e) "Colonial" : as c) above, but having special reverse types and Latin legends which emphasise the privileged status of the issuing city as a Roman "colonia" founded for the settlement of veterans.

f) "Alliance" : special, usually very large, "medallic" pieces, commemorating commercial or ceremonial alliances between cities.

g) "Client-kingdom" : issues of tribes or kingdoms, subject to Roman domination but permitted to produce their own coinage for local usage.

Under Domitian a large number of eastern mints issued bronze coins. The British Museum collection contains bronze coins of Domitian and Domitia from more than one hundred eastern cities, and from Asia Minor alone more than 105 cities issuing bronze coins under Domitian were counted by the compilers of the von Aulock Sylloge Index[16]. However, individual issues of eastern bronzes were usually small and intermittent, and their areas of circulation were very much more restricted than the issues of coinage produced in Rome[17]. Of the categories of "Greek Imperial" bronze coinage outlined above, the "official", "provincial" and "client-kingdom" issues had the widest circulation, although they rarely travelled far from the provinces which issued them. The remaining classes of eastern bronze coinage were of even more localised circulation and usage. Basically, they were produced only for the internal requirements of the issuing city.

Numismatic evidence

From the above brief outline of coinage production in the Roman Empire in the time of Domitian, it is easy to see which issues were the "most important". The widely circulating and voluminous issues of silver denarii, together with the more valuable but less common gold aurei, all from the mint of Rome, provided the staple currency of the Empire. These were backed up, in the central and western regions of the Empire, by large issues of bronze coinage in sestertii, dupondii and asses, also from Rome. These principal denominations of coinage from Rome should provide the main evidence for an understanding of imperial monetary history (or even "monetary policy") in this period. They also certainly supply the most important numismatic evidence for the Empire's finances. The surveys of Domitian's coinage, which form the central part of this work, will therefore concentrate on these particular coins, but the other denominations from Rome, including the precious metal half pieces (quinarii) and the smallest bronzes, will also be considered for whatever information they may provide on organisation of coinage production and mint output and policy.

The eastern "Greek Imperial" coinages, particularly the silver issues and the bronzes which might be classified as "official", could also provide information towards an understanding of the overall organisation of coinage production and for the government's management of finances in the eastern provinces. However, the influence of these coinages was much more limited than that of the great Roman issues. Also, there is not yet available a comprehensive catalogue of Domitian's eastern coinages; nor is there sufficient data on finds and hoards for quantitative surveys of these coins to be undertaken. They are therefore outside the scope and capacity of the present work.

To make use of the numismatic or historical evidence provided by any series of coinage issues it is first necessary to establish the firmest possible chronological arrangement of the coins. Only when it is known at what time, or at least in what order, the separate issues of the various denominations were produced, does it become possible to put forward suggestions on the policy behind mint output. We can see whether a metal or a denomination was issued continuously or only intermittently, and this helps us to understand the nature of the coinage. But it should not always be assumed that regularity of issue denotes importance, and that infrequency of issue indicates the opposite. One denomination might be issued regularly, but in very small quantities, whereas another may appear in only occasional issues, but each of these issues could comprise very large numbers of coins.

The only way to confirm the status of any issue of coinage is to estimate its volume, relative or absolute. A major drawback of the existing catalogues is that, if they provide any information at all on the extent of issue of coins, it is on degrees of rarity. Such judgements on particulars of rarity are of interest to coin dealers and collectors. However, although it is generally of value to know, for example, that certain pieces (eg. silver and gold "multiples" and coins with special "commemorative" types) are either exceedingly, very, or just moderately, rare, it should be just as important to the numismatist, and it is without doubt much more important to the historian (especially the economic historian) to know which coins are very common. A catalogue of known issues and varieties provides the basic framework of mint activity, but only by obtaining estimates of coin emission can we determine the extent of operation within the mint.

Information on the quality of the coinage is also important. The weight and metrology of, in particular, the precious metal issues, reveal the standards being applied and the relationship between denominations. Any abrupt changes in standards of fineness should denote major policy decisions, and the extent to which standards were observed might indicate the level of supervision operating at the mint at a given time. Recent analyses of Roman imperial silver coinage by D.R. Walker have revealed that Domitian undertook such major reforms of standards that his reign should now be considered one of the most significant in the development of the imperial coinage[18]. Also, the new information available on metrology has the additional value of providing scientific evidence to confirm the chronological arrangement of undated issues.

The designs on the faces of Roman imperial coins have for a very long time been a popular subject of study. The legends and types provide invaluable evidence for chronology and they can sometimes also be used to interpret the history of the period and the ideology of the issuing authorities. The value to the historian of interpretative typological studies has long been recognised, although numismatists have been criticised for concentrating too much of their attention on them[19]. The major doubt expressed by historians is that the subtleties of propaganda sometimes identified by numismatists on coin designs would not necessarily have been intelligible to the recipients of the messages (the coin users); but what really matters for our purposes is the intention of the design, not whether it was always comprehended. It is essential to assess in a critical manner the evidence of coin types, and especially to distinguish between types which might have had a particular relevance to the issuer rather than designs copied, sometimes perhaps unthinkingly, from previous issues. However, any noticeable changes in types might indicate shifts in the programme of imperial propaganda or in the policies which the coin designs were sometimes employed to advertise. The types might also reflect the degree to which the emperor himself was involved in the selection of designs, or how much the die cutters were attempting to satisfy what they believed to be his tastes. The recording of imperial names and numbered titles in the coin legends might also provide information on the emperor's attitude towards the coinage as a medium for propaganda.

It has been argued that for Roman imperial coins of the first century AD reverse types provide the key to defining the activities of the separate _officinae_ (workshops) into which the mint was divided[20]. The number of _officinae_ can be estimated when the substantive reverse types have been recognised; and an outline picture of the internal mint organisation and structure might then be proposed, into which the other types may be placed. Additional information on the organisation of the mint may be gained from a close scrutiny of the dies with which the coins were struck. The dies themselves no longer exist but they can often be identified on the surviving coins. Die studies can reveal whether or not two or more reverse types shared the same obverse die, or whether the same dies were employed for different denominations or across successive issues. Die studies can also, of course, be used to estimate mint output.

NOTES

1. <u>BMCRE</u> II, p. lxx, xcvii; catalogue numbers <u>BMC</u> Domitian 513-520.

2. <u>BMC</u> Domitian 251-8.

3. In AD 88, <u>BMC</u> 126.

4. M.H. Crawford, <u>JRS</u> 1970, 42-5.

5. Roman quadrantes have been recorded from the excavations at Antioch and Athens : D.B. Waage, <u>Antioch on the Orontes</u>, IV.2. (Princeton 1952), 95; M. Thompson, <u>The Athenian Agora</u>, II. (Princeton 1954), 11.

6. N.A. Frolova, <u>The Coinage of the Kingdom of Bosporus, AD 69-238</u> (B.A.R. Int. ser. 56, Oxford, 1979), 94-6, 103.

7. N.A. Frolova, "The Bosporus and Rome at the end of the 1st century AD and the beginning of the 2nd, in the light of numismatic data", <u>Vestnik Drevnei Istorii</u> 2 (1968), 133-143.

8. Roman denarii are virtually never found in the region; eastern provincial silver coins of the period are also absent.

9. Asia: <u>BMCRE</u> II, p. 351-3. Coins of Domitian as Emperor dated AD 81 have been recorded (eg. <u>Cohen</u> 666), but these require confirmation, whereas tetradrachms of Domitian as Caesar dated 81 can be verified. Egypt: J.G. Milne, <u>Catalogue of Alexandrian Coins</u> (Oxford 1971), 14-15. Syria: W. Wruck, <u>Die syrische Provinzialprägung von Augustus bis Trajan</u> (Stuttgart 1931), 133. Tarsus: G.F. Hill, <u>British Museum Catalogue of Greek Coins, vol. 21, Lycaonia, Isauria and Cilicia</u> (London 1900), 186. Caesarea: D.R. Walker, <u>Metrology</u> I, 127-8. Lycia: D.R. Walker, <u>Metrology</u> I, 130.

10. This is the traditional reckoning (see, eg. H. Mattingly, <u>Roman Coins</u> (2nd ed. London 1960), 201). D.R. Walker (<u>Metrology</u> I, 137) believes the Syrian tetradrachm of this period was valued at four denarii.

11. D.R. Walker, <u>Metrology</u> I, 130.

12. D.R. Walker, <u>Metrology</u> I, 120.

13. One of the clearest examples is provided by the massive issues of Syrian tetradrachms produced in the late 60s AD coinciding with the Jewish war - see D.R. Walker, <u>Metrology</u> III, 115-7.

14. <u>BMC</u> 251, 255.

15. eg. <u>BMC Galatia etc.</u>, p.180-182 (Domitian).

16. P.R. Franke, W. Leschorn and A.U. Stylow, <u>Sammlung von Aulock Index</u> (Berlin 1981), Prägetabellen 1-12.

17. See T.B. Jones, "A Numismatic Riddle : the so-called Greek Imperials", <u>Proceedings of the American Philosophical Society</u> 107 (1963), 308-347.

18. <u>Metrology</u> I, 120-121.

19. The most famous criticism was penned by A.H.M. Jones, "Numismatics and History", in <u>ERCHM</u>, 13-33; answered (for Roman imperial coinage) by C.H.V. Sutherland, "The Intelligibility of Roman Imperial Coin Types", <u>JRS</u> 49 (1959), 46-55, and again in <u>The Emperor and the Coinage</u> (London 1976), 96-121. M.H. Crawford ("Roman coin types and public opinion", in C.N.L. Brooke et al.(ed.), <u>Studies in Numismatic Method presented to Philip Grierson</u> (Cambridge 1983), 47-64) has recently argued that the reverse designs on new coins would hardly have been noticed by the population; the only really important type for the coin user was the mark of authority (the obverse bust), and the diversity of reverse types was little more than an incidental by-product resulting from the historical development of coinage production.

20. See, eg. D.W. MacDowall, "The organisation of the Julio-Claudian mint at Rome", in R.A.G. Carson and C.M. Kraay (ed.), <u>Scripta Nummaria Romana</u> (Essays for C.H.V. Sutherland) (London 1978), 32-57. The association of <u>officinae</u> with reverse types was earlier noted by R.A.G. Carson, "System and Product in the Roman Mint", in <u>ERCHM</u>, 227-239.

CHAPTER 2

THE GOLD AND SILVER COINAGE OF ROME, AD 81-96

Introduction

The issues of gold and silver coinage produced by the mint of Rome during the reign of Domitian can be divided into three distinct periods. The basis for this division was revealed by the recent metrological survey of Roman imperial silver coins by D.R. Walker[1].

The earliest group of issues is listed below under the title First Period. This period covers the first few months of Domitian's reign in late 81 and early 82, during which the silver content of the denarius remained approximately at the level to which it had declined in the reigns of Domitian's immediate predecessors, Vespasian and Titus[2].

In 82 there was a major readjustment in the silver content of the denarius, and this marks the beginning of the next phase of precious metal coining, which is here termed the Second Period. In this Period, from 82 to 85, the precious metal coinage is generally heavier and the silver content of the denarius is appreciably greater than at any other time in Domitian's reign[3].

The period from 85 to the end of the reign (96) has been labelled Domitian's Third Period. During this Period the silver content of the denarius was maintained at a lower level than that which it had enjoyed in the years 82-85, though it was still a noticeably finer coin than the denarius of the First Period of 81-82[4].

The metrological changes in the denarius in 82 and 85 have thus provided a framework within which to investigate the pattern of precious metal coining in the reign of Domitian. A further elucidation of this three-period programme will be provided by a closer examination of all the precious metal issues of the reign, which will be set out in tables listed year by year. The tables will be of two kinds : the Tables of issues, arranged chronologically and designed to identify the coins; and the Analysis tables, the purpose of which is to investigate and confirm the physical composition of the coins.

Tables of issues

The arrangement of the Tables which list the various issues (groups of coins minted within certain well defined limits) has been designed to emphasise any significant changes or developments in the coinage, characterised by such features as legend content, legend direction and type content.

The first column in each Table lists the issues, numbered separately under each year of Domitian's reign. For example, in the year 81 the separate issues are numbered from 1 to 3, with numbers 2 and 3 subdivided into 2a, 2b and 3a, 3b. In the text, the issues are identified by the year, plus the sequential number of the issue:- eg. AD 81, issue no. 3b = 81.3b. The second column lists the denominations employed for each issue. The letters AU denote that specimens of gold aurei are known to have been struck; the letters AR indicate examples of silver denarii, ARQ examples of silver quinarii (half-denarius pieces), and AUQ examples of the gold quinarius (half-aureus piece, represented in Domitian's reign by just one issue in 88). The legends (inscriptions on both sides of the coin) are listed in the third column, which begins with an illustration of the direction of the lettering. Die-axes are not noted; the die-axis for all coins from the mint of Rome in the reign of Domitian is ↑↓ or thereabouts. The final column in the Tables provides a list of the *RIC* references for each issue. Because these Tables are not intended to be read simply as a revision of the standard catalogues, no attempt will be made to account for every piece noted in *RIC* or the other standard catalogues (*BMCRE* II and *Cohen*)[5]. However, where coins (that are not just obvious hybrids or forgeries) have been recorded in these catalogues with legends that conflict with the sequence of legends recorded in the lists of issues in the Tables, these pieces will be discussed in short notes beneath each Table.

At the base of each Table is a list of the obverse and reverse types (designs) employed on the issues within the Table, unless this has already been indicated. In the listing of attributes (of eg. deities) the object in the right hand is always described first. For some series of issues the types used for the separate issues are grouped together at the end because the employment of a particular type from a familiar group (eg. the *pulvinaria*[6] reverse types of 81-82, or the four standard Minerva reverse types used consistently from 83-96) is not relevant to the immediate purpose of the Tables, which is the chronological arrangement of all issues. In this section of the Tables the issues in which a particular type is used are indicated within brackets placed after the type description. In groups where no brackets are included the types are presumed to have been employed on all issues within the group. The appearance of new obverse or reverse types can often be an important indication of mint activity, and in periods when typological changes are frequent this will be emphasised; but when regular groups of types are used the presence or absence of a particular element may simply be an accident of survival. The quantitative analysis based on hoard surveys and examination of other finds will show how a study of the extent of usage of reverse types within an issue can give clues towards an understanding of mint organisation. The quantitative analysis also helps to confirm the isolation of variant types, which are listed within the Tables in which they occur.

Analysis Tables

The purpose of the tables headed *Analysis* is to illustrate certain physical aspects of the coins within each issue or group of issues identified in the Tables of issues. The average weights for aurei, and the percentage of silver content for denarii, are listed so that when they are compared with the figures on sizes of issues from the quantitative analysis it will be possible to investigate the relationship between the apparent volume of coin emission and the quality of the coinage. The Analysis figures show the similarities between coins of the issues listed within a particular group, and at the same time they point to the differences (or similarities) between separate groups.

In the Analysis tables the first column lists the issues numbered according to their arrangement in the Tables of issues. The tables are then divided into two parts, dealing separately with aurei and denarii. For aurei the first column lists the average weights of the coins from each issue which were recorded in the report on the Zemun hoard from Yugoslavia; the number of coins involved is noted within brackets. The Zemun hoard has been singled out for this use because it is by far the largest well-recorded hoard of aurei from the period. It was apparently buried very soon after the reign of Domitian, so it provides an excellent sample for estimating the weights of Domitian's aurei as well as the sizes of issues. What is more, these weights can be used to assist in the arrangement of the undated coins because they are on the whole consistent, within the three-period framework established for denarii. The second column, which is included simply for comparison with the Zemun figures, lists the average weights of aurei from a selection of museum collections[7].

For denarii only one set of figures is provided. These show the average percentage of silver contained in the coins of each issue according to the results revealed by Walker's survey on metrology. The averages have been calculated from the numbers of specimens noted in brackets. Because the fineness of the silver was a major factor in determining the pattern of survival of denarii these figures will be of vital importance when compared with the results of the quantitative analysis. Also, the degree of fineness of the denarii is again a useful indicator for the arrangement of undated issues.

First Period, AD 81-82

Dated issues (pl.I,1-11)

Issue	Denom	Legends (obv  outwardly, rev  inwardly)	RIC
81.1 (pl.I,1-2)	AR	IMP CAESAR DOMITIANVS AVG TR P COS VII	1-5
81.2a (pl.I,3-4)	AU AR	IMP CAES DOMITIANVS AVG PONT COS VII DES VIII P P	6-9
81.2b	AR	IMP CAES DOMITIANVS AVG PONT TR P COS VII DES VIII P P	10-10A
81.3a	AU AR	IMP CAES DOMITIANVS AVG P M COS VII DES VIII P P	13-15
81.3b (pl.I,5-10)	AU AR	IMP CAES DOMITIANVS AVG P M TR P COS VII DES VIII P P	16-23
variants: i)	AU AR	IMP CAES DOMITIAN AVG PONT (2a,b rev)	
ii)	AR	IMP CAES DIVI VESP F DOMIT(IAN) AVG P M (3a?, 3b rev) (pl.I,9-10)	
82.1 (pl.I,11)	AU AR	IMP CAES DOMITIANVS AVG P M TR POT COS VIII P P	24-31

Types

obv
- i) Head of Domitian, laureate, facing right
- ii) Head of Domitian, laureate, facing left (81.3b)

rev AU AR :-
- i) Draped table or seat, above which a horizontal thunderbolt (usually winged)
- ii) Draped table or seat with a frame decorated with either one palmette (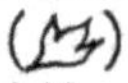) and six corn ears (), or three crescents with globes (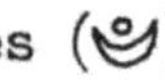).
- iii) Dolphin coiled around anchor
- iv) Tripod, on which a dolphin (earliest denarii also have a wreath and two ravens above tripod)
- v) Two curule chairs, above which a wreath
- vi) Altar with flame in centre and horns left and right
- vii) Minerva advancing right, brandishing javelin and holding shield (Minerva standard type 1) (81.2b, 3a,3b; 82.1)
- viii) Minerva standing left, holding Victory and spear (81.2b,3a,3b; 82.1)

Notes: 81.2a,3a... This rev legend can also be read : P P COS VII DES VIII.

81.3a...... RIC 11,12 (=Cohen 54,55: no P P in rev legend) are errors; their rev legends should read as 2a and 3a above.

variant(i)... AU(*rev* 2a), *Cohen* 57(Paris); AR(*rev* 2b), *RIC* 10B (listed in *ASFN* 1884,p.179) perhaps requires confirmation

variant(ii).. IMP CAES DIVI VESP F DOMITIAN AVG P M is the commonest variant legend used in AD 81. It has been recorded on a denarius with *obv* issue 3a (B.Boric-Breskovic, *Numismatica* 1979, 88), but the published illustration of this coin is not sufficiently clear to confirm that it belongs to this issue and not issue 3b. Many examples can be confirmed having this *obv* legend combined with *rev* legend 3b. The *obv* reading IMP CAES DIVI VESP F DOMIT AVG PONT (with *rev* type curule chairs) occurs on a denarius (Institut für Antike Numismatik, Vienna).

82.1......... *BMC* 25n (= Vierordt sale, 5 March 1923, lot 1129: not illustrated) with *obv* legend lacking P M requires confirmation.

Analysis

Issue	Aurei - weights		Denarii
	Zemun	museums	% silver
81.1			92.5(4)
81.2a	-	7.00(2)	-
81.2b			92.0(1)
81.3a	-	6.96(1)	93.62(2)
81.3b	7.34(2)	7.18(10)	90.25(12)
82.1	-	7.35(3)	91.03(8)

These issues, which are dated by Domitian's titles to the years 81 and 82, were all produced within a period of probably less than twelve months after Domitian's accession on September 13, 81. These are the only dated issues of gold and silver from Domitian's First Period of coinage.

The issues of 81 were all struck within a period of only three and a half months. The coins have been divided into a number of separate issues and sub-divisions because in this period the legends changed quite rapidly in order to incorporate or re-arrange the titles which the new emperor was rapidly acquiring[8]: IMPERATOR, AUGUSTUS/TRIBUNICIA POTESTAT - POTIFEX (MAXIMUS) / PATER PATRIAE, CONSUL DESIGNATUS VIII. The legends thus developed as follows:-

AD 81 IMP CAESAR DOMITIANVS AVG ⟷ TR P COS VII

↓ ↓

IMP CAES DOMITIANVS AVG PONT
(IMP CAES DOMITIAN AVG PONT)
(IMP CAES DIVI VESP F DOMIT AVG PONT) ⟷ COS VII DES VIII P P

↓ ↓

IMP CAES DOMITIANVS AVG P M
(IMP CAES DIVI VESP F DOMIT(IAN) AVG P M) ⟷ TR P COS VII DES VIII P P

↓ ↓

AD 82 IMP CAES DOMITIANVS AVG P M ⟷ TR POT COS VIII P P

We do not know exactly when these separate titles were added to the coin dies, so it is not possible to speculate on the time limits of each issue. However, it appears from the records of the Arval brothers that Domitian did not become Pontifex Maximus until after the end of October[9]. Therefore, only the very first issue should have been struck before this date. The abbreviation Pont presumably stands for Pontifex Maximus. Under Augustus it did not - on coins he was Pont before the death of Lepidus (eg. BMC 548 : 10-6(?) BC); but Nero appears as Pont (eg. BMC 393 : AD 66) after having been Pontifex Max (eg. BMC 9 : AD 55-56). Thus it seems likely that all the coins of issues 81.2 and 81.3 were struck in the last two months of the year.

It is not possible to gauge the time span for emission of the coins in issue 82.1, because we do not know the exact date for the reform which ended Domitian's First Period of coinage (separating issues 82.1 and 82.2). The absence of a number for Domitian's Tribunicia Potestas is not helpful. The fact that the first issue of the Second Period has Domitian TR POT instead of TR POT II (which he acquired on September 13/14, 82) might suggest that the reform took place before this date. But the first issue of 83 also neglects to number Domitian's Tribunicia Potestas.

The dated issues of the First Period have been grouped together in a single table because of the obvious similarities they share. The reverse types were all used in the reign of Titus except for one (Minerva standing left holding Victory). The selection of types for use in each particular issue was probably not of any great significance, but it is perhaps worth noting the two Minerva types are not known to have been used until issue 81.2b. The other types are all repeats from the pulvinaria series of Titus' reign which relate to the offering of vows to the gods voted by the Senate[10]. The occasion for the employment of such types would normally be the aftermath of a natural disaster[11]. The appearance of the two Minerva types, and especially the introduction of the new one, can be construed as the first sign that Domitian was asserting a personal influence on the mint, because it was well known that Minerva was the patron-goddess of the new emperor[12].

The style of portraiture on all these issues is the same as that displayed on the coinage minted for Domitian as Caesar in the reign of Titus. It is characterised by a small, neat head, facing right (pl. XII,1-3). There are, however, a few exceptional denarii in issue 81.3b with a left-facing portrait, all apparently struck from the same die (pl. I,10).[13] This particular head is more like a portrait of Titus than Domitian, and it is closest in style to the left-facing heads minted during the reign of Domitian's brother (cf. pl. XII,4-5). In fact, so close in appearance are these two portraits that the Domitian die may have been re-cut from an old die of Titus, or if not, both dies must surely have been produced by the same die cutter.

The denarii with the left-facing head belong to the group of coins which have the variant obverse legend: IMP CAES DIVI VESP F DOMITIAN AVG P M . There is no evidence to suggest that these coins were not minted at Rome[14], and there are reverse die links between them and coins with the regular obverse legend[15].

Apart from considerations of type content and style, the coins of Domitian's First Period have other features which link them closely to the issues of Titus. It has already been noted that the denarii have a similar silver content to their predecessors. According to Walker[16], the denarii minted by Titus in AD 80 average 91.37% silver content, which is very close to the fineness of Domitian's coins (92.5% in 81, 92.0% in 82). The same also applies to their dimensions and weights, which adhere closely to the standards operating under Titus[17].

Regarding internal mint organisation, an examination of dies revealed that shared obverse dies invariably linked together coins with the same reverse type. Not a single die link was found connecting coins with different reverse types, but denarii and aurei with the same reverse types did share obverse and reverse dies. These findings suggest that production of denarii and aurei was organised within strictly separated _officinae_, identified by reverse types.

Undated issue 1 : AD 81 - early 82 (pl.I,12)

Issue	Denom	Legends	RIC
81-82 (pl.I,12)	ARQ	IMP CAES DOMITIANVS AVG P M ↶ out VICTORIA AVGVST ↷ in, ↶ out, or ↺ out	42,44
	obv	Head of Domitian, laureate, facing right	
	rev	Victory holding wreath and palm, advancing right or seated left on throne.	

This issue of silver quinarii has usually been attributed to the period 81-83[18]. Walker analysed one piece and found it to contain only 85% silver[19]. Having presumed that this coin should have been minted within the years 82-83, in the height of Domitian's Second Period when the denarius was at its peak of fineness, he understandably failed to offer an explanation for this unusually low reading[20]. However, a recent analysis of the quinarii from this issue in the British Museum yielded readings almost as low as Walker's :-

BMC 55 = 89.7% silver
BMC 56 = 88.3% silver[21]
BMC 57 = 89.6% silver

It therefore seems certain that these quinarii were struck in Domitian's First Period, before the major reform of 82. They could not have been issued later in the reign because the extremely low (for Domitian) silver content, and the absence of the title _Germanicus_ preclude a date after 83.

The portrait type on these quinarii is early, and the reverse designs employ the usual Victory types used for this denomination. One unusual feature is the flexibility of reverse legend direction.

Second Period, AD 82-85

The Second Period spans approximately three years of minting activity, and it is in many ways the most interesting phase in the development of coinage in Domitian's reign. The first issue of precious metal coinage in this Period was struck in 82, between Domitian's first major reform of the currency and the end of that year.

AD 82 (later) (pl.I,13-14)

Issue	Denom	Legends (obv ↶ outwardly, rev ↷ inwardly)	RIC
82.2 (pl.I,13-14)	AU AR	IMP CAES DOMITIANVS AVG P M TR POT IMP II COS VIII DES VIIII P P	32-33b
	obv	Head of Domitian, laureate, facing right	
	rev AU	Bust of Minerva, helmeted, facing left, sometimes with sceptre over right shoulder	
	rev AR	Fortuna standing left, holding rudder and cornucopiae	
Notes: The rev legend variant with ..DES IX.. exists on aurei (eg. BMC 33)			

Analysis

Issue	Aurei - weights: Zemun	Aurei - weights: museums	Denarii: % silver
82.2	7.72(17)	7.70(7)	97.0(2)

There are many features which distinguish this issue from the earlier issue of 82 and the issues of 81. Indeed, the differences are so dramatic that they can be said to represent a revolutionary change in minting policy.

Firstly, the reverse types of the previous period disappear[22], and they are replaced by two new types. The design used for gold is a helmeted bust of Minerva, while for silver a Fortuna type appears for the first time in the reign. The use of different reverse types for aureus and denarius obviously indicates a strict separation of reverse dies between the denominations, but an examination revealed that obverse dies were shared by both denominations (and therefore both reverse types). These factors denote a marked change in internal mint practice compared with the First Period.

The style of portraiture on the obverse remains largely the same as that of the earlier issues of the reign, but there are the first indications that a new portrait was being introduced (eg. pl.I,14). The new style has a larger head with less markedly 'Flavian' features, giving the portrait a rather younger appearance. This suggests that the die engravers were attempting a new portrait with the emphasis on a differentiation of the features of Domitian from those of his brother and from those displayed on his own coins as Caesar which had dominated the earliest portraits of his reign[23].

However, the most important difference between this issue and the earlier ones is not to be found in type content or style but in the intrinsic quality of the coinage. As a comparison of the Analysis tables shows, the aurei from museums and from the Zemun hoard reveal an abrupt rise in weight. A similar increase (though less marked) can also be detected in the weights of denarii[24], but, more importantly, according to Walker's metrological survey this small increase in denarius weight was accompanied by a dramatic increase in silver content. Thus we have the first dated issue of the Second Period.

Undated issue 2 : AD 82-83 (pl.I,15-23)

Issue	Denom	Legends	RIC
82-83			
(a) (pl.I,15)	AU AR	IMP CAES DOMITIANVS AVG P M ↶ out IVPPITER CONSERVATOR ↶ out obv Head of Domitian, laureate, facing right rev Eagle standing front on thunderbolt, wings spread, head left	40
(b) (pl.I,16)	AR	IMP CAES DOMITIANVS AVG P M ↶ out SALVS AVGVST ↷ in obv Head of Domitian, laureate, facing right rev Salus seated left on throne, holding corn ears	41
(c) (pl.I,17)	AU	DIVVS AVGVSTVS VESPASIANVS ↶ out DIVA DOMITILLA AVGVSTA ↶ out obv Head of Divus Vespasian, radiate, facing right rev Bust of Diva Domitilla, draped, r., hair in long plait	Titus 69
(d) (pl.I,18)	AU	DIVVS TITVS AVGVSTVS ↶ out IVLIA AVGVSTA DIVI TITI F ↶ out obv Head of Divus Titus, radiate, facing right rev Bust of Julia, draped, r., hair massed in front above forehead and plaited in bun behind	216
(e) (pl.I,19)	AU	IMP CAES DOMITIANVS AVG P M ↶ out DOMITIA AVGVSTA IMP DOMIT ↶ out obv Head of Domitian, laureate, facing right rev Bust of Domitia, draped, r., hair massed in front above forehead and knotted in long plait behind	210

(f) (pl.I,20) AU AR — DOMITIA AVGVSTA IMP DOMIT ↺ out / CONCORDIA AVGVST ↺ out — 212

obv Bust of Domitia, draped r., as above

rev Peacock standing right

(g) (pl.I,21) AU AR — DOMITIA AVGVSTA IMP DOMIT ↺ out / DIVVS CAESAR IMP DOMITIANI F ↺ out — 213

obv Bust of Domitia, draped, r., as above

rev Naked infant boy seated on globe, surrounded by either seven stars or one crescent and six stars

---

(h) (pl.I,22) AR — DOMITIA AVGVSTA IMP DOMIT ↺ out / PIETAS AVGVST ↻ in — 214

obv Bust of Domitia, draped, r., as above

rev Pietas seated l., sceptre in l. hand, facing standing child

---

(i) (pl.I,23) AR — DIVA DOMITILLA AVGVSTA ↺ out / FORTVNA AVGVST ↻ in — Titus 71

obv Bust of Diva Domitilla, draped, r., hair same as Domitilla in (c) above

rev Fortuna standing left, holding rudder and cornucopiae

Notes: (f) The variant obv legend ending ...DOMITIANI recorded in BMC 60n. and 61n. (RIC 212n., 212B) cannot be confirmed:- Cohen 3 is plated; Montagu sale 1896, lot 244 has a portrait clearly belonging to a later issue of Domitia and is therefore also false. The variant rev legend ending ...AVGVSTI recorded in BMC 61n. is not clear on the only quoted example (Ratto sale, 8 Feb. 1928, lot 2488).

(c-i) In addition to the numerous obvious hybrids there are many other examples of these coins in the standard catalogues which are plated forgeries:-
Divus Vespasian/Diva Domitilla, RIC Titus 69 (AR = Cohen 2, requires confirmation); Divus Titus/Julia, RIC 216a (AU, modern forgery); Domitian/Domitia, RIC 210 (AR = Cohen 3, plated); Domitian/Domitia, RIC 211 (AR = Cohen 4: rev legend variant DOMITIA AVGVSTA, plated); Domitia/PACI AVGVST, RIC 213A (AR, plated); Diva Domitilla/PACI AVGVSTAE, RIC Titus 72 (AR, plated); Diva Domitilla/PIETAS AVGVST, RIC Titus 73 (AR = Cohen 4, plated). A "Becker" forgery of the Diva Domitilla (FORTVNA AVGVST type) also exists (Hill, Becker 160).

Analysis

Issue 82-83	Aurei - weights Zemun	museums	Denarii % silver	
(a)	7.77(17)	7.63(8)	97.37(2) 98.05(2)*	(a)
(b)			98.37(2) 97.90(1)*	(b)
(c)	-	7.48(4) (c–d)		
(d)	7.69(2)			
(e)	-	7.72(15) (e–g)		
(f)	7.82(4)		97.75(1) 98.20(1)*	(f)
(g)	7.76(2)		-	(g)
(h)			98.30(1)*	(h)
(i)			97.90(1)*	(i)

* These coins were analysed recently at the British Museum (I. Carradice and M. Cowell, "An analysis..", 169).

There are numerous reasons for these coins to be alotted a date early in the Second Period of Domitian's reign. The fineness of the denarii that have been analysed (types a,b,f,h,i) indicates that these coins at least must have been minted after the reform of AD 82. The weights of the aurei (types a,c,d,e,f,g) are also sufficiently high to confirm that these coins must also have been produced after the reform. Meanwhile, all the coins with Domitian's titles in their legends (types a,b,e,f,g,h) could only have been struck before late AD 83 when the name Germanicus was adopted and added to the regular titulature on coinage[25]. The obverse legend direction on all the coins and the style of Domitian's portrait (types a,b,e), which is still dominated by the small head of the earliest style, are also consistent with a date early in the Second Period. Finally, portrait similarities and die links bind many of the types together; it therefore seems reasonable to assume that all of these coins were produced within the period late 82 to late 83.

A date for the coins of types (a) and (b) early in the Second Period is made even more secure by the existence of die links connecting them with coins of the dated issue 82.2. Denarii with the Salus reverse type have been found to share obverse dies with aurei of issue 82.2, and Iuppiter Conservator aurei also die link with denarii of the dated issue. On the other hand, obverse die links between the Salus and Iuppiter Conservator coins are not evident. The logical inference from this evidence is that types (a) and (b) were contemporary, but produced quite separately.

The designs on these two coins are both new for Domitian's reign. The eagle of Jupiter type with the legend IVPPITER CONSERVATOR probably refers to Domitian's memorable escape from the Capitol in AD 69 when he was amongst the Flavian company besieged by the supporters of Vitellius[26]. He later credited his escape to Jupiter, in the precincts of whose temple he had concealed himself. Apart from this coin design Domitian also commemorated his salvation by erecting a temple to Jupiter Custos[27]. The Salus type with legend SALVS AVGVST is also probably alluding to this same event; it seems a natural partner for the *Iuppiter Conservator* coins. The remaining types of this series (c-i) all relate to Domitian's family. Types (c), (d) and (e) appear to have been struck only in gold; although many denarii have been quoted in catalogues and sale lists they are invariably plated or they are modern forgeries. On the other hand, the two Domitia types (f and g) were certainly produced in both metals, while the remaining Domitia type (h) and the Diva Domitilla coins (type i) seem only to have been struck in silver. These coins are all rare, although, no doubt because thay have always been especially popular with collectors, ancient plated forgeries appear to be common, as also are modern forgeries of these types.

The early date (82-83) suggested for this whole series is especially appropriate for the types (c,d,g,i) which celebrate deified members of Domitian's family. The deification of his father, brother, sister (or mother) and his son obviously increased the new emperor's distinction, even if he himself was responsible for most of the *consecrationes*. The aureus types (c) and (d), commemorating Domitian's deified father[28] and brother, accompanied respectively by their deified daughter (or wife) and living daughter, are obvious partners. They are joined by a third gold-only type (e), celebrating the living emperor and his empress Domitia *Augusta*, to complete the illustrious sub-group. The Diva Domitilla denarius with Fortuna reverse (type i) is attributed to the reign of Titus in the standard catalogues, but the recent analysis of the British Museum piece (*BMC* Titus 137) suggests that this coin could not possibly have been minted before the reform of 82[29]. Also, the portrait style is virtually identical to that on the Diva Domitilla aureus (type c), and the Fortuna on the reverse is the same as the denarius reverse type on issue 82.2 (pl.I,14). This Diva Domitilla denarius issue was therefore produced in 82-83 and it represents an interesting addition to Domitian's early "family" group.

The remaining types of the series (f,g,h) are all devoted to Domitian's wife. The portrait of Domitia is the same as that used for the aureus (type e) she shares with Domitian (cf. pl.I,19-23). The two reverse types which were used on both gold and silver are particularly appropriate for the empress. On one (f) a peacock, the bird of Jupiter's wife, Juno, appears together with the legend *Concordia August* stressing the union of emperor and empress. The second type (g) depicts Domitian and Domitia's deified son. Having died in infancy the boy is represented as a child-god playing in the heavens[30]. The third reverse type (h), which is confined to denarii, illustrates Domitia's dutiful affection (*pietas*) for her child. It is presumably no coincidence that the same type appears on sestertii of Domitia bearing the legend *DIVI CAESAR MATRI*[31]. The sestertii would have been minted in 81 or 82 because the mint of Rome appears to have issued no bronze coinage in 83, and the absence of a reference to the name *Germanicus* precludes a later date. It therefore seems that two roughly contemporary issues of "Domitia" coinage were produced early in the reign, one in precious metals, the other in bronze (cf. the similarity of portraiture, pl. XII,21-22)[32]. Regarding production of the "Domitia" group (types f-h), it was noticed that obverse dies are shared between coins with different reverse types and between aurei and denarii. They appear to form a closely knit sub-group.

Altogether, these "Family" coins form quite a remarkable

group. They provide a fascinating gallery of Flavian portraits. They also illustrate the importance of dynastic continuity to the new emperor. It is especially ironic that Domitian should have taken such care to honour his family. His relationship with his father had been by no means smooth[33], and he had apparently resented his brother with an intensity that developed into open hostility during Titus' reign[34]. Domitian is supposed to have done little to honour the memory of his popular brother (apart from deifying him)[35], but here Titus appears with the rest of the Flavian house, including even Domitilla who had died at least twelve years before Domitian became emperor[36].

AD 83 (pl.I,24 - pl.II,4)

Issue	Denom	Legends (obv outwardly, rev inwardly)	RIC
83.1 (pl.I,24-25)	AR ARQ	IMP CAES DOMITIANVS AVG P M TR POT COS VIIII P P	34-35
83.2 (pl.II,1-4)	AU AR	IMP CAES DOMITIANVS AVG P M TR POT II COS VIIII (or IX) DES X P P	36-38
83.3	AU	IMP CAES DOMITIAN AVG GERMANICVS P M TR P III COS IX DES X P P	HCC 13

obv Head of Domitian, laureate, facing right

rev AU AR :-

i) Minerva advancing right, brandishing javelin and holding shield (Minerva standard type 1) (1,2)

ii) Minerva standing right on base decorated with two prows, holding javelin and shield, owl at her feet (Minerva standard type 2)* (2,3)

iii) Minerva standing left, holding thunderbolt and spear, shield at her feet (Minerva standard type 3) (2)

iv) Minerva standing left, holding spear (Minerva standard type 4) (1,2)

ARQ Winged caduceus upright (1)

Notes: 83.1 BMC 36, an aureus with rev type cornucopiae, COS VIIII, has been omitted; it is a barbarous copy of COS IIII coins of Vespasian (eg. BMC Vespasian 196-7)

83.2 RIC 39 lists a denarius (= Cohen 602) with obv legend IMP CAES DOMITIANVS AVG GERMANIC, head laureate, draped, r., rev Minerva type 4; but in fact the coin has obv facing left, and it is a plated hybrid (as NC 1946, p.21, no.44 - Zurich).

* This Minerva type is always accompanied by an owl. The type is usually described as "Minerva on prow", but the usual type has Minerva and the owl standing on a statue base which comprises a column (decorated with two figures) adorned with two prows, ie. a columna rostrata (see H. Dressel, Die römische Medaillone, 10-14). I have, however, observed one example (a denarius in Oxford from issue 92.1) which clearly shows a normal prow.

Analysis

Issue	Aurei - weights Zemun	museums	Denarii % silver
83.1			-
83.2	7.73(10)	7.68(4)	97.0(1)
83.3	-	7.64(1)	

Issues 83.1 and 2 date from the period January to mid-September (TR POT - TR POT II); 83.3 was produced within the remainder of the year. The metallurgical composition of these coins is consistent with the pattern established for the Second Period coinage. The aurei are heavy; the denarii and quinarii (Walker = 97.75% silver (1 coin); BMC 38 = 98.5% silver) are extremely fine.

There are some significant developments in typological content. In the first issue two new types are introduced for the first time in the reign. On denarii a new standing Minerva (standard type 4), facing left and leaning on a spear, joins the more aggressive type 1, which reappears after being absent in issue 82.2; and on quinarii a winged caduceus replaces the usual Victory types. The caduceus type was only used on this single issue of quinarii by the mint of Rome, but the new Minerva type became part of a series of Minerva reverse types that was to dominate the mint's production of denarii for the rest of the reign. This series of four standard Minerva types[37] appears for the first time in its complete form in the second issue of 83. It was perhaps a reflection of Domitian's personal influence that these four images of his favourite deity should be employed as designs on the silver coinage to the virtual exclusion of all other types. They no doubt copied well known statue types and it is interesting that the aggressive aspect of Minerva is dominant[38].

The consistent use of the four standard Minerva reverse types from now on suggests that production of denarii, and sometimes of aurei, was organised on the basis of a four *officinae* system, with each *officina* identified by reverse type[39]. In issue 83.2 obverse die links were observed connecting denarii with different reverse types. Therefore, internal mint organisation again appears to have differed slightly from the procedure operating in the First Period.

The obverse portraiture on the first two issues of 83 is the same as for the previous issues with the early, small head still the dominant style. Similarly, the obverse legend remains the same. But this apparent immobilisation of the obverses of Domitian's coins was soon to end. At this time the emperor himself was engaged in a military campaign in Germany, and the outcome of this war was destined to have the most profound and lasting effect on the coinage of Domitian. It was not until the following year that the Roman mint felt the full repercussions of Domitian's success against the Chatti in Germany, but the issues of 84 were apparently anticipated by a third issue in 83. Only one specimen, an aureus, from this issue is known to exist, but, apart from the fact that it is unique, there seems no reason to question its authenticity[40]. Stylistically it is a fine example of an aureus from the mint of Rome, and it shares its obverse die with an aureus from the first issue of 84 (BMC 46). The obverse legend includes the earliest known reference on Roman coinage to Domitian's adoption of the title Germanicus following his victories over the Chatti[41]. The reverse, which uses the standard Minerva type 2, has a legend combining the titles COS IX (AD 83) and TR P III, which is the only example of this combination[42]. This is also the latest known coin from Domitian's reign which notes his designation as consul for the following year.

AD 84 (pl.II,5-11)

In 84 there were three dated issues of precious metal coinage. The first two issues, which included both gold and silver coins, can be grouped together.

Issue	Denom	Legends		RIC
84.1 (pl.II,5)	AU AR?	IMP CAES DOMITIAN AVG GERMANICVS P M TR POT III IMP V COS X P P	↺ out ↻ in	45,46 46b,47a
84.2a (pl.II,6-9)	AU AR	IMP CAES DOMITIANVS AVG GERMANIC P M TR POT III IMP V COS X P P	↻ in ↻ in	46a,c,47,48 48a,49,50
84.2b (pl.II,10)	ARQ	IMP CAES DOMITIAN AVG GERMANICVS P M TR POT III IMP V COS X P P	↻ in ↻ in	51

obv Head laureate, facing right (1,2a,2b)
Head laureate, facing right, with aegis (2a)
Bust draped, head laureate, facing left (2a)

rev AU AR Minerva 1 2 3 4 (1,2a)
AU AR Eagle on thunderbolt (2a)
AU Helmeted bust of Minerva facing right (2a)
ARQ Victory advancing right (2b)

Notes: 84.1 ... The only denarius of this issue that I have been able to confirm in publication is an example of RIC 47a in the Salaşuri hoard. The legends on this coin might have been mis-read, in which case this issue would have been restricted to gold aurei.

84.1-2a Coins quoted with obv legend IMP CAES DOMITIANVS AVG GERMANICVS cannot be confirmed : RIC 46b (= Riv.It 1914, p.178), RIC 47a (= Cohen 353), read ..DOMITIAN.; RIC 45 (= Cohen 354,355) lack references. Cohen 356 (= RIC 46) is an aureus with variant obv legend IMP CAES DOMITIANVS GERMANICVS (Paris).

84.2a .. Cohen 351 with rev legend ..IMP VI.. cannot be verified; Cohen 352 (also listed as ..IMP VI..) actually reads ..IMP V..(Paris).

Analysis

Issue	Aurei - weights: Zemun	Aurei - weights: museums	Denarii % silver
84.1	7.85(1)	7.75(2)	-
84.2a	7.82(3)	7.62(5)	98.75(2)

These issues were produced between January and mid-September 84. The coins, like those of the dated issues of 83, all conform to the standards of the Second Period in terms of weight and fineness. Attention is therefore again focused on stylistic and typological developments.

The title Germanicus which Domitian added to his official names now appears on both metals as part of the obverse legend. In the first issue it is spelt out in full, but in the second issue it is shortened to GERMANIC, except for the issue of quinarii (2b). Issues 84.1 and 84.2 are not usually listed separately in catalogues[43], but a comparison of obverses (pl.XII,8-9) shows that there are firm stylistic grounds for dividing them into successive issues. The legend in the first is inscribed outwardly from right to left and is accompanied by the early style of portrait of Domitian[44], whereas in the second issue, and for the first time on precious metal coinage in Domitian's reign, the obverse legend is inscribed inwardly from left to right[45]. From now onwards this becomes the standard form of legend inscription for both obverses and reverses. The portraiture of this issue (84.2) is also very different. The early style virtually disappears and the new style, which had been foreshadowed by earlier, isolated examples, becomes dominant. The larger head of the emperor is now cut in a bold and more elaborate style, and in most examples the aegis of Minerva, which is draped over his left shoulder, protrudes in front of, and sometimes also behind, the neck. Particularly striking is the less common portrait type with a left-facing draped bust of Domitian (pl.II,8-9) which recalls in style the left-facing head of issue 81.3b (cf. pl.I,10). It is possible that these left-facing portraits of 81 and 84 may all have been the work of the same die engraver, who by the year 84 was able to produce a stylish bust with the personal features of Domitian, suitably idealised, now much more recognisable[46].

The four standard Minerva types, which comprised the series first established in full in 83, are used on the reverses in both these issues of 84. The type with an eagle on thunderbolt, which was introduced for the Iuppiter Conservator coins of 82-83, reappears in the second issue, together with an unusual type depicting a bust of Minerva in Attic helmet facing right, which is used here for the first and only time in the reign[47]. These last two types are the only reverses which are sometimes accompanied by the left-facing obverse bust. For the silver quinarii, which were only produced in the second issue, the usual design of a Victory advancing right is used.

The remaining issue of 84 was struck only in gold:-

Issue	Denom	Legends	RIC
84.3 (a) (pl.II,11)	AU	IMP CAES DIVI VESP F DOMITIAN AVG ↻ in GERMANICVS COS X ↻ in	-
	obv	Bust draped, head laureate, facing left	
	rev	Germania, mourning, seated r. on shield; below, broken spear (standard Germania type)	
84.3 (b)	AU	IMP CAES DIVI VESP F DOMITIAN AVG ↻ in DE GERMAN ↻ in	-

obv	Bust draped, head laureate, facing left
rev	Captive seated right at foot of trophy

Notes: (a) Not in RIC or BMC; Santamaria sale, 25 May, 1926, lot 281. Also two aurei from the Zemun hoard, and another from Friume, Portugal (M. Ramires, "Tesouro monetario Romano de Friume", Nummus 1954, 74-80). Cohen 139 with obv DOMITIANVS AVGVSTVS has been omitted; this is clearly a misreading of an aureus from later in the reign.

(b) Not in RIC or BMC; Münzhandlung Basel, sale 6 (1936), lot 1639 (weight 7.50 g.)

Analysis

Issue	Aurei - weights	
	Zemun	museums
84.3 (a)	7.61(2)	-
84.3 (b)	-	-

These two coin types undoubtedly belong together because the only known examples share the same obverse die. The reverse designs refer explicitly to Domitian's victorious campaign against the Chatti. The captive and trophy type (b) is similar to the designs used by Titus to celebrate his victories in Judaea[48], and the mourning Germania type (a) represents Germania Capta, the personification of the defeated German people. This Germania type became a standard reverse design on the aureus for the rest of Domitian's reign. The only obverse type used for this issue is the draped left-facing bust, executed in a notably fine style, as employed for issue 84.2a. The coins of issue 84.3 also have the unusual obverse legend with ..DIVI VESP F.. which is used for the first time on the precious metal coinage since 81.

Although this issue has been designated 84.3, it was not necessarily the third issue of 84 in order of production. However, the style of portraiture and the obverse legend direction suggest that these coins are more closely related to issue 84.2a than to the earlier issue of 84. The weights of the two Zemun coins of type (a) are both slightly lower than might have been expected for aurei of 84 according to the sequence of weights for the Second Period, but this could be just a coincidence. There is no reason to question the authenticity of these coins nor their attribution to the mint of Rome. It can be said that they represent a very limited issue in an unusual style. The issue may in fact have been produced largely for commemorative purposes, related to Domitian's recent victories in Germany[49].

AD 85 (first part) (pl.II,12-16)

The issues of 85 have been divided into two separate sections because in this year the second major readjustment in the quality of Domitian's coinage took place. The first three issues of 85 belong to the first part of the year before the reform.

Issue	Denom	Legends	RIC
85.1a (pl.II,12-13)	AU AR	IMP CAES DOMITIANVS AVG GERMANIC ↻ in P M TR POT IIII IMP VIII COS XI P P ↻ in	52-57
85.1b (pl.II,14)	ARQ	IMP CAES DOMITIAN AVG GERMANICVS ↻ in P M TR POT IIII IMP VIII COS XI P P ↻ in	58-59
85.2 (pl.II,15)	AU AR	IMP CAES DOMIT AVG GERM P M TR P IIII ↻ in IMP VIIII COS XI CENSORIA POTESTAT P P ↻ in, ↺ out	66b,c
85.3 pl.II,16	AR	IMP CAES DOMIT AVG GERM P M TR P IIII ↻ in IMP VIIII COS XI CENS POTES P P ↻ in	66a

<u>obv</u> Head laureate, facing right (1a,1b)
Head laureate, facing right, with aegis (1a,2,3)

<u>rev</u> AU AR Minerva 1 2 3 4 (1a,2)
AU AR Eagle on thunderbolt (1a)
AU AR Germania (2,3)
ARQ Victory advancing right (1b)
ARQ Victory seated left (1b)

Notes: 85.2 Reverse legend directions are : ↻ and ↺ for Minerva types; ↺ only for Germania.
<u>RIC</u> p.161n. (=<u>ASFN</u> 1884, p.179,74), an aureus with <u>rev</u> legend ..CENSOR POT.. and <u>obv</u> IMP CAES DOMITIANVS AVG seems very doubtful; it certainly requires confirmation.

85.3 <u>RIC</u> 66a mistakenly lists the <u>rev</u> legend ..CENS POT..; the coin, which is in London, reads ..CENS POTES..
<u>RIC</u> 65 (= <u>Cohen</u> 176) is not in Paris; only coins with <u>rev</u> type Germania have so far been confirmed in this issue.

Analysis

Issue	Aurei - weights Zemun	Aurei - weights museums	Denarii % silver
85.1a	7.72(2)	7.61(3)	98.92(3)
85.2	-	7.53(3)	98.00(1)*
85.3	-	-	97.50(1)*

* In Walker, <u>Metrology</u> I, p.96, the denarius of issue 85.2 = no.1042, the denarius of issue 85.3 = no.1041

The first issue of 85 has the same obverse legend as issue 84.2. The aurei and denarii use the shortened title GERMANIC, whereas the quinarii have GERMANICVS. The portraiture also follows the same pattern. The new "elaborate" style, often with aegis, dominates the aurei and denarii (eg. pl.II,12), whereas the old, small-head portrait is retained on quinarii (pl.II,14). There is a simple explanation for the lack of stylistic progression on the quinarius. The two specimens of issue 85.1b in the British Museum (<u>BMC</u> 76,77) were both struck from the same obverse die as the collection's sole example from issue 84.2b (<u>BMC</u> 50A), suggesting perhaps that no new obverse dies were produced in preparation for the obviously limited emission of this particular denomination in 85.

The reverse types of issue 85.1 are also the same as those used on the coins of issue 84.2. It was observed that obverse die links exist between coins with different reverse types and between aurei and denarii. Issue 85.1 must have been struck between January and April, because in April Domitian assumed the office of Censor[50], and consequently, the remaining issues of 85 all had to include the emperor's new title.

The issue with the full reading CENSORIA POTESTAT has been placed earliest in the series which includes the censorial title, because it would be logical for the office to be emphasised at first, whereas it could later be abbreviated when it had become a familiar element in the imperial titulature. For this issue (85.2) the reverse legend is sometimes inscribed outwardly from left to right. Perhaps this break with the now established convention might have some connection with the unusually long legend. All known examples of this issue have the new portrait style on the obverse, together with aegis. The reverse typology shows an interesting development. The four Minerva types remain in use but the eagle of Jupiter has disappeared and its place has been taken by the Germania type which was first introduced on the special aurei of issue 84.3. Reverse types in issue 85.2 are shared by both aurei and denarii.

Issue 85.3 is represented by very few confirmed examples. Stylistically the issue is identical with issue 85.2, but the reverse legend has the shortened title CENS POTES and in arrangement it returns to the normal form of left to right inwardly. Portraiture is again limited to the new style with aegis, and there is a reduction in the number of reverse types with apparently only the Germania being employed. The analysis by Walker showed that these coins clearly belong to the restoration period, but that they were the last to be struck at that standard[51]. In Walker's list the different legends of the four coins dated April-September 85 which were analysed are not pointed out. In fact Walker no. 1041 = RIC 66a but with legend CENS POTES (as BMC 82); Walker no. 1042 = RIC 66b (CENSORIA POTESTAT). These two coins stand out in marked contrast to the two remaining pieces ascribed to the period April-September 85 (nos. 1043-4) whose silver content was considerably lower and whose legends read CENS POT. A recent analysis of British Museum denarii confirmed this pattern[52]:-

BM 1982-10-1-3 (CENSORIA POTESTAT) = 97.9% silver

BMC 82 (CENS POTES) = 98.7% silver

BMC 78-80 (CENS POT) = 94.5%, 92.8%, 90.6% silver

Third Period, AD 85-96

After the third issue of 85 the silver standard of the Second Period was abandoned. The exact date of this change in policy is not known, but it certainly took place between April (Domitian became Censor) and September (Domitian became TR P V)[53]. The new standard was the same as that introduced by Nero in 64, which meant a substantial reduction in the silver content of the denarius, although the new level was still noticeably higher than that operating in Domitian's First Period, AD 81-82. At the same time there was a slight reduction in the weight of both the aureus and the denarius. These new standards for precious metal coinage were rigorously maintained for the rest of Domitian's reign[54], a factor which greatly facilitates the making of comparisons between the sizes of issues.

AD 85 (second part) (pl.II,17-21)

After the adoption of the new precious metal coinage standards three more issues were produced in 85. Issue 85.4 was minted before mid-September (TR P V); issues 85.5 and 6 were produced between mid-September and the end of the year.

Issue	Denom	Legends* (obv ↻ inwardly, rev ↺ inwardly)	RIC
85.4 (pl.II,17)	AU AR	IMP CAES DOMIT AVG GERM P M TR P IIII IMP VIIII COS XI CENS POT P P	62-64
85.5a (pl.II,18-19)	AR	IMP CAES DOMIT AVG GERM P M TR POT V IMP VIIII COS XI CENS POT P P	68-69
85.5b (pl.II,20)	AU AR	IMP CAES DOMIT AVG GERM P M TR P V IMP VIIII COS XI CENS POT P P	70-72
85.6 (pl.II,21)	AU AR	IMP CAES DOMIT AVG GERM P M TR P V IMP XI COS XI CENS P P P	72a,b

obv Head laureate, facing right (4,5a,5b,6)
Head laureate, facing right, with aegis (4,5a)

rev AU Germania (4,5b,6)
AR Minerva 1 2 3 4 (4,5b,6)
AR Minerva seated left (5a)
AR Germania (5a)

Notes:
* This form of legend arrangement is used for the remainder of the reign; there is only one exception (in issue 88.3)

85.4 HCC 27 confirms the existence of aurei in this issue. RIC 60,61 (=Cohen 28,24) are hybrid forgeries: TR P IIII and CENS P P P are incompatible (see Buttrey, CJ 1975, 31-2). RIC 67 (= Cohen 25 - no reference, issue 5b-6, rev CENS P P P) is plausible; it may belong to a group of variants similar to those of AD 87-89, but it requires confirmation.

85.5a The only coins of this issue are the silver multiples or money medallions, BMC 83 (Minerva seated rev - eight denarius?), BMC 85 (Germania rev - five denarius?).

Analysis

Issue	Aurei - weights		Denarii
	Zemun	museums	% silver
85.4	-	7.47(1)	92.87(2)
85.5b	7.54(2)	7.49(2)	93.25(2)
85.6	7.57(1)	-	-

In these issues the legend formula for Domitian's denarii reaches the regular form which was to last until the end of the reign. In issues 4 and 5 the censorial title of Domitian is abbreviated to CENS POT, and in issue 6 it is further reduced to CENS P, following his adoption of the title Censor Perpetuus[55]. The reverse legend has now arrived at the limit of its development, as had the obverse in issue 85.2. On the denarius, from now until the end of the reign (apart from on isolated exceptions) only the numerals of the titles change.

The types employed are the standard series of four Minerva varieties for silver and the Germania type for gold. The only exceptions are the special types on the two commemorative silver multiples which make up issue 85.5a. The larger (eight denarius?) piece has a very elaborate seated Minerva type (pl.II,18) which is reminiscent of the seated Athena type popularised by the coinage of Lysimachus of Thrace which dates back to the third century BC. The rather smaller (five denarius piece ?) medallion has the normal Germania type (pl.II, 19), which from this date is otherwise used only on gold aurei. These two pieces also have the extended obverse legend with TR POT instead of TR P. The style of portraiture is the same as that employed on the earlier issues of 85, although from issue 5b onwards the aegis is no longer included (cf. pl.XII,10,11,15).

By far the most significant difference between the coins of issues 85.4-6 and the coins of the earlier issues of 85 is to be seen in their weights and fineness. The denarii of the later issues analysed by Walker had an average silver content 5½ % lower than the earlier issues[56]. Also, according to the weights of the Zemun coins there is a visible reduction in the weight of the aureus[57]. The three Zemun aurei representing these later issues of 85 are the first since the coins of the First Period to have an average weight of less than 7.6g.

AD 86 (pl.III,1-8)

There are five separate issues of precious metal coins that can be dated to the year 86. The first two issues were produced between January and mid-September; the remaining three issues, divided by the emperor's acceptance of two more imperatorial acclamations, were all produced between mid-September and the end of the year.

Issue	Denom	Legends	RIC
86.1 (pl.III,1-4)	AU AR ARQ	IMP CAES DOMIT AVG GERM P M TR P V IMP XI COS XII CENS P P P	73-78
86.2 (pl.III,5-6)	AU AR ARQ	IMP CAES DOMIT AVG GERM P M TR P V IMP XII COS XII CENS P P P	79-84

86.3 (pl.III,7)	AU AR	IMP CAES DOMIT AVG GERM P M TR P VI IMP XII COS XII CENS P P P	85-86
86.4	AU AR	IMP CAES DOMIT AVG GERM P M TR P VI IMP XIII COS XII CENS P P P	87
86.5 (pl.III,8)	AU AR	IMP CAES DOMIT AVG GERM P M TR P VI IMP XIIII COS XII CENS P P P	88-90

obv Head laureate, facing right

rev AU Germania
AU AR Minerva 1 2 3 4
ARQ Victory advancing right (1,2)
ARQ Victory seated left (1)*

Notes: 86.1-5 RIC p.163 n* (AU with rev GERMANICUS COS XII) is an invention; the coin, which was published in BNS 1884, p.131, is an ordinary aureus of AD 92-94 (COS XVI).
* D.H.E. Whitehead, NC 1974, 180-1. This coin is not, as the author suggests, a hybrid.

Analysis

Issue	Aurei - weights: Zemun	Aurei - weights: museums	Denarii % silver
86.1	7.57(5)	7.54(8)	93.6(5)* (86.1–86.5)
86.2	7.59(5)	7.52(3)	
86.3	7.38(2)	-	
86.4	7.62(2)	-	
86.5	7.58(1)	7.51(3)	

* The fineness of the denarius is now so regular that the silver percentages of the separate issues have not been listed. Instead, for this and for future years, the average silver percentage for all the issues within each group is given

These issues of 86 all follow the same pattern. The obverses have the same laureate, right-facing portrait of Domitian without aegis. The "new" portrait of the years 82-85 has become the standard form, though now without the "elaborate" qualities which characterised the dies which included the aegis. The same reverse types are used for all these issues; they are the standard Minerva series, which is here used on both silver and gold, and the Germania type, which is confined, as is usual, to aurei[58]. The quinarii, which were restricted to the first two issues, also use standard reverse types.

The persistent use in this year of the same series of four Minerva reverse types in its entirety in each issue of denarii and aurei confirms the organisational importance of this group[59]. The Germania aurei appear just as regularly, so they must also be brought into a consideration of the *officina* system, which seems to have been mobilised in full for each separate issue. The overall impression gained from the issues of 86 is that they were the product of a mint which had undergone a prolonged series of systematic changes but has now settled into a uniform system of production. From now until the end of the reign the main interest in the precious metal coinage is in its strict observance of changes in the numbered titles of the emperor. The frequency with which these changes takes place from now on determines the arrangement of the separate issues.

AD 87 (pl.III,9-13)

Issue	Denom	Legends	RIC
87.1 (pl.III,9-11)	AU AR ARQ	IMP CAES DOMIT AVG GERM P M TR P VI IMP XIIII COS XIII CENS P P P	91-97
87.2 (pl.III,12)	AU AR ARQ	IMP CAES DOMIT AVG GERM P M TR P VII IMP XIIII COS XIII CENS P P P	100-5
		obv: Head laureate, facing right Head laureate, facing left (1 - rare) rev: AU Germania* AU AR Minerva 1 2 3 4 ARQ Victory advancing right ARQ Victory seated left	
variant: (pl.III,13)	AR	DOMITIANVS AVG GERMANICVS COS XIII+ across field (Minerva 4)	BMC 100

Notes: 87.1-2 The variant RIC 98 (=Cohen 26 : IMP CAES DOMIT AVG GERMANIC COS XIII / CENS P P P , Minerva 4) has been omitted; the coin (in Paris) is a plated forgery. It is possible that other variants of these issues may exist, but any such recorded may also be plated forgeries.

87.2 Cohen 65, rev COS XIII across field, Minerva 3 (mistakenly listed, RIC 99, as Minerva 4) requires confirmation.

* The Germania type has so far not been verified on denarii : Cohen 225 (which was also alleged to have a variant obv type) is not in Paris (as Cohen); Cohen 226 (RIC 103) lacks a reference; BMC p.322n* (= Martinetti sale, 18 Nov. 1907, lot 1791) was mistakenly noted as a denarius - it is in fact an aureus.

\+ The rev inscription of BMC 100 is unclear, but HCC 36, which has the same obv and rev dies, definitely reads COS XIII

Analysis

Issue	Aurei - weights		Denarii
	Zemun	museums	% silver
87.1	7.62(7)	7.49(6)	93.62(6)
87.2	-	7.60(2)	

Apart from one variant type which omits imperatorial and tribunician titles (BMC 100), the coins of 87 are divided easily into two issues, one dated before and one dated after mid-September when Domitian's tribunician number changed from VI to VII. In style and legend form the two issues follow the same pattern as the issues of 86, and once again the entire Minerva series is used for aurei as well as denarii, while the Germania type is restricted to aurei. One interesting feature on the obverse is the isolated reappearance of a left-facing head of Domitian (pl.III,10) in issue 87.1. The silver quinarii have the usual Victory types.

AD 88 (pl.III,14-23)

The coins dated firmly to 88 fall into three main issues:-

Issue	Denom	Legends	RIC
88.1 (pl.III,14-17)	AU AR AUQ ARQ	IMP CAES DOMIT AVG GERM P M TR P VII IMP XIIII COS XIIII CENS P P P	107-13
88.2 (pl.III,18)	AR	IMP CAES DOMIT AVG GERM P M TR P VII IMP XV COS XIIII CENS P P P	114
		obv Head laureate, facing right Head laureate, facing right, with aegis* (1) rev AU Germania AR Minerva 1 2 3 4 AUQ ARQ Victory advancing right (1) ARQ Victory seated left (1)	
variant: (pl.III,19)	AR	IMP CAES DOMIT AVG GERM P M TR P VII COS XIIII across field (Minerva 2 3 4)	106
88.3 (a) (pl.III, 20-21)	AU AR ARQ	DOMITIANVS AVGVSTVS GERMANICVS (obv) IMP CAES DOMIT AVG GERM P M TR P VIII (obv) COS XIIII LVD SAEC FEC (rev) obv Head laureate, facing right rev Herald advancing right, holding wand and shield	119 117-8
88.3 (b) (pl.III,23)	AU AR	DOMITIANVS AVGVSTVS GERMANICVS (obv) IMP CAES DOMIT AVG GERM P M TR P VIII (obv) obv Head laureate, facing right rev Within wreath, a column inscribed LVD-SAEC-FEC in three lines; COS XIIII across field	115
88.3 (c) (pl.III,22)	AR	IMP CAES DOMIT AVG GERM P M TR P VIII (obv) obv Head laureate, facing right rev Herald standing left, facing incense burner and column inscribed COS-XIIII-LVD-SAEC-FEC (in 5 lines)	116
variant: (pl.III,20)	AR	IMP CAES DOMIT AVG GERM P M TR P VIII ∩ out (obv) obv Head laureate, facing left; rev three types (a,b and c) as above RIC 117a, 115a, 116a	

Notes:	*	This obv type is known only on the large commemorative gold piece (RIC 108), perhaps worth five aurei, of issue 88.1
	88.1-2	RIC 106a (Riv.It 1891,p.24), rev COS XIIII CENS PER P P (Minerva 2); RIC 110a (Cohen 233, but not in Paris), and RIC 111a (Cohen 241, but not in Vienna), rev IMP XIIII COS XIIII CENS P P P, with variant obv legend IMP CAES DOMIT AVG GERMAN P M TR P VII all require confirmation. If any can be verified they will represent another branch of variants.

Analysis

Issue	Aurei - weights Zemun	museums	Denarii % silver
88.1	7.50(3)	7.35(1)	93.25(14)
88.2			
88.3	7.59(2)	7.46(4)	

The first two issues of 88 were produced before mid-September, the third issue was minted after. Issue 88.1 has the usual types for each denomination: Germania for aurei, the Minerva series for denarii, and the two Victory types for quinarii in silver. The gold quinarius which was included in this issue for the first (and apparently the only) time in the reign also employs one of the standard Victory types. Issue 88.2 was confined to denarii. Both issues use the standard legend formulae, although the variant reverse with the consular number struck across the centre of the field, which first appeared in the previous year, is retained.

The third issue of 88 introduces a whole new series of reverse types, accompanied by variations in the legends and obverse type. The reason for this novelty is that at this time the Secular Games were being celebrated and the types and legends were designed to commemorate the event. The types depict the herald of the games, the commemorative column erected for the games, and sometimes both, together with an incense burner. The reverse legend has the phrase COS XIIII LVD SAEC FEC inscribed either around or across th field and on the column. The denarii use the standard obverse legend, but occasionally a left-facing head is employed with the associated legend inscribed outwardly from right to left and with the usual DOMIT extended to DOMITIAN. Aurei, meanwhile, have the new shortened legend DOMITIANVS AVGVSTVS GERMANICVS, and from this date until the end of the reign they never again share the same legends as the denarii.

AD 88-89 (pl.IV,1-11)

Between mid-September 88 and mid-September 89 a number of issues of coinage were produced which, because Domitian did not take the consulship for 89, cannot be (by their titles) more closely dated. The exception is issue 88.3, which has been dated to 88 by the event (the Secular Games - celebrated in October of that year) commemorated on its reverse types. The remaining issues can be divided into two separate groups.

The first group (A) displays only one of Domitian's titles, the consulship, but the second group (B) provides all his titles and can therefore be arranged into a chronological series according to the progression of his imperatorial acclamations, which proceed from 16 to 21 in this twelve month period. These issues are classified formally as 88-89 B.1-5, but a diploma dated November 7, 88, records Domitian as IMP XVII, so issue B1 was produced entirely before this date and issue B2 (IMP XVII) should also have begun by this time, although it might have extended a little later, perhaps into early 89 [60]. The remaining issues (B3-5) should all be dated to 89. They record Domitian's imperatorial acclamations gained in a year which began with the suppression of the revolt of Antonius Saturninus and another war against the Chatti, and later included campaigns against the Marcomanni and Quadi, the ending of the long struggle against the Dacians, and finally the celebration of a double triumph.

Issue	Denom	Legends	RIC
88-89 A (pl.IV,1-12)	AU	DOMITIANVS AVGVSTVS GERMANICVS COS XIIII	123-8
variants:-			
(pl.IV,3)	AR	IMP CAES DOMIT AVG GERMANIC COS XIIII CENS P P P across field	120
(pl.IV,4)	AR	IMP CAES DOMIT AVG GERM COS XIIII CENS PER P P across field	BM
(pl.IV,5)	AR	IMP CAES DOMITIAN AVG GERMANICVS or IMP CAESAR DOMITIAN AVG GERMANIC or IMP CAESAR DOMITIANVS AVG GERMANICVS COS XIIII across field	121-2
		obv Head laureate, facing right* rev AU Germania AU Domitian in triumphal quadriga AU AR Minerva 1 2 3 4	
88-89 B1 (pl.IV,6)	AR	IMP CAES DOMIT AVG GERM P M TR P VIII IMP XVI COS XIIII CENS P P P	129-30
88-89 B2 (pl.IV,7)	AR	IMP CAES DOMIT AVG GERM P M TR P VIII IMP XVII COS XIIII CENS P P P	131-4
88-89 B3 (pl.IV,8)	AR	IMP CAES DOMIT AVG GERM P M TR P VIII IMP XVIII COS XIIII CENS P P P	135-6a
88-89 B4 (pl.IV,9-10)	AR	IMP CAES DOMIT AVG GERM P M TR P VIII IMP XIX COS XIIII CENS P P P	137-41
88-89 B5 (pl.IV,11)	AR	IMP CAES DOMIT AVG GERM P M TR P VIII IMP XXI COS XIIII CENS P P P	142
		obv Head laureate, facing right rev AR Minerva 1 2 3 4 AR Victory advancing right (B4)	

Notes:		
	88-89 A	Denarii with the same legends as the aurei of this issue have been quoted (RIC 125,126) from Cohen (Cohen 143,141, without references), but they require confirmation.
	*	The aurei from this issue listed by Cohen as having bare-headed obverse portraits (Cohen 140,145) require confirmation.
	88-89 B2	BMC p.330 n150 mentions a coin from this issue with variant obv legend ..DOMITIANVS.. from Musée Crozatier, Le Puy. This coin is now confirmed; another example recently appeared in Numismatic Fine Arts sale 6, 27-28 Feb.1979, lot 685.
	B5	A denarius with rev legend ..IMP XX COS XIV..(Nordheim Sale, 3 Dec.1929, lot 132 - now in British Museum) is a plated forgery.

Analysis

Issue	Aurei - weights		Denarii
	Zemun	museums	% silver
88-89 A	7.57(18)	7.50(16)	93.29(16)
88-89 B1-5			

The aurei of group A use the reduced legend form DOMITIANVS AVGVSTVS / GERMANICVS COS.. which from now becomes the standard legend formula for Domitian's gold until the end of the reign. Also, a new reverse design, with Domitian standing in a triumphal quadriga, presumably commemorating the double triumph of 89 [61], is introduced to complete the series of standard reverse types of Domitian's later years (four Minerva types, Germania and Quadriga). The denarii of this group are similar to the variants recorded from 87 and 88, but this was apparently the last occasion on which such pieces were produced to interrupt the otherwise stereotyped pattern of precious metal issues. The denarius issues of group B form a well defined series and they conform to the standard pattern except that in the fourth issue a Victory type is added to the usual series of Minerva reverses. This particular type was regularly used on Domitian's quinarii but only this once on a denarius issue.

Undated issue 3 : AD 88-89 (?) (pl.IV,12-13)

Two undated coin types belonging to the "Family" category can be assigned tentatively to the years 88-89.

Issue	Denom	Legends	RIC
88-89 (?)			
(a) (pl.IV,12)	AU	DOMITIA AVG IMP DOMITIAN AVG GERM CONCORDIA AVGVST,(AVGVSTA) or (AVGVSTI)	215-5B
	obv	Bust of Domitia (large), draped r., hair massed high in front above forehead and knotted in long plait behind	
	rev	Peacock standing right	

(b) (pl.IV,13)	AU	IVLIA AVGVSTA DIVI TITI FILIA	218-8A
		obv Bust of Julia (large), draped r. or l.*, hair massed high in front above forehead and knotted in long plait behind rev Peacock standing front, with tail spread.	

Notes: (a) This coin was probably struck only in gold. The denarius (?) referred to in BMC 249n. requires confirmation.

(b) It is possible that these types were also struck on denarii (eg. Cohen 7; Mazzini pl.85 = Magnaguti sale 2, 1949, lot 607), but the authenticity of any such pieces requires confirmation. RIC 217 (= Cohen 5 : rev CONCORDIA AVGVSTI, facing peacock type) is undoubtedly false, combining a legend of Domitia with the type of Julia. As with the previous "family" issue of 82-83, plated forgeries abound, and modern forgeries also exist (eg. "Becker" : Hill, Becker 161).

* Cohen 8, in Zagreb (RIC 218A), was from the Zemun hoard (Ljubic p.13,no.26).

Analysis

Issue	Aurei - weights	
	Zemun	museums
88-89(?) (a)	7.58(4)	7.61(6)
88-89(?) (b)	7.57(2)	7.51(4)

These aurei have many features which distinguish them from the "family" coins of 82-83 which, according to style, legends, weight and fineness, clearly belonged in the Second Period of Domitian's coinage. The two coins listed here under 88-89(?) share the same portrait style (pl.XII,20,24) which is very different from the other portraits of Julia and Domitia (cf. pl.XII,19,21), their obverse legends are inscribed in the later convention of left to right inwardly, and coin type (a) includes Domitian's title GERM for Germanicus, a name which the emperor had not yet acquired when the other series was struck. These coins therefore undoubtedly represent a later group. The examples from this issue in the Zemun hoard were lighter in weight than the Zemun examples from the earlier "family" group; they should therefore not have been issued later in the Second Period (ie. 83-85), but rather at some time in the Third Period. The death of Julia by the year 90 provides a *terminus ante quem* for coin type (b)[62]; it is therefore suggested that on the basis of the Zemun weights these coins can be placed in the years 88-89(?).

AD 89 (pl.IV,14-15)

Issue	Denom	Legends	RIC
89 (pl.IV,14-15)	AR	IMP CAES DOMIT AVG GERM P M TR P VIIII IMP XXI COS XIIII CENS P P P.	143-6
		obv Head laureate, facing right rev Minerva 1 2 3 4	

Analysis

Issue	Denarii - % silver
89	93.5 (3)

This issue of denarii was produced between mid-September and the end of December 89. It conforms to the usual pattern for a Third Period denarius issue, having the standard obverse portrait, the four regular Minerva reverse types, and the conventional legend formulae.

AD 90 (pl.IV,16-17)

Issue	Denom	Legends	RIC
90 (pl.IV, 16-17)	AR ARQ	IMP CAES DOMIT AVG GERM P M TR P VIIII IMP XXI COS XV CENS P P P	147-51
		obv Head laureate, facing right rev AR Minerva 1 2 3 4 ARQ Victory seated left	

Analysis

Issue	Denarii - % silver
90	93.7 (5)

This issue of denarii and quinarii, produced between January and mid-September 90, contains no irregularities.

AD 90-91 (pl.IV,18-21)

Issue	Denom	Legends	RIC
90-91 A (pl.IV,18-20)	AU	DOMITIANVS AVGVSTVS GERMANICVS COS XV	160-5
90-91 B (pl.IV,21)	AR	IMP CAES DOMIT AVG GERM P M TR P X IMP XXI COS XV CENS P P P	152-5
		obv Head laureate, facing right Head bare, facing right (A)* rev AU Germania AU Domitian in triumphal quadriga AU AR Minerva 1 2 3 4	

Notes: * The appearance of this new obverse type in this issue is based on only one confirmed example (Cohen 154, an aureus in Paris); an allegedly similar piece, Cohen 149, is not in London (as Cohen).

Analysis

Issue	Aurei - weights		Denarii
	Zemun	museums	% silver
90-91 A	7.61(59)	7.54(20)	
90-91 B			93.55(5)

Domitian was not Consul in 91 so that, whereas the denarii of issue 90-91 B are dated by the emperor's tribunician title to the period mid-September 90 to mid-September 91, the aurei (A) could have been issued at any time from January 90 to December 91. The issues in both gold and silver conform to the standard patterns for the Third Period. The Minerva series is once again used for aurei as well as denarii. The only unusual feature is the introduction of a new, bare-headed portrait of Domitian on the obverse in the gold issue 90-91 A. This type was not properly established until the next aureus issue dated 92-94 [63]; the coin which apparently confirms the use of this type in this issue must be considered an isolated forerunner.

Undated issue 4 : AD 90-91(?) (pl.IV,22)

Issue	Denom	Legends	RIC
90-91(?) (pl.IV,22)	AU	DIVA IVLIA AVGVSTA	220
	obv	Bust of Diva Julia (large), facing right, hair massed high in series of ridges at front and coiled up behind.	
	rev	Diva Julia seated in funeral car drawn right by two elephants.	

Analysis

Issue	Aurei - weights	
	Zemun	museums
90-91(?)	7.72(1)	-

Although there is no firm evidence for the dating of this exceedingly rare issue, a strong case can be argued for placing it within the period 90-91. It was obviously produced at a later date than the third group of undated coins from Domitian's reign, which have been attributed to the years 88-89(?), because Julia is now deified. It is known that Julia was no longer alive in 90 [64], and two dated issues of sestertii for Diva Julia were struck in 90-91 and 92-94. The reverse type employed on this issue of aurei was chosen to commemorate Julia's consecration and it is therefore probable that the issue was struck soon after she became a Diva, so a date of 90-91, parallel to the first Diva Julia sestertius issue, has been proposed.

AD 91 (pl.IV,23-24)

Issue	Denom	Legends	RIC
91 (pl.IV,23-24)	AR	IMP CAES DOMIT AVG GERM P M TR P XI IMP XXI COS XV CENS P P P	156-9

obv	Head laureate, facing right
rev	Minerva 1 2 3 4

Analysis

Issue	Denarii - % silver
91	92.94 (4)

This issue, of denarii only, was produced between mid-September and the end of December 91, and it contains no irregularities.

AD 92 (pl.IV,25-pl.V,2)

Issue	Denom	Legends	RIC
92.1 (pl.IV,25-V,1)	AR ARQ	IMP CAES DOMIT AVG GERM P M TR P XI IMP XXI COS XVI CENS P P P	166-70
92.2 (pl.V,2)	AR	IMP CAES DOMIT AVG GERM P M TR P XI IMP XXII COS XVI CENS P P P	-
	obv	Head laureate, facing right Head laureate, facing right, with aegis (1)*	
	rev	AR Minerva 1 2 3 4 ARQ Victory seated left (1)	

Notes: 92.1 This issue also includes silver medallions : RIC 167 (= BMC 191, five denarius piece ?); Cohen 275, and Riv.It 1898,p.44 (a four denarius ? piece struck from the same pair of dies as BMC 191.
92.2 See I.A. Carradice, ZPE 28 (1978), 159-60.
* Confined to the silver medallion Cohen 275

Analysis

Issue	Denarii - % silver
92.1	93.64 (7)
92.2	-

These two issues were produced between January and mid-September 92. The second issue records Domitian's twenty second (and final) imperatorial acclamation, which he must have received for victories against the Suebi and Sarmatians, probably announced at the end of the summer campaigning season. This issue, which was only recently recognised, is represented by very few examples so it probably came into production only shortly before the start of Domitian's next tribunician year (mid-September 92).

Both of these issues conform to the usual pattern for silver issues of the period except that issue 92.1 includes some silver medallions, and one of these pieces (Cohen 275) employs for its obverse type a portrait of Domitian with aegis. During a die investigation of denarii from issue 92.1 it was found that every obverse die link connected coins with the same reverse type (though not necessarily the same reverse die). The absence of any obverse die links across different reverse types suggests a firm separation of production between each officina, identified by its use of a particular Minerva reverse type. This indicates a return to the mint practice (ie. separation of obverse as well as reverse dies) operating in the First Period, 81-82.

AD 92-93 (pl.V,3)

Issue	Denom	Legends	RIC
92-93 (pl.V,3)	AR	IMP CAES DOMIT AVG GERM P M TR P XII IMP XXII COS XVI CENS P P P	171-4
		obv Head laureate, facing right rev Minerva 1 2 3 4	
Notes: 92-93		RIC p.174n* mentions a denarius of this issue (BMC 199) with rev type temple with eight columns, but this coin is a plated forgery; another example in the Hunterian collection (HCC 84), and no doubt all other examples, is also plated.	

Analysis

Issue	Denarii - % silver
92-93	93.37 (6)

Domitian did not take the consulship for 93 so these denarii are dated by his tribunician title to the period mid-September 92 to mid-September 93. They have all the usual features of denarii of this period of the reign.

AD 92-94 (pl.V,4-5)

Issue	Denom	Legends	RIC
92-94 (pl.V,4-5)	AU	DOMITIANVS AVGVSTVS GERMANICVS COS XVI	181-5a
		obv Head laureate, facing right Head bare, facing right rev Minerva 1 2 3 4 Germania Domitian in triumphal quadriga	
variant:	AU	DOMITIANVS AVGVSTVS GERMANICVS obv Head bare, facing right; rev Dom. in triumphal quad.	-*
Notes: *		Cohen 138; Canessa sale 1923 (Caruso coll.) no. 272; Ars Classica xvii, October 1934, nos. 744-5. Variant, with obv	

DOMITIANVS AVG, recorded from the Zirkowitz hoard, Pichler p.26, 11.

Analysis

Issue	Aurei - weights	
	Zemun	museums
92-94	7.62(9)	7.53(14)

The aurei of this period are dated only by the consular title of the emperor, therefore, because Domitian declined to take the consulship in 94 as well as 93, these coins could have been issued at any time between January 92 and December 94. The most interesting feature of these coins is the fine bare-headed portrait of the emperor (pl.XII,17). In this issue it was apparently confined to aurei with the quadriga reverse type, and the variant coins also couple this new bare-headed portrait with the quadriga reverse[65]. On these particular pieces the reverse legend omits Domitian's consular title, but the evidence suggests that they can be linked with the COS XVI issue. The obverse portrait is identical to the one employed with the dated quadriga reverses, whereas the bare-headed portrait on the later dated issues (eg. pl.V,11) has a less imposing appearance, as also do the bare-headed portraits on the denarii attributed to the years 95-96? (pl.V,17-22). Furthermore, the quadriga reverse is not known to have been used in the issues which can be dated after 92-94.

AD 93-94 (pl.V,6-7)

Issue	Denom	Legends	RIC
93-94 (pl.V,6-7)	AR	IMP CAES DOMIT AVG GERM P M TR P XIII IMP XXII COS XVI CENS P P P	175-8
		obv Head laureate, facing right rev Minerva 1 2 3 4	

Analysis

Issue	Denarii - % silver
93-94	93.36 (7)

These denarii were produced within the period mid-September 93 to mid-September 94. The issue contains no irregularities.

AD 94 (pl.V,8)

Issue	Denom	Legends	RIC
94 (pl.V,8)	AR	IMP CAES DOMIT AVG GERM P M TR P XIIII IMP XXII COS XVI CENS P P P	179-80
		obv Head laureate, facing right rev Minerva 1 2 3 4	

Analysis

Issue	Denarii - % silver
94	94.0 (2)

These denarii were produced between mid-September and the end of December 94. Again there are no unusual features.

AD 95 (pl.V,9-10)

Issue	Denom	Legends	RIC
95 (pl.V,9-10)	AR ARQ	IMP CAES DOMIT AVG GERM P M TR P XIIII IMP XXII COS XVII CENS P P P	186-9
		obv Head laureate, facing right rev AR Minerva 1 2 3 4 ARQ Victory seated left	

Analysis

Issue	Denarii - % silver
95	94.0 (5)

Domitian once more took the consulship (for the seventeenth and final time) in 95. These coins can therefore be dated within the period January to mid-September 95. Once again the issue conforms in every way to the usual standards for a denarius issue from this part of the reign.

AD 95-96 (pl.V,11-17)

Issue	Denom	Legends	RIC
95-96 A (pl.V,11-12)	AU	DOMITIANVS AVGVSTVS GERMANICVS COS XVII	198-202
95-96 B (pl.V,13-17)	AR	IMP CAES DOMIT AVG GERM P M TR P XV IMP XXII COS XVII CENS P P P	190-6
		obv Head laureate, facing right Head bare, facing right Head laureate, facing right, with aegis (B) rev AU Germania AU AR Minerva 1 2 3 4 AR Winged Minerva advancing left holding javelin and shield AR Female figure advancing left holding bird and caduceus (Pax ?)* AR Altar with two statues and two eagles	
Notes: 95-96A RIC 203 (=BMC 229) records an aureus with rev type:- Temple of two columns flanked by two Victories. Apart			

from the unique rev design this coin also has a variant obv legend (IMP CAES DOMIT AVG GER COS XVII CENS PER P P) and a most unusual obv type with an aegis and a very odd portrait of Domitian. Its irregular nature was recently confirmed by analysis which revealed it to have a metallurgical composition very different from Domitian's normal aurei. It therefore must be false.

* The existence of this type (RIC 196 : "strange and uncertain reverse") in this issue is confirmed by H. Cahn, NC 1946, p.22 no.50.

Analysis

Issue	Aurei - weights Zemun	museums	Denarii % silver
95-96 A	7.65(2)	7.40(6)	
95-96 B			94.02(10)

The aurei of issue A were produced between January 95 and September 18th. 96 when Domitian was killed[66]; the denarii (B) date from the emperor's tribunician year, mid-September 95 to mid-September 96. The issues continue to employ the principal types in gold and silver except that the Quadriga reverse from the aureus series is no longer in evidence. In addition, on denarii a number of new reverse types are introduced : a winged Minerva (Minerva Victrix), a Pax (?), and an altar type. Other interesting features are the reintroduction of the aegis as a variant obverse (but apparently for only one reverse type)[67], and the continued use of the bare-headed portrait of Domitian, which is now employed on both denominations, though its use seems to have been somewhat restricted[68].

Undated issue 5 : AD 95-96(?) (pl.V,18-22)

Issue	Denom	Legends	RIC
95-96(?) (pl.V,18-22)	AR	DOMITIANVS AVG GERM or IMP CAES or IMP CAESAR (obv)	204-8

obv Head bare, facing right

rev Temple of four columns (Serapis)
Temple of four columns, no pediment (Cybele)
Temple (round?) of four columns, no pediment (Minerva)
Temple of six columns (Jupiter)
Temple of eight columns

Analysis

Issue	Denarii - % silver
95-96(?)	94.0(2)

This series of undated denarii with various temple[69] reverse designs is generally attributed to the last years of Domitian's reign, 94-96. However, it can be argued that these coins should be dated more narrowly to the years 95-96. The series is linked together by shared obverse dies and in style the portraits are close to the bare-headed types on the gold issue dated 95-96 (cf. pl.V,11). Also, a group of monumental and architectural types appeared on sestertii of Domitian dated 95-96 [70]. It would be appropriate that this series of denarii were issued at the same time as the "monumental" bronzes and also the "altar" denarius of the dated issue 95-96 (significantly, the only denarius type of issue 95-96 to be combined with the bare-headed obverse portrait).

AD 96 (pl.V,23)

Issue	Denom	Legends	RIC
96 (pl.V,23)	AR	IMP CAES DOMIT AVG GERM P M TR P XVI IMP XXII COS XVII CENS P P P	197-7B
	obv	Head laureate, facing right	
	rev	Minerva 1 3 Winged Minerva Pax (?)	

(Analysis)[71]

These final denarii from Domitian's reign should all have been produced in 96 between September 13/14, when the emperor's sixteenth tribunician year began, and September 18, when he was murdered. It is possible that some of the coins could have been struck from dies prepared in anticipation of his attaining TR POT XVI, but there is no evidence to confirm this practice in this period. Regarding types, only two of the standard Minerva series of reverse designs are known to have been used, but it is possible that examples from the other types (2 and 4) are simply awaiting discovery[72]. In addition, the winged Minerva and the Pax (?) reverse types from the previous denarius issue are retained. Only the standard laureate portrait of Domitian appears to have been used as the obverse type.

Summary 1 Gold and Silver Issues AD 81-96 (Domitian and Domitia)

The following list of issues illustrates the development of legends on gold and silver coins throughout the reign of Domitian. These legends have formed the basis of the chronological arrangement of his coinage, and any changes in their composition and direction or method of inscription can be observed here, alongside other factors, such as bust types and production of denominations.

Bust types:
- A - Head laureate, facing right
- B - Head laureate, facing left
- C - Bust draped, head laureate, facing left
- D - Head laureate, facing right, with aegis
- E - Head bare, facing right
- * - only on medallions

Year/Issue	Denom	Bust	Standard legends (obverse first)	
81.1	AR	A	IMP CAESAR DOMITIANVS AVG TR P COS VII	↺ out ↻ in
81.2a	AU AR	A	IMP CAES DOMITIANVS AVG PONT COS VII DES VIII P P	↺ out ↻ in
81.2b	AR	A	IMP CAES DOMITIANVS AVG PONT TR P COS VII DES VIII P P	↺ out ↻ in
81.3a	AU AR	A	IMP CAES DOMITIANVS AVG P M COS VII DES VIII P P	↺ out ↻ in
81.3b	AU AR	AB	IMP CAES DOMITIANVS AVG P M TR P COS VII DES VIII P P	↺ out ↻ in
82.1	AU AR	A	IMP CAES DOMITIANVS AVG P M TR POT COS VIII P P	↺ out ↻ in
81-82	ARQ	A	IMP CAES DOMITIANVS AVG P M VICTORIA AVGVST	↺ out ↻ in, ↺ out, ↷ out
82.2	AU AR	A	IMP CAES DOMITIANVS AVG P M TR POT IMP II COS VIII DES VIIII P P	↺ out ↻ in
82-83 (a-e)	AU AR	A	IMP CAES DOMITIANVS AVG P M (various undated)	↺ out ↻ in, ↺ out
82-83 (f-h)	AU AR	-	DOMITIA AVGVSTA IMP DOMIT (various undated)	↺ out ↻ in
83.1	AR ARQ	A	IMP CAES DOMITIANVS AVG P M TR POT COS VIIII P P	↺ out ↻ in
83.2	AU AR	A	IMP CAES DOMITIANVS AVG P M TR POT II COS VIIII DES X P P	↺ out ↻ in

Year/Issue	Denom	Bust	Standard legends	
83.3	AU	A	IMP CAES DOMITIAN AVG GERMANICVS P M TR P III COS IX DES X P P	↶ out ↷ in
84.1	AU AR?	A	IMP CAES DOMITIAN AVG GERMANICVS P M TR POT III IMP V COS X P P	↶ out ↷ in
84.2a	AU AR	ACD	IMP CAES DOMITIANVS AVG GERMANIC P M TR POT III IMP V COS X P P	↷ in ↷ in
84.2b	 ARQ	A	IMP CAES DOMITIAN AVG GERMANICVS P M TR POT III IMP V COS X P P	
84.3a-b	AU	C	IMP CAES DIVI VESP F DOMITIAN AVG GERMANICVS COS X / DE GERMAN	
85.1a	AU AR	AD	IMP CAES DOMITIANVS AVG GERMANIC P M TR POT IIII IMP VIII COS XI P P	
85.1b	 ARQ	A	IMP CAES DOMITIAN AVG GERMANICVS P M TR POT IIII IMP VIII COS XI P P	
85.2	AU AR	D	IMP CAES DOMIT AVG GERM P M TR P IIII IMP VIIII COS XI CENSORIA POTESTAT P P	
85.3	AR	D	IMP CAES DOMIT AVG GERM P M TR P IIII IMP VIIII COS XI CENS POTES P P	
85.4	AU AR	AD	IMP CAES DOMIT AVG GERM P M TR P IIII IMP VIIII COS XI CENS POT P P	
85.5a	AR	AD*	IMP CAES DOMIT AVG GERM P M TR POT V IMP VIIII COS XI CENS POT P P	
85.5b	AU AR	A	IMP CAES DOMIT AVG GERM P M TR P V IMP VIIII COS XI CENS POT P P	
85.6	AU AR	A	IMP CAES DOMIT AVG GERM P M TR P V IMP XI COS XI CENS P P P	
86.1	AU AR ARQ	A	IMP CAES DOMIT AVG GERM P M TR P V IMP XI COS XII CENS P P P	
86.2	AU AR ARQ	A	IMP CAES DOMIT AVG GERM P M TR P V IMP XII COS XII CENS P P P	
86.3	AU AR	A	IMP CAES DOMIT AVG GERM P M TR P VI IMP XII COS XII CENS P P P	
86.4	AU AR	A	IMP CAES DOMIT AVG GERM P M TR P VI IMP XIII COS XII CENS P P P	
86.5	AU AR	A	IMP CAES DOMIT AVG GERM P M TR P VI IMP XIIII COS XII CENS P P P	

Year/Issue	Denom		Bust	Standard legends
87.1	AU	AR ARQ	AB	IMP CAES DOMIT AVG GERM P M TR P VI IMP XIIII COS XIII CENS P P P
87.2	AU	AR ARQ	A	IMP CAES DOMIT AVG GERM P M TR P VII IMP XIIII COS XIII CENS P P P
88.1	AU AUQ	AR ARQ	AD*	IMP CAES DOMIT AVG GERM P M TR P VII IMP XIIII COS XIIII CENS P P P
88.2		AR	A	IMP CAES DOMIT AVG GERM P M TR P VII IMP XV COS XIIII CENS P P P
88.3	AU		A	DOMITIANVS AVGVSTVS GERMANICVS COS XIIII LVD SAEC FEC / -
		AR ARQ	AB	IMP CAES DOMIT AVG GERM P M TR P VIII COS XIIII LVD SAEC FEC / -
88-89A	AU		A	DOMITIANVS AVGVSTVS GERMANICVS COS XIIII
88-89B1		AR	A	IMP CAES DOMIT AVG GERM P M TR P VIII IMP XVI COS XIIII CENS P P P
88-89B2		AR	A	IMP CAES DOMIT AVG GERM P M TR P VIII IMP XVII COS XIIII CENS P P P
88-89B3		AR	A	IMP CAES DOMIT AVG GERM P M TR P VIII IMP XVIII COS XIIII CENS P P P
88-89B4		AR	A	IMP CAES DOMIT AVG GERM P M TR P VIII IMP XIX COS XIIII CENS P P P
88-89B5		AR	A	IMP CAES DOMIT AVG GERM P M TR P VIII IMP XXI COS XIIII CENS P P P
88-89?	AU		-	DOMITIA AVG IMP DOMITIAN AVG GERM CONCORDIA AVGVST etc.
89		AR	A	IMP CAES DOMIT AVG GERM P M TR P VIIII IMP XXI COS XIIII CENS P P P
90		AR	A	IMP CAES DOMIT AVG GERM P M TR P VIIII IMP XXI COS XV CENS P P P
90-91A	AU		AE	DOMITIANVS AVGVSTVS GERMANICVS COS XV
90-91B		AR	A	IMP CAES DOMIT AVG GERM P M TR P X IMP XXI COS XV CENS P P P
91		AR	A	IMP CAES DOMIT AVG GERM P M TR P XI IMP XXI COS XV CENS P P P

Year/Issue	Denom	Bust	Standard legends
92.1	AR ARQ	AD*	IMP CAES DOMIT AVG GERM P M TR P XI IMP XXI COS XVI CENS P P P
92.2	AR	A	IMP CAES DOMIT AVG GERM P M TR P XI IMP XXII COS XVI CENS P P P
92-93	AR	A	IMP CAES DOMIT AVG GERM P M TR P XII IMP XXII COS XVI CENS P P P
92-94	AU AR	AE	DOMITIANVS AVGVSTVS GERMANICVS COS XVI / GERMANICVS
93-94	AR	A	IMP CAES DOMIT AVG GERM P M TR P XIII IMP XXII COS XVI CENS P P P
94	AR	A	IMP CAES DOMIT AVG GERM P M TR P XIIII IMP XXII COS XVI CENS P P P
95	AR ARQ	A	IMP CAES DOMIT AVG GERM P M TR P XIIII IMP XXII COS XVII CENS P P P
95-96A	AU	AE	DOMITIANVS AVGVSTVS GERMANICVS COS XVII
95-96B	AR	ADE	IMP CAES DOMIT AVG GERM P M TR P XV IMP XXII COS XVII CENS P P P
95-96?	AR	E	DOMITIANVS AVG GERM / IMP CAESAR (undated)
96	AR	A	IMP CAES DOMIT AVG GERM P M TR P XVI IMP XXII COS XVII CENS P P P

Legend direction: The legend on both obverses and reverses from issue 84.2 until the end of the reign is almost always inscribed ↻ inwardly. There are only two exceptions: 1) the reverses of some of the (rare) coins of issue 85.2, which have the extended legend ending ..CENSORIA POTESTAT P P ; 2) the obverses on a rare group of denarii from issue 88.3 which also have a variant legend with ..DOMITIAN..and the unusual bust type B. These exceptions have their legends inscribed ↺ outwardly.

Summary 2 - Domitian's Three Periods of precious metal coinage

Table A Weight and Fineness of Domitian's gold and silver issues

Issue	Aureus - weight		Issue	Denarius - % silver
	Zemun	Museums		Walker
First Period				
			81.1	92.50
81.2a	-	7.00	81.2a	-
			81.2b	92.00
81.3a	-	6.96	81.3a	93.62
81.3b	7.34	7.18	81.3b	90.25
82.1	-	7.35	82.1	91.03
average	7.34(2)	7.18(16)		91.13(27)
Second Period				
82.2	7.72	7.70	82.2	97.00
82-83a	7.77	7.63	82-83a	97.37
			b	98.37
82-83c	-			
d	7.69	7.48		
e	-		82-83e	-
f	7.82	7.72	f	97.75
g	7.76		g	-
			h	98.30*
			i	97.90*
			83.1	-
83.2	7.73	7.68	83.2	97.00
83.3	-	7.64		
84.1	7.85	7.75	84.1	-
84.2a	7.82	7.62	84.2a	98.75
84.3a	7.61	-		
b	-	-		
85.1a	7.72	7.61	85.1a	98.92
85.2	-	7.53	85.2	98.00
85.3	-	-	85.3	97.50
average	7.75(60)	7.65(52)		98.01(17)

Table A (continued)

Issue	Aureus - weight Zemun	 Museums	Issue	Denarius - % silver Walker
Third Period				
85.4	-	7.47	85.4	92.87
85.5b	7.54	7.49	85.5b	93.25
85.6	7.57	-	85.6	-
86.1	7.57	7.54	86.1-5	93.60
86.2	7.59	7.52		
86.3	7.38	-		
86.4	7.62	-		
86.5	7.58	7.51		
87.1	7.62	7.49	87.1-2	93.62
87.2	-	7.60		
88.1	7.50	7.35	88.1-3	93.25
88.3	7.59	7.46		
88-89A	7.57	7.50	88-89A-B	93.29
88-89?a	7.58	7.61		
b	7.57	7.51		
			89	93.50
			90	93.70
90-91A	7.61	7.54	90-91B	93.55
90-91?	7.72	-		
			91	92.94
			92.1	93.64
			92.2	-
			92-93	93.37
92-94	7.62	7.53		
			93-94	93.36
			94	94.00
			95	94.00
95-96A	7.65	7.40	95-96B	94.02
			95-96?	94.00
			96	-
average	7.63(125)	7.54(96)		93.51(101)

Fineness: The fineness calculations in the above table are all taken from Walker's figures except for those marked *, which denotes analyses of British Museum denarii that were recently examined by the British Museum Research Laboratory.

Table A illustrates the impact on the aureus and the denarius of the changes in standards adopted by the Roman mint in 82 and 85; changes which have enabled us to divide the reign of Domitian into three separate Periods of coining. There is a clear consistency between all the issues of gold and silver within these Periods

The aurei in the Zemun hoard are obviously the best guide to the weights of gold coins. They should in theory show a steady increase in wear in accordance with the length of time they were in circulation. Thus, the earliest coins should be the most worn, and the latest coins the least worn. According to the recorded weights this is indeed confirmed, but only if the three Periods are considered separately. The heaviest coins date from the Second Period because, although these had circulated longer than the Third Period aurei and should therefore have incurred greater wear, they were originally struck to a heavier weight standard. Of the Third Period coins in Zemun only the issues of the 90's, in other words the "newest" coins of Domitian, can rival the Second Period aurei in weight. Within the Third Period itself, however, the coins reveal in general a gradual, if slight, increase in weight over the ten years of issue. Not surprisingly, the lightest Zemun aurei of Domitian are the two issued in 81 because these are the "oldest" and they were struck when the lowest standards of the reign were operating.

The weights of aurei from museum collections agree perfectly well with the Zemun figures. These coins show less uniformity in weight because they come from various sources and therefore have very different degrees of wear (although any badly damaged or seriously worn pieces were excluded from the list). In each Period the average weights of museum aurei are slightly less than the average Zemun weights, because the possible circulating life of all the Zemun coins of Domitian was short and therefore they should all be of above average condition. However, the overall chronological pattern of weights is the same for both sets of figures, and their consistency has helped confirm the placement of undated issues.

The analyses of denarii reveal an even more impressive uniformity within the three separate coining Periods. The exact position of the two reforms, in 82 and 85, has been established, and this is clearly illustrated on Table A; and now that the full significance of the three-Period division of Domitian's precious metal coinage has been illustrated it should be possible, with the aid of the revised catalogue of issues, to investigate the pattern of coinage emission throughout the fifteen years of the reign.

NOTES

1. D.R. Walker, Metrology I, III.

2. D.R. Walker, Metrology I, 95.

3. D.R. Walker, Metrology I, 96,115.

4. D.R. Walker, Metrology I, 97-9, 115-6.

5. The appropriate time for a complete revision of the catalogue of Domitian's Roman coinage will be the publication of a new edition of RIC II. A number of articles have been written since the publication of RIC II and BMCRE II listing new types and variants, including coins of Domitian, eg. : L.G.P. Messenger, NC 1926, 322-335, NC 1933, 1-7, NC 1948, 85-8; C.H.V. Sutherland, NC 1940, 255--264, NC 1944, 1-26; A.A. Boyce, ANS Museum Notes 1947, 21-33; H.A. Cahn, NC 1946, 7-27; H.W. Parke, NC 1947, 150-9; C.M. Kraay, ANS Museum Notes 1960, 109-116; I. Carradice, Num.Circ. 1980, 306. Numerous additional new types and variants have also been published in coin hoard reports since the 1920s.

6. See BMCRE II, lxxxv.

7. The collections from which these figures were compiled are : Berlin, Cambridge, Glasgow, London, Oxford, Paris, Vienna. Brackets again indicate the total number of coins from which the average weights have been calculated. For obvious reasons, badly damaged and exceptionally worn pieces were omitted.

8. On the dating of these titles see T.V. Buttrey, Chronology, 34-6.

9. M. McCrum and A.G. Woodhead, Select Documents.., 21-2. It is assumed that the Arval Brethren would not have failed to celebrate Domitian's election as Pontifex Maximus. Their records for the early weeks of the reign are complete up to the entry which can be dated October 30th. This particular entry is incomplete, but it does not appear to be a celebration of Domitian's election as Pontifex Maximus.

10. See BMCRE II, lxxii f., lxxxv.

11. In this instance the great fire of AD 80 has been proposed (BMCRE II, lxxxv).

12. See eg. Suetonius, Dom 15.

13. The three examples which I have been able to compare (from Milan, Stockholm and Vienna) show the same obverse die.

14. The Roman mintage of these pieces has been questioned by A.S. Robertson (HCC I, clvi).

15. A coin with this legend (obv head r.) from New York shares rev die with two denarii having the standard legend of 81.2b and 81.3b (Londonthorpe hoard).

16. Metrology I, 94.

17. A comparison of weights of denarii revealed the following : -
Titus, AD 80, ave. wt. 3.21 g. (Walker, 39 coins).
Domitian, AD 81, ave. wt. 3.20 g. (Walker, 20 coins).
Domitian, 82.1, ave. wt. 3.13 g. (Walker, 8 coins).
Titus's aurei in BMCRE II and HCC I have ave. wt. 7.20 g. (17).

18. RIC II, p.158; BMCRE II, p.309-310 (AD 81-84).

19. Metrology I, p. 100 (no. 1151 = RIC 44).

20. Metrology I, 117

21. I. Carradice and M. Cowell, "An analysis..", 172.

22. The only First Period aureus or denarius type which later reappeared in Domitian's reign was the Minerva standard type 1. From 83 this again became a regular type, especially on denarii.

23. It is not uncommon for the early portraits of a new emperor to bear a strong resemblance to those of his predecessor. One explanation for this is that many of the earliest coins were struck from old dies which were hurriedly re-cut to adapt the features of the former portrait to that of the new emperor.

24. Ten denarii from museum collections weighed an average 3.29 g. (Berlin, London, Milan, Oxford, Paris, Vienna).

25. For the date of the title Germanicus on coins see T.V. Buttrey, Chronology, 52-6.

26. Suetonius, Dom 1,2.

27. Tacitus, Histories, 3,74; Suetonius, Dom. 5. He had already (in Vespasian's reign) built a shrine to Jupiter Conservator (Tacitus, Histories, 3,74).

28. In RIC II (p. 124) Mattingly attributed coin type (c) to the reign of Titus, alongside the many Divus Vespasianus denarii of 80-81, but in BMCRE II, p. lxxxiv, he rightly re-attributed it to Domitian's reign on grounds of style.

29. I. Carradice and M. Cowell, "An analysis..", 171-2.

30. This type recalls the image of the baby Divus Caesar described by Martial, 4,3.

31. RIC 440, BMC 501.

32. Note also the contemporary production of aes coins of Divus Titus. See below, p. 117.

33. Tacitus, Histories 4,51-2.

34. Suetonius, Titus 9,3; Dom 2,3.

35. Suetonius, Dom 2,3.

36. Both Domitillae (Domitian's mother and sister) were dead before Vespasian became emperor in AD 69 (Suetonius, Vesp 3).

37. See pl.II,1-4. I have followed Mattingly's BMCRE catalogue in numbering the types 1 to 4 : BMC 39, 40, 42, 44. Mattingly numbers them in a slightly different order in his introduction: BMCRE II, lxxxv f.

38. For a recent examination of this series see L. Morawiecki, Klio 1977, 185-193.

39. This interpretation obviously has to be reconsidered when different or additional reverse types and variants are introduced.

40. The coin is in the Hunterian collection, Glasgow (HCC Domitian 13 : weight 7.64 g.).

41. T.V. Buttrey, Chronology, 54-5; P.A. Holder, "Domitian and the title Germanicus", LCM 2.7 (1977), 151.

42. I have ignored Cohen 590. This denarius was recorded as having rev legend TR P III IMP V COS VIIII, type, Elephant walking l; but, presuming it was read correctly, this coin must be a hybrid forgery combining an early obv of Domitian with a rev of Titus (with botched legend).

43. eg. BMCRE II, p. 307-9; RIC II, p. 159-60.

44. The illustrated coin (BMC 46, aureus) has the same obv die as HCC 13 from issue 83.3.

45. Although on Domitian's aes coinage the obverse legend had been inscribed in this manner since the start of the reign.

46. On the production of portraits from imagines in Domitian's reign, see M. Alföldi, in Overdruk uit Festoen, 15-22. An interesting example of popular familiarity with Domitian's portrait is provided by the identification of a graffito from the Domus Tiberiana: H. Jucker, "Graffito einer Domitiansbüste", Schweizer Münzblatter 23. 89 (Feb. 1973), 11-13.

47. This particular type is extremely rare. The few specimens I have compared (BMC 45; RN 1893, 41 (pl.1,3); Münzhandlung Basel sale 15 (1955), lot 750) all share the same rev die. In style the type differs from the earlier bust of Minerva (issue 82.2) in that she wears an Attic, not Corinthian, helmet; but it is also noticeable that the head is larger - a stylistic development paralleled in the obverse portraits of Domitian.

48. eg. BMC Titus 36-41; these coins have the same style of trophy as Domitian's, but they have two seated captives.

49. Compare the unusual and exceedingly rare sestertii also issued at this time (see below, p.115).

50. T.V. Buttrey, CJ 1975, 26-34.

51. D.R. Walker, Metrology I, 96-7

52. I. Carradice and M. Cowell, "An analysis..", 172-3.

53. D.R. Walker, Metrology I, 115.

54. "The mean fineness of the coinage of the last 11 years of the reign remains exactly the same" (D.R. Walker, Metrology I, 115).

55. T.V. Buttrey, CJ 1975, 26-34.

56. D.R. Walker, Metrology I, 96-7. The British Museum pieces recently analysed showed a similar reduction (see above, n.52).

57. This reduction is less noticeable in coins from museums where the drop in weight appears very slight, but museum specimens, coming from various sources and having uneven degrees of wear, are not as reliable as the Zemun coins for purposes of comparison.

58. For issue 86.4 I have not seen any examples of the Germania type, but at this time the standard designs form such a regular group that it is unlikely that any one type would have been omitted from a single issue.

59. Hoard evidence has confirmed that all four Minerva types appear in virtually every issue in both metals; any remaining gaps will surely be filled in time (see below, p. 146-7).

60. See T.V. Buttrey, Chronology, 38.

61. Suetonius, Dom 6,1.

62. See below, n.64.

63. In the sale of coins from the Fins d'Annecy hoard (Raymond Serrure sale, Paris, 25 May, 1894), two aurei from 90-91 were recorded with the bare-headed obv type, but these may have been described in error. Of the 59 aurei of this issue recorded in detail from the Zemun hoard not one had a bare-headed obv type.

64. In Martial 6,3 and 13 (published in 90) Julia is referred to as already deified; and her name was omitted from the vows of the Fratres Arvales for the safety of the imperial family on 3 Jan. 90 (CIL VI, 2067).

65. Note also that Cohen 154 (the only confirmed bare-headed aureus from issue 90-91) has the same combination of types.

66. Suetonius, Dom 17,3.

67. BMC 237n., winged Minerva rev type (another example in the Cyprus hoard : NC 1977, 28).

68. On aurei it has been recorded with three of the Minerva reverses (Cohen 165, 167, BMC 226A), but on denarii it is known only with the Altar reverse type.

69. The identifications of the cult statues with the temples listed here are based on Mattingly in BMCRE II, p. lxxxviii.

70. See I. Carradice, "Coins, monuments..."

71. No coins of this issue were analysed by Walker.

72. Because this issue was produced within such an extremely short period of time there are insufficient specimens available for a judgement to be made on how many types, both obv and rev, might have been prepared for production.

CHAPTER 3

SURVEY OF DENARII

Introduction : Hoard survey

This is the first time that a detailed survey of hoards has been undertaken in order to investigate the size of individual issues of coinage in the early imperial period. For this reason, and because of the specially important position held by the denarius in the coinage and finances of the period, it has been considered necessary to define in detail the methods employed in the denarius survey, and to explain the criteria used for including material[1].

The main purpose of this survey is to establish a pattern of denarius emission, with estimates of issue sizes. The basic information for the survey is provided by coin hoard reports; there are insufficient records of loose finds of denarii (many of which in any case represent the remains of disturbed hoards) to construct a comparable survey[2]. From the hoards the denarii minted between AD 81 and 96 will be listed chronologically according to issues. The denarii are the most suitable of Domitian's coins for a quantitative study because they were minted only in Rome, they circulated virtually throughout the Empire, and they are the coins which occur most frequently in hoards of the second century, from which period the bulk of the data is taken. The reign of Domitian is particularly well fitted for a survey such as this because his coinage (and especially his denarii) exhibits a profusion of numbered titles which facilitates the accurate identification and dating of individual issues. Altogether, between 81 and 96 Domitian's denarii record eleven consulships, sixteen tenures of tribunician power, and sixteen of the Emperor's twenty-two imperatorial acclamations. Thus the categorising of individual coins for Domitian's reign presents few problems, and even the coins that lack numbered titles can usually be dated within quite narrow time periods. However, once these coins are extracted from a hoard report and are offered as evidence in a survey of an historical period many difficulties can arise, and these must be recognised and explained before the coins themselves can be used.

The initial problem to overcome is in proving whether or not the coins of any particular hoard can justifiably be included in the survey[3]. In other words, can they be shown to be a representative sample, and if so, of what exactly are they representative? An isolated hoard denotes the burial of a sample of coinage at a specific place and approximate date by a person or persons unknown. It does not by itself indicate its usefulness as a sample. It might have constituted the most valuable monetary possessions of the depositor, but this does not mean necessarily that all coin-owners in the Roman world at that time would have possessed an identical or even a similar sample of Roman currency[4]. A number of separate hoards is required, and if this can be achieved the contents of these hoards can reasonably be regarded collectively as a representative sample of the coinage buried at a particular time in certain areas. The greater the number of hoards that can be considered, the more useful will be the information they collectively yield. However, there are still problems.

Firstly, there is the difficulty of unbalanced geographical distribution. A number of hoards from the same region may reveal much information on the coinage buried in that area, but the circumstances which forced an individual in one region to deposit his coinage are unlikely to have been duplicated simultaneously in all of the regions in which that coinage was circulating. Hence, during the second century we find a concentration of coin hoards in those frontier regions most susceptible to external threats, especially the Danube area[5]. Similarly, the circumstances which induced the burial of coin hoards were not in existence continuously throughout the second century, or indeed for any period. On the contrary, there were concentrations of coin-burying activity confined to certain periods during which security was least assured, while more peaceful times produced correspondingly less burying. Therefore, the conditions which induced coin-burying should inevitably have left us with an unbalanced pattern of coin hoard distribution in both location and date of deposit. This would appear to be a major obstacle to a quantitative survey of the coinage as it suggests that the circumstances governing the eventual deposition of the evidence were unrelated and far removed from those under which it was first produced and issued (that is, the management and working of the mint). However, as the hoards that will be considered in this survey were buried over a long period of time after their (Domitianic) contents were issued, it is likely that by the natural process of circulation the coinage from Rome would have found its way to the furthest reaches of the Empire[6]. Also, much of the coinage originally minted, including the denarii, would probably have been sent direct to the armies in those threatened frontier areas, where a proportion of it must surely have remained. The main question then is: would this coinage have survived in an approximately equal proportion to its original volume of issue?

Because no mint records survive from the Roman period it is not possible to compare the survival of coins with emission figures. However, it has been shown that in other periods, for which mint records are extant, a close correlation can be found to exist between the original volume of output and the survival of coins in hoards[7]. There is no reason why, in normal circumstances, the same should not be possible for the Roman imperial period. Therefore, in principle, the pattern of coinage originally issued should be reflected in the amounts now being recovered from the earth in hoards, provided that a sufficient number of hoards from different regions and periods is examined. But there are some important conditions affecting the survival of coins in circulation, and these have to be taken into consideration when selecting material for inclusion in the survey, and again when interpreting the data.

Above all, special care has to be taken when dealing with

coinage whose survival might have been affected by special circumstances such as official debasements or large scale withdrawals of coins from circulation. Obviously it would be dangerous to use indiscriminately hoards buried during or after a period when coins of the same denomination but inferior quality were being issued, because the factors determining the survival of these coins would then be their quality, weight and condition, rather than the quantities in which they were originally issued.

According to the principles of the so-called "Gresham's Law"[8], finer coins already in circulation are driven out (by export abroad, hoarding and melting down) by the arrival of poorer quality, and hence less intrinsically valuable, new coinage[9]. A series of debasements which took place in the second century, under Trajan (107), Antoninus Pius (148), Marcus Aurelius (161, 170), Commodus (180, 190) and Septimius Severus (the "great" debasement of 194/5), should all have affected the circulation of Domitian's silver coinage[10]. It has been said that Domitian's denarii defied Gresham's Law by remaining in circulation unhindered until the reign of Antoninus Pius[11], but this claim can be shown to be incorrect. It resulted from an assumption that the coinage of Domitian can be treated in a general manner, without consideration of possible differences in fineness between coins within the reign[12]. In fact, Domitian's finest silver coins (ie. the denarii of the Second Period) could have been expected to begin disappearing from circulation at least as early as the reform of currency by Trajan, which is usually dated to 107, at the same time as Trajan's recall of earlier currency noted by Cassius Dio (68, 15, 3) and the associated production of "Restoration" issues[13]. In the subsequent debasements of the second century, culminating with the great debasement of Septimius Severus, Domitian's denarii from the Third and eventually the First Periods would also gradually have been driven out of circulation. Further declines in the silver standard in the third century would then have disposed of any remaining precious metal coins of Domitian, although by this time most of his currency would have already disappeared, except for the issues of the First Period. The effects of these debasements should therefore have been felt at different times by the issues of the separate Periods of Domitian's coinage, and hence the burial dates of the hoards have to be noted as carefully as possible (see Appendix 1), so that the data can be listed chronologically in a way that should reveal the true pattern of survival and, at the same time, expose any inconsistencies.

Another difficulty relating to the location of hoards should be mentioned. Roman coins penetrated far beyond the frontiers of the Roman world[14], but it is likely that the coins which arrived at the most distant regions would be less representative of the body of coinage produced by the mint than the coins circulating within the Empire. The reason for this is that although Roman money was considered to be of value abroad it was not issued directly for exportation, and so the factors governing its appearance in distant lands would not normally be conditioned by the regular production of the mint. The more distant finds of Roman coins from Scandinavia, Russia and India will therefore be omitted, and the survey will be confined to hoards from within the Empire and from central Europe where the native tribes were in more direct contact with the Romans.

In addition to the chronological and geographical distribution of coin finds there remains one more major influence on the suitability of the evidence. This is the accessibility and reliability of the hoard reports which provide the basic information for the survey. There are two stages during which information on a coin hoard may become distorted. The first stage is during its recovery and prior to publication. It is a well known fact that many hoards, particularly ones discovered many years ago, were incomplete by the time their contents came to be identified in a report. This problem does not usually arise when a hoard is discovered in the course of archaeological excavations, but it is a common feature with hoards uncovered by chance - the category to which most hoards belong. Luckily, it is often possible to determine whether the extraction of coins from a hoard has been undertaken selectively or in a haphazard manner. The presence of any coins of exceptional quality or great rarity should be sufficient evidence that a hoard was not plundered selectively (or at least not effectively). Otherwise, a comparison with other hoards of similar date should expose obvious irregularities. If a hoard has been plundered selectively it cannot usually be used for survey purposes, but a hoard which has suffered a random extraction of coins will still have a representative sample which is perfectly adequate for study[15].

The second stage in which information on a hoard may become distorted, or indeed may be lost altogether, is its identification and subsequent appearance (or non-appearance) in published form. The standard of hoard reports varies from country to country and this tends to affect the apparent distribution pattern of hoards, so that some regions are represented by many well-recorded hoards whereas others, where there is apparently no reason for them to be less well-represented, have yielded very few (and these often inadequately published). It is just not possible to compare a balanced number of hoards from all over the Roman world, so we must depend on a very small number of hoards representing vast areas of the Empire to corroborate the evidence from regions where we have no shortage of well recorded hoards (eg. Britain and the Danube).

In conclusion, there are a number of problems associated with the collection of data for a hoard survey. However, the difficulties are not as great as they might at first appear so long as each hoard is regarded with a critical eye. Every hoard has its own history which extends throughout the periods before its deposition and after its recovery[16]. In order to study a hoard usefully it is necessary to take into account all of the information available on this history, but, with or without this information, the hoard must demonstrate its own usefulness by surviving comparison with other hoards found in both similar and differing circumstances. Thus, the key to conducting a survey lies in obtaining a pattern or patterns of regularity, and these should be exposed adequately by a systematic organisation and tabulation of the data.

The Hoards

The hoards of denarii which have been included in this survey are arranged in both a chronological and geographical order. Chronologically they are divided according to the reign to which the last coin in the hoard can be dated. It should not be assumed that a hoard was buried immediately after the date of the latest coin it contains, or that the composition reflects the coinage circulating at, or just before, the date of burial. Some hoards were apparently gathered together sporadically and much of their contents may have been put aside much earlier than would be assumed from their date of burial. However, the date of the latest coin is the most convenient chronological peg to use, and any wildly anomalous hoards will be easily identified when listed alongside their contemporaries.

The hoards have been divided into the following three regions:-

A : North-western Europe (including Britain and the Rhine).
B : Central, eastern and southern Europe (including the Danube).
C : Other areas (including the East and Africa).

Within each reign the hoards are arranged chronologically in the three groups, A, B and C. The list is confined to hoards which contain more than five denarii minted during the reign of Domitian[17].

	Hoard	Region : Country	Reign when buried	Date of last coin
1	Acarnania	B : Greece	Nerva	97
2	Lavenham	A : Britain	Trajan	103-111
3	Verulamium	A : Britain	Trajan	112-117
4	Egypt	C : Egypt	Trajan	112-117
5	Mallerstang	A : Britain	Hadrian	134-138
6	Swaby	A : Britain	Hadrian	137
7	Castagnaro	B : Italy	Hadrian	126
8	Erla	B : Austria	Hadrian	134-138
9	Tiszanagyrev	B : Hungary	Hadrian	134-138
10	Murabba 'Ât	C : Israel	Hadrian	119-122
11	Volubilis	C : Morocco	Hadrian	119-122
12	Eleutheropolis	C : Israel	Hadrian	134-138
13	Middels Osterloog	A : West Germany	Ant.Pius	140-144
14	Londonthorpe	A : Britain	Ant.Pius	153-154
15	Dîmbău	B : Romania	Ant.Pius	143
16	Vyskovce	B : Czechoslovakia	Ant.Pius	152-153
17	Visa	B : Romania	Ant.Pius	155-156
18	Salaşuri	B : Romania	Ant.Pius	158
19	Tipasa	C : Algeria	Ant.Pius	143
20	Allerton Bywater	A : Britain	M.Aurelius	164-169
21	Stockstadt-am-Main	A : West Germany	M.Aurelius	167-168
22	Edwinstowe	A : Britain	M.Aurelius	179-181
23	Osiek	B : Yugoslavia	M.Aurelius	164-165
24	Mocsolad	B : Hungary	M.Aurelius	164-165
25	Kurd-gyulaji	B : Hungary	M.Aurelius	164-165
26	Lengowo	B : Poland	M.Aurelius	165-166
27	Sotin	B : Yugoslavia	M.Aurelius	165-166
28	Apetlon II	B : Austria	M.Aurelius	166-167
29	Szombathely	B : Hungary	M.Aurelius	176-177
30	Simionesti	B : Romania	M.Aurelius	177-180
31	Bîrgaoani	B : Romania	M.Aurelius	177-180
32	Barway	A : Britain	Commodus	181
33	Bletchley	A : Britain	Commodus	183
34	Briglands	A : Britain	Commodus	186-187
35	Bargercompascuum	A : Holland	Commodus	187-188

36	Parava	B : Romania	Commodus	183-184
37	Przewodowa	B : Poland	Commodus	186-187
38	Sascut	B : Romania	Commodus	187
39	Handley	A : Britain	Sept.Sev.	194-195
40	Chmielow Piaskowy	B : Poland	Sept.Sev.	193
41	Puriceni	B : Romania	Sept.Sev.	194
42	Magura	B : Romania	Sept.Sev.	196
43	Vidin	B : Bulgaria	Sept.Sev.	201-207

44	Abergele	A : Britain	Sept.Sev.	201-206
45	Muswell Hill	A : Britain	Sept.Sev.	209
46	Darfield	A : Britain	Caracalla	213
47	Tell Kalak	C : Jordan	Elagabalus	222
48	Falkirk	A : Britain	Alex.Severus	230
49	East England	A : Britain	Alex.Severus	231-235
50	Turkey	C : Turkey	Traj.Decius	249-251
51	Réka Devnia	B : Bulgaria	Traj.Decius	249-251

In the above list a line has been drawn to separate the hoards buried after the great debasement of Septimius Severus (AD 194/5) from those whose contents suggest that they were assembled before that event. It has already been mentioned that the coinage "reform" of Severus was the last of a series of second century debasements which would have affected the survival in circulation of Domitian's denarii. As this particular debasement was the most drastic so far, and was accompanied by a great increase in output of new denarii, suggesting a large scale recoinage programme[18], it was bound to have had the most profound effect on all circulating denarii, including Domitian's. The Magura and Vidin hoards (nos. 42 and 43) each contained only one recorded coin struck later than 194/5, so although these two hoards were apparently buried after Severus's debasement their composition is effectively the same as the earlier Severan hoards and very different from the later hoards. They are therefore included with the hoards buried before the debasement.

The division between the pre-194/5 hoards and post-194/5 hoards is maintained for the following table (Table B) which records the number of denarii of Domitian from each issue of the reign which were identified in the reports of the 51 hoards in the survey.

Table B Frequency of denarii of Domitian, AD 81-96, in hoards

	Hoard		Issues							
			81.1	2a	2b	3a	3b	82.1	82.2	82-83
Nerva	B	1	1	-	-	-	-	-	-	-
Trajan	A	2	-	-	-	1	1	1	-	-
	A	3	-	-	-	-	-	-	-	-
	C	4	-	-	-	-	-	-	-	1
Hadrian	A	5	-	-	-	-	-	-	-	1
	A	6	-	-	-	1	1	2	-	-
	B	7*	1	-	-	-	2	2	-	-
	B	8	-	-	-	-	4	-	-	1
	B	9	-	-	-	-	-	-	-	-
	C	10	-	-	-	-	-	-	-	-
	C	11	-	-	-	-	-	-	-	1
	C	12	-	-	-	-	1	-	-	-
Ant. Pius	A	13	-	-	-	-	-	-	-	-
	A	14	-	-	-	-	2	-	-	-
	B	15	-	-	-	1	1	-	-	-
	B	16	1	-	-	-	4	1	-	-
	B	17	-	-	-	-	-	1	-	-
	B	18	3	1	-	4	2	6	-	-
	C	19	-	-	-	-	-	-	-	-
M. Aurel.	A	20	-	-	-	-	1	-	-	-
	A	21	-	-	-	-	2	-	-	-
	A	22	-	-	-	-	-	-	-	-
	B	23	1	-	-	-	4	3	-	-
	B	24	1	-	-	-	10	4	-	-
	B	25	-	-	-	-	2	1	-	-
	B	26	1	-	-	-	2	-	-	-
	B	27	-	1	-	-	3	1	1	-
	B	28	1	-	-	-	-	-	-	-
	B	29	-	-	-	-	-	-	-	-
	B	30	-	-	-	-	-	-	-	-
	B	31	2	-	-	-	1	-	-	-
Commodus	A	32	-	-	-	-	1	1	-	-
	A	33	-	-	-	1	1	-	-	-
	A	34	-	-	-	-	-	-	-	-
	A	35	-	-	-	-	-	-	-	-
	B	36	-	-	-	-	1	-	-	-
	B	37	-	-	-	-	1	-	-	-
	B	38	-	1	-	-	3	1	-	-
Sept. Sev.	A	39	-	-	-	-	3	-	-	-
	B	40	-	-	-	-	2	1	-	-
	B	41	1	-	-	-	3	-	-	-
	B	42	1	1	-	1	6	2	-	1
	B	43	-	-	-	-	2	-	-	-
Total 1-43			14	4	-	9	66	27	1	5
Later	A	44-6	1	-	1	-	2	1	-	-
	C	47	1	-	-	-	6	1	-	-
	A	48-9	-	-	3	-	9	2	-	-
	C	50	-	-	-	-	-	-	-	-
	B	51	8	-	1	2	80	17	-	1
Total 44-51			10	-	5	2	97	21	-	1

Table B (continued)

Hoard		83.1	83.2	84.1	84.2	85.1	85.2	85.3	85.4	85.5	85.6
		Issues									
B	1	-	-	-	1	-	-	-	-	-	-
A	2	-	-	-	-	-	-	-	-	-	-
A	3	-	-	-	-	-	-	-	-	-	-
C	4	-	2	-	-	-	-	-	-	-	-
A	5	-	-	-	-	-	-	-	-	-	-
A	6	-	-	-	-	-	-	-	-	1	-
B	7*	-	2	-	-	-	1	-	-	2	1
B	8	-	1	-	-	-	1	-	-	-	-
B	9	-	-	-	-	-	-	-	-	-	-
C	10	-	-	-	-	-	-	-	-	1	-
C	11	-	-	-	-	-	-	-	-	-	-
C	12	-	-	-	-	-	1	-	-	-	-
A	13	-	-	-	-	-	-	-	-	-	-
A	14	-	-	-	-	-	-	-	-	-	-
B	15	-	-	-	-	-	-	-	-	-	-
B	16	-	1	-	-	-	-	-	1	-	-
B	17	-	-	-	-	-	-	-	-	-	-
B	18	-	-	1	-	-	-	-	-	1	-
C	19	-	-	-	-	-	-	-	-	-	-
A	20	-	-	-	-	-	-	-	-	-	1
A	21	-	-	-	-	-	1	-	-	-	-
A	22	-	-	-	-	-	-	-	-	-	-
B	23	-	-	-	-	-	-	-	-	-	-
B	24	-	-	-	-	-	-	-	-	-	-
B	25	-	-	-	-	1	-	-	-	-	2
B	26	-	-	-	-	-	-	-	-	-	-
B	27	-	-	-	-	-	-	-	-	-	-
B	28	-	-	-	-	-	-	-	-	-	-
B	29	-	-	-	-	-	-	-	-	-	-
B	30	-	-	-	-	-	-	-	-	-	-
B	31	-	-	-	-	-	-	-	-	-	-
A	32	-	-	-	-	-	-	-	-	-	-
A	33	-	-	-	-	-	-	-	-	-	-
A	34	-	-	-	-	-	-	-	-	-	-
A	35	-	-	-	-	-	-	-	-	-	-
B	36	-	-	-	-	-	-	-	-	-	-
B	37	-	-	-	-	-	-	-	-	-	-
B	38	-	-	-	-	-	-	-	-	-	-
A	39	-	-	-	-	-	-	-	-	-	-
B	40	-	-	-	-	-	-	-	-	-	-
B	41	-	-	-	-	-	-	-	1	-	-
B	42	-	-	-	-	-	-	-	-	-	-
B	43	-	-	-	-	-	-	-	-	-	-
1-43		-	6	1	1	1	4	-	2	5	4
A	44-6	-	-	-	-	-	-	-	-	-	-
C	47	-	-	-	-	-	-	-	-	-	-
A	48-9	-	-	-	-	-	-	-	-	-	-
C	50	-	-	-	-	-	-	-	-	-	-
B	51	-	-	-	-	-	-	-	-	-	-
44-51		-	-	-	-	-	-	-	-	-	-

Table B (continued)

Hoard		Issues									
		86.1	86.2	86.3	86.4	86.5	87.1	87.2	88.1	88.2	88.3
B	1	-	-	-	-	-	-	-	-	-	-
A	2	1	-	-	-	-	-	-	-	-	1
A	3	-	-	-	-	-	1	-	-	-	1
C	4	1	1	1	-	1	2	-	2	-	-
A	5	-	-	-	-	1	-	-	-	-	-
A	6	-	-	-	-	-	1	-	-	1	1
B	7*	-	1	-	-	-	-	2	5	-	1
B	8	-	-	-	-	-	2	-	2	-	-
B	9	-	-	-	1	-	-	-	-	-	-
C	10	-	-	-	-	-	1	-	-	-	-
C	11	2	-	-	1	-	-	-	1	-	-
C	12	-	-	-	-	-	-	1	-	1	-
A	13	1	1	-	-	-	-	-	-	-	-
A	14	1	1	-	-	-	-	-	3	-	-
B	15	-	-	-	-	-	-	-	1	-	1
B	16	2	3	-	-	-	-	1	6	-	1
B	17	-	-	-	-	-	-	-	-	-	-
B	18	2	-	-	1	-	6	-	8	-	1
C	19	-	-	-	-	-	1	-	1	1	-
A	20	-	-	-	-	-	-	-	-	-	-
A	21	-	-	-	-	-	2	2	3	1	-
A	22	-	-	-	-	-	-	-	3	-	-
B	23	2	-	-	-	2	2	1	4	-	3
B	24	-	1	-	-	-	-	1	1	-	4
B	25	-	-	-	-	-	-	-	11	2	-
B	26	-	1	1	-	-	-	1	-	-	-
B	27	1	-	-	-	-	2	-	7	-	1
B	28	-	-	-	-	-	-	-	-	-	-
B	29	-	-	-	-	-	-	1	2	-	1
B	30	-	-	-	-	-	-	-	-	-	-
B	31	-	-	-	-	-	-	3	2	-	-
A	32	-	-	1	-	-	-	-	1	-	-
A	33	-	-	-	-	-	1	-	1	-	-
A	34	-	-	-	-	-	-	-	1	-	1
A	35	-	-	-	-	-	-	-	-	-	-
B	36	-	-	-	-	-	-	-	-	-	-
B	37	-	1	-	-	-	-	1	-	-	1
B	38	-	-	-	-	-	2	-	-	-	3
A	39	1	-	-	-	-	2	-	-	-	-
B	40	-	-	-	-	-	-	-	-	-	-
B	41	-	-	-	-	-	1	-	3	-	-
B	42	1	-	-	-	1	1	2	9	-	4
B	43	-	-	-	-	-	1	-	2	-	-
1-43		15	10	3	3	5	28	16	79	6	25
A	44-6	-	-	1	-	-	-	-	2	-	-
C	47	1	-	-	-	-	-	-	-	-	-
A	48-9	-	1	-	-	-	-	1	3	-	-
C	50	-	-	-	-	-	1	1	-	-	-
B	51	3	1	-	1	-	2	1	14	-	1
44-51		4	2	1	1	-	3	3	19	-	1

Table B (continued)

Hoard		88-89 A	88-89 B1	B2	B3	B4	B5	89	90	90-91	91
B	1	-	-	-	-	2	-	-	1	1	-
A	2	1	-	-	-	6	-	1	5	1	-
A	3	-	-	-	-	-	-	-	3	1	-
C	4	-	-	-	-	1	-	-	5	6	3
A	5	-	-	-	-	1	-	-	2	1	-
A	6	-	-	2	-	1	-	1	2	1	-
B	7*	-	-	3	-	9	-	1	9	12	7
B	8	-	-	2	-	7	-	1	6	7	3
B	9	1	-	-	-	1	-	-	2	3	-
C	10	-	-	-	1	1	-	-	-	-	1
C	11	-	-	-	-	-	-	2	-	5	-
C	12	-	-	1	-	2	-	-	2	1	1
A	13	-	-	-	-	1	-	-	1	-	-
A	14	-	-	-	-	3	-	1	3	4	2
B	15	-	-	-	-	3	-	-	1	1	-
B	16	-	-	-	-	14	-	-	7	9	3
B	17	-	-	1	-	-	-	-	-	1	1
B	18	-	1	3	1	16	-	4	14	16	10
C	19	1	-	-	-	-	-	-	-	-	-
A	20	1	-	-	-	1	-	-	-	-	-
A	21	2	-	1	-	10	2	1	2	5	3
A	22	-	1	2	-	1	-	1	2	3	-
B	23	-	-	1	1	4	-	2	3	3	1
B	24	-	-	-	1	4	-	2	9	2	2
B	25	-	-	-	-	2	-	2	-	11	-
B	26	-	-	-	-	1	-	-	1	1	1
B	27	-	-	1	-	5	-	-	2	4	3
B	28	-	-	-	-	1	-	1	1	-	-
B	29	-	-	2	-	5	-	-	4	5	2
B	30	-	-	-	-	-	-	-	2	-	1
B	31	-	-	-	-	6	-	-	2	2	1
A	32	-	-	1	-	1	-	-	1	2	1
A	33	-	-	-	-	2	-	-	1	4	-
A	34	-	-	-	-	1	-	-	-	-	-
A	35	-	-	-	-	1	-	-	-	2	-
B	36	-	-	-	-	1	-	-	2	-	-
B	37	-	-	-	-	2	-	2	4	1	1
B	38	-	-	-	-	4	-	-	1	-	1
A	39	-	-	-	-	5	-	-	-	1	-
B	40	-	-	-	-	-	-	-	-	-	-
B	41	-	-	-	-	4	-	-	1	2	1
B	42	-	-	1	1	15	-	-	7	7	3
B	43	-	-	-	-	1	-	-	1	-	-
1-43		6	2	21	5	145	2	22	109	125	52
A	44-6	-	-	-	-	1	-	-	1	5	3
C	47	-	-	-	-	-	-	-	2	2	-
A	48-9	1	-	-	-	2	-	3	3	5	-
C	50	-	-	-	-	-	-	-	1	3	3
B	51	-	-	4	-	18	-	4	14	12	8
44-51		1	-	4	-	21	-	7	21	27	14

Table B (continued)

Hoard		92.1	92.2	92-93	93-94	94	95	95-96	95-6?	96	Total
		Issues									
B	1	2	-	1	-	-	3	2	-	-	14
A	2	4	-	2	5	-	2	2	-	-	34
A	3	-	-	-	-	-	-	1	-	-	7
C	4	10	-	4	10	1	1	5	-	2	59
A	5	1	-	1	2	-	-	-	1	-	11
A	6	1	-	7	3	-	1	-	-	-	27
B	7*	18	-	15	10	3	11	9	-	1	128
B	8	7	-	9	4	1	4	6	-	-	68
B	9	1	-	2	-	-	2	3	-	-	16
C	10	-	-	-	1	-	-	-	-	-	6
C	11	1	-	1	1	-	-	3	-	-	18
C	12	2	-	3	1	-	-	-	-	-	17
A	13	-	1	-	-	-	-	5	-	-	10
A	14	7	-	9	2	1	-	7	-	-	46
B	15	-	-	-	-	-	-	1	-	-	10
B	16	20	-	10	5	2	3	14	-	-	108
B	17	-	-	1	-	-	-	2	-	-	7
B	18	14	-	32	25	1	8	20	-	-	201
C	19	1	-	1	-	-	-	-	-	-	6
A	20	-	-	1	-	-	-	1	-	-	6
A	21	8	-	6	4	-	4	10	-	-	69
A	22	2	-	3	-	-	1	-	-	-	19
B	23	5	-	5	5	2	4	5	-	-	63
B	24	9	-	6	4	2	8	5	-	1	77
B	25	6	-	9	17	-	8	3	1	-	78
B	26	2	-	2	2	-	-	2	-	-	18
B	27	11	-	10	7	2	2	5	-	-	69
B	28	2	-	1	-	-	-	1	-	-	8
B	29	5	1	7	5	2	3	2	-	-	47
B	30	1	-	1	-	-	2	-	-	-	7
B	31	1	-	2	3	-	1	1	-	-	27
A	32	-	-	-	1	-	-	-	-	-	11
A	33	-	-	-	2	-	-	1	-	-	14
A	34	3	-	-	1	-	-	-	-	-	7
A	35	-	-	1	1	-	-	1	-	1	7
B	36	-	-	2	-	-	-	3	-	-	9
B	37	6	-	6	1	-	1	-	-	-	28
B	38	1	-	2	2	1	3	1	-	3	29
A	39	-	-	5	-	1	-	1	-	-	19
B	40	1	-	-	1	-	1	1	-	-	7
B	41	4	-	7	2	-	1	6	-	-	37
B	42	3	-	8	7	-	4	3	-	-	89
B	43	-	-	2	1	-	-	2	-	-	12
1-43		159	2	184	135	19	78	134	2	8	1550
A	44-6	3	-	5	-	-	2	4	-	-	32
C	47	2	-	1	2	-	2	1	-	-	21
A	48-9	6	-	6	4	-	-	1	-	1	51
C	50	-	-	3	1	1	1	2	-	-	17
B	51	26	4	23	19	2	15	15	-	-	296
44-51		37	4	38	26	3	20	23	-	1	417

Survival of denarius issues, AD 81-96

Table B gives a clear picture of the distribution of denarii recorded in the sample of hoards. The pattern which emerges is quite impressively consistent. There is an obvious difference in the survival rate of the finer and less fine coins between the early and late hoards, but within each chronological period the hoards do contain a similar sample of coins. To illustrate more clearly the pattern of survival of coins from different periods of the reign, the denarii of Domitian can be divided into seven phases of minting, of approximately equal duration, and the proportion of coins surviving from each of these phases can be tabulated (Table C) and illustrated on histograms (Figure 1).

Phases of minting:
1 = AD 81 - AD 82, no. 1
2 = AD 82, no. 2 - AD 85, no. 3
3 = AD 85, no. 4 - AD 87
4 = AD 88 - AD 89
5 = AD 90 - AD 91
6 = AD 92 - AD 94
7 = AD 95 - AD 96

Table C

Hoards	Phases of minting							
	1	2	3	4	5	6	7	Total
Nerva-Trajan	4 3.5%	4 3.5%	8 7.0%	15 13.2%	26 22.8%	39 34.2%	18 15.8%	114
Hadrian	14 4.8%	9 3.1%	18 6.2%	49 16.8%	65 22.3%	95 32.7%	41 14.1%	291
Ant. Pius	27 7.0%	2 0.5%	22 5.7%	72 18.6%	73 18.8%	132 34.0%	60 15.5%	388
M. Aurelius	41 8.4%	3 0.6%	26 5.3%	109 22.4%	78 16.0%	161 33.1%	70 14.4%	488
Commodus	11 10.5%	- -	6 5.7%	23 21.9%	21 20.0%	30 28.6%	14 13.3%	105
Sept. Sev.	23 14.1%	1 0.6%	11 6.7%	45 27.6%	23 14.1%	42 25.8%	19 11.7%	164
Hoards 44-51	135 32.4%	1 0.2%	14 3.4%	53 12.7%	62 14.9%	108 25.9%	44 10.6%	417

Figure 1

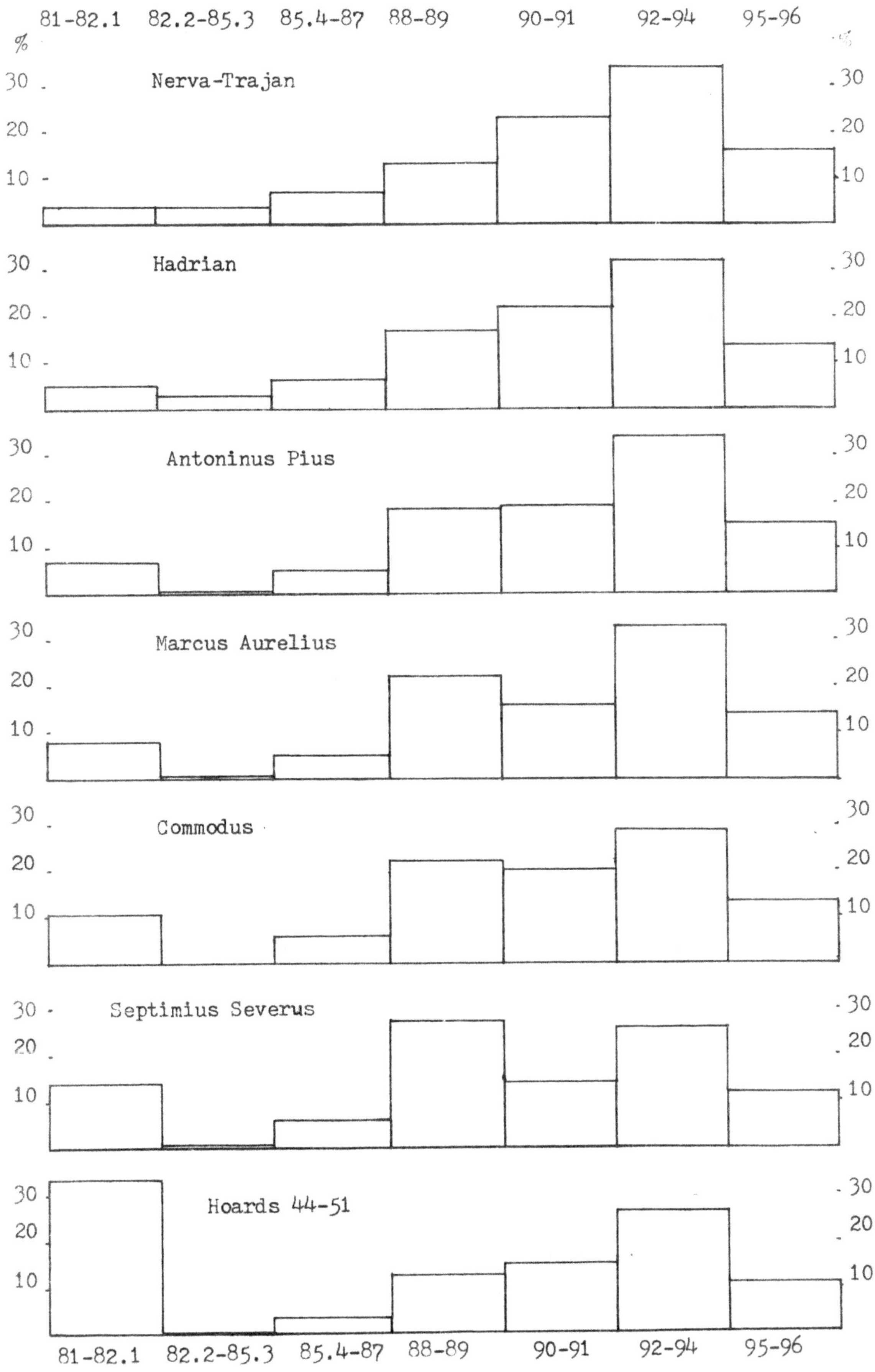
81-82.1
82.2-85.3
85.4-87
88-89
90-91
92-94
95-96
%
30
20
10
Nerva-Trajan
Hadrian
Antoninus Pius
Marcus Aurelius
Commodus
Septimius Severus
Hoards 44-51

In Figure 1 the issues of the First Period (81-82.1), which comprise the first column in the histograms, show a steady proportionate increase against the later issues until, after the debasement of Septimius Severus, they dramatically become the commonest surviving denarii of the reign. At the same time the issues of the Second Period (82.2-85.3), comprising the second column in the histograms, are poorly represented in the early hoards and then they virtually disappear altogether after the reign of Hadrian. Together, the many issues of the Third Period (85.4-96) are well represented in hoards throughout the survey, but they gradually become proportionately less common than First Period coins towards the end of the second century and into the third century. Within the Third Period each phase of minting into which the Period has been divided, represented by the third to the seventh columns in the histograms, shows, with just one exception, a proportionately consistent pattern of survival. The exceptional issues (88-89) appear to have been hoarded in larger numbers in the second half of the second century than in earlier or later periods, but otherwise the pattern of survival of Third Period coins is identical for every period of hoard burying.

The denarii of the Third Period were all struck to the same standard of fineness, so a consistent pattern of survival would be expected. They also, with only one major exception, share the same reverse types, so it would be difficult to imagine how any issues could be singled out for selective hoarding in a manner which might distort the pattern. It is worth noting that the one issue whose types stand out in contrast to the regular "Minerva" denarii of the Third Period is the "Secular Games" issue 88.3, but it was not the hoarding of these particular coins that has caused the irregularity of the column 88-89 on the histograms. A glance at the Frequency Tables (Table B) shows that these are not represented in hoards in any great numbers, but two other issues of the period, 88.1 and 88-89B4, certainly do stand out. These issues have no obvious external features to distinguish them from any others, so their increased appearance in hoards may have something to do with the availability of coins in the areas from which most of the later second century hoards come. Therefore, in order to test the effect that geographical location of hoards may have had on the survival of coins for the whole survey, a further table (Table D, with accompanying diagram, Figure 2) has been prepared, with the hoards divided according to regions A, B and C. The hoards from the reigns of Nerva, Trajan and Hadrian have been grouped together because they shared a very similar pattern in Figure 1, and it is necessary to combine them in order to obtain a sufficiently large statistical sample[19].

In Figure 2 the pattern of denarius survival appears more confused than in the histograms of Figure 1. This is not surprising because the samples involved are much smaller and therefore, inevitably, less reliable. Nevertheless, there are some striking consistencies

The First Period issues show a steady increase, and then a rapid rise in hoards 44-51, in all regions. The Second Period issues from all regions are initially quite scarce, and they soon disappear everywhere. For the Third Period the groups of issues 92-94 and 95-96 also show an almost identical pattern of survival for each region. The remaining groups of issues merit a closer examination.

Table D Geographical distribution and survival of denarius issues

Hoards		Phases of minting 1	2	3	4	5	6	7	Total
Nerva-Hadrian	A	7	1	5	17	16	26	7	79
		8.9%	1.3%	6.3%	21.5%	20.3%	32.9%	8.9%	
	B	10	7	9	35	51	73	41	226
		4.4%	3.1%	4.0%	15.5%	22.6%	32.3%	18.1%	
	C	1	5	12	12	24	35	11	100
		1.0%	5.0%	12.0%	12.0%	24.0%	35.0%	11.0%	
Anton. Pius	A	2	-	4	8	10	20	12	56
		3.6%	-	7.1%	14.3%	17.9%	35.7%	21.4%	
	B	25	2	17	61	63	110	48	326
		7.7%	0.6%	5.2%	18.7%	19.3%	33.7%	14.7%	
	C	-	-	1	3	-	2	-	6
		-	-	16.7%	50.0%	-	33.3%	-	
Marcus Aurelius	A	3	1	5	30	15	24	16	94
		3.2%	1.1%	5.3%	31.9%	16.0%	25.5%	17.0%	
	B	38	2	21	79	63	137	54	394
		9.7%	0.5%	5.3%	20.1%	16.0%	34.9%	13.7%	
Commodus	A	4	-	2	10	11	9	3	39
		10.3%	-	5.1%	25.6%	28.2%	23.1%	7.7%	
	B	7	-	4	13	10	21	11	66
		10.6%	-	6.1%	19.7%	15.2%	31.8%	16.7%	
Sept. Severus	A	3	-	3	5	1	6	1	19
		15.8%	-	15.8%	26.3%	5.3%	31.6%	5.3%	
	B	20	1	8	40	22	36	18	145
		13.9%	0.7%	5.5%	27.8%	15.3%	25.0%	12.5%	
Hoards 44-51	A	19	-	3	12	17	24	8	83
		22.9%	-	3.6%	14.5%	20.5%	28.9%	9.6%	
	B	108	1	8	41	34	74	30	296
		36.5%	0.3%	2.7%	13.9%	11.5%	25.0%	10.1%	
	C	8	-	3	-	11	10	6	38
		21.1%	-	7.9%	-	29.0%	26.3%	15.8%	

Figure 2

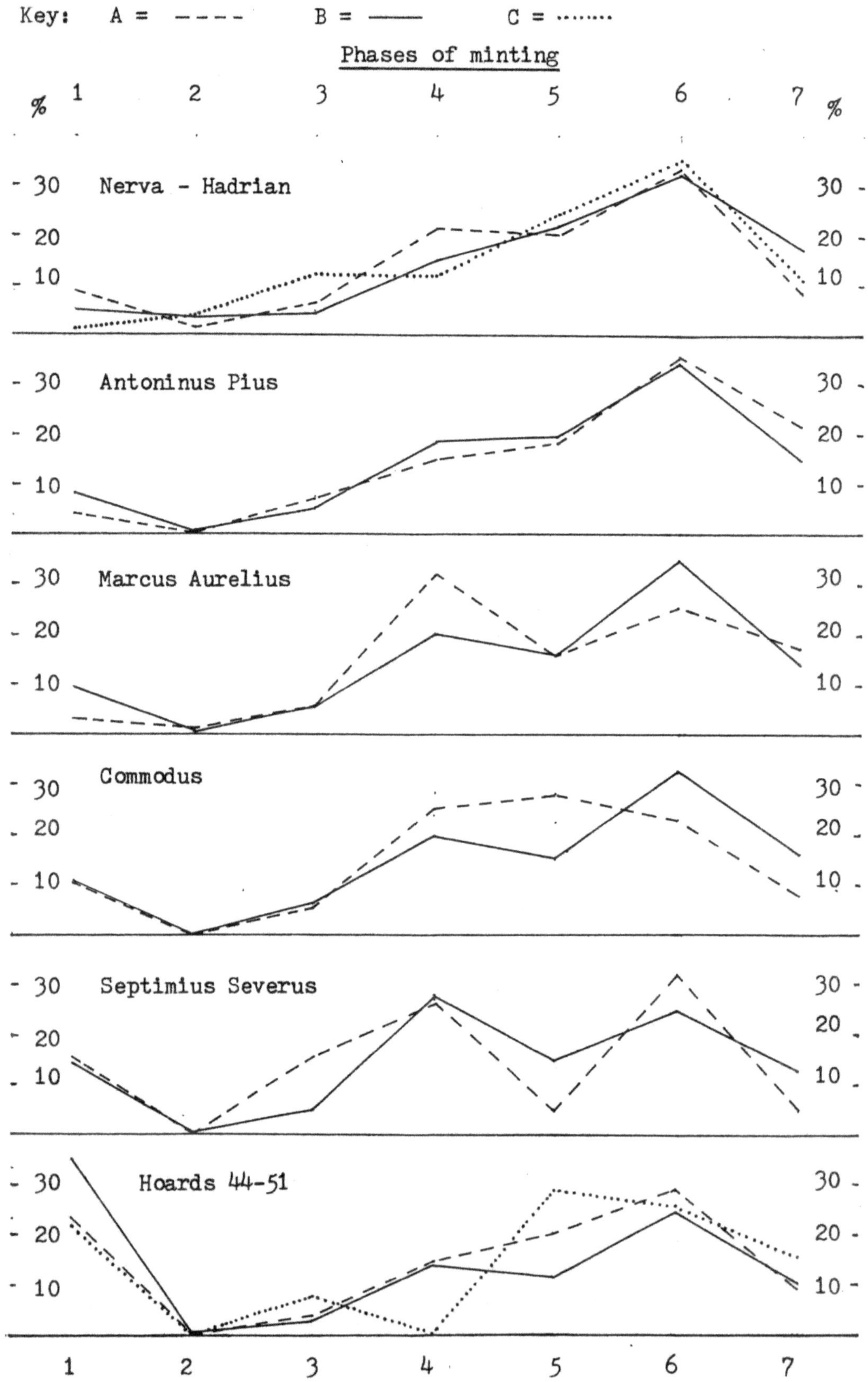
Key: A = ---- B = —— C = ...
Phases of minting
% 1 2 3 4 5 6 7 %
30 Nerva - Hadrian 30
20 20
10 10
30 Antoninus Pius 30
20 20
10 10
30 Marcus Aurelius 30
20 20
10 10
30 Commodus 30
20 20
10 10
30 Septimius Severus 30
20 20
10 10
30 Hoards 44-51 30
20 20
10 10
1 2 3 4 5 6 7

The pattern of survival for the issues 90-91 can be discussed in similar terms to those of 85.4-87. Regions A and B are very consistent apart from when the sample from A is unreliably small (under Commodus and Septimius Severus). These issues in region C in the post-Severus debasement period are unusually common, but again this sample (38 coins) is not by itself necessarily a reliable indicator.

The years 88-89 contained the issues which interrupted the otherwise consistent pattern in Figure 1. Figure 2 does not reveal any obvious trends that could provide a definite explanation for their irregularity, but a close examination of the regional differences does permit certain tentative suggestions. The hoards of region A from the second century mostly show a high proportion of coins from 88-89, although the pattern is not entirely consistent because the samples are by no means ideal. The hoards of region B provide a larger and therefore better sample. They reveal a definite and steadily increasing rise in the hoarding of the 88-89 issues in the second half of the second century, and because this region provides much the largest sample, these hoards are mostly responsible for the pattern reached in Figure 1. What then is the explanation for the increase in hoarding of these particular issues ?

One possibility is that these issues simply became increasingly available to the hoarders of region B as the second century progressed. The great majority of denarii from region B buried in the reign of Hadrian come from two hoards from Italy and Austria, whereas the B hoards buried in later reigns come predominantly from further east, often beyond the Danube. Perhaps large numbers of denarii from the issues of 88-89 were originally exported outside the Empire, for example as subsidies to tribes assisting in the defense of the Danube frontier. These coins later appear in ever increasing numbers in hoards for two reasons : 1) the main hoard-burying area is now the Danube; 2) many of these coins had gradually drifted back inside the Empire by way of trade in the period after the frontiers were stabilised (after Hadrian). This suggested reconstruction of the history of these issues is only tentative, and further research into the nature of individual hoards would be needed to test its plausibility. Nevertheless, it is worth noting that in the two periods for which data on region C was useable (Nerva - Hadrian and hoards 44-51), the hoards of this region, which was furthest removed from the European frontiers of the Empire, are the only hoards in which the issues of 88-89 are less well represented than both those of 85.4-87 and 90-91. This would seem to indicate that if an explanation does exist for the phenomenon of the 88-89 issues, it lies in the distribution of coinage to the northern "military" areas[20].

It should be emphasised that the inconsistencies revealed by the "regionalised" Figure 2 and the histograms of Figure 1 are not really very substantial. Variations of more than 10% in the survival of issues between separate regions are very rare. Almost all the wider discrepancies occur when one or more of the samples is dangerously small. It is much more significant that the different regions more often than not contain a very similar sample of coinage (with variations of less than 5% of their total content). It has to be admitted that the survey is dominated by coins buried in the frontier regions A and (especially) B, but the definite consistencies that have been revealed between hoards of all regions suggest that this sample is by no means unrepresentative[21]. The same overall chronological pattern of survival is clearly revealed by the hoards of each reign. Particularly impressive is the consistency of the First Period, Second Period, and later Third Period coin distributions. Therefore, it is justifiable to say that, collectively at least, the hoards in this survey provide a fair indication of the quantities of denarii of Domitian circulating in various periods following his death.

Size of issues according to survival rate

Using the figures provided by the hoard survey, the relative size of each denarius issue can now be estimated. Tables B and C and the histograms (Figure 1) indicated that the major turning points for the survival of denarii of Domitian were the reigns of Hadrian/Antoninus Pius and, more especially, the debasement of Septimius Severus. The hoards buried before the end of Hadrian's reign include proportionately more coins of Domitian's Second Period, and less coins of the First Period, than all later hoards; and the hoards buried after Severus's debasement include many more coins of the First Period than were to be found in the earlier hoards. Therefore, in order to take account of the different circumstances affecting the survival of denarii, the estimations of issue sizes are set out in three tables (Tables E, F and G), dealing separately with hoards 1-12 (buried in the reigns of Nerva to Hadrian), hoards 1-43 (Nerva to the debasement of Septimius Severus) and hoards 44-51 (later hoards). Because the number of coins surviving from many of the individual issues was so small, the size of each issue is best expressed as a percentage against the largest issue in the Table (ie. normalised) rather than as a percentage of the total number of coins.

In Tables E, F and G lines have been drawn to denote the separation of the three groups of issues : First Period (81-82.1), Second Period (82.2-85.3), and Third Period (85.4-96). Within these groups the individual issues should have had an equal chance of survival, so their relationship to each other would remain unchanged throughout the 150 years during which all the hoards were deposited. However, because the metallurgical composition of the coins of each group is different, the earlier withdrawal of finer coins makes comparisons between issues from different Periods very dangerous. Obviously, the most reliable figures should be those recorded in Table E, because the hoards which contributed these figures were buried before the removal of Domitian's finest coins had fully taken effect. Perhaps this sample should have excluded hoards buried later than Trajan's reign, because the withdrawal of Domitian's finest coins presumably dates from then[22], but such a sample would have been unrealistically small. Even with the reign of Hadrian added only twelve hoards could be included in Table E, the total sample is therefore still very small (405 coins) and some issues will be under-represented because they happened not to be present, whereas they probably would have appeared in a larger sample. Table F is based on a much larger sample, and it must provide the best evidence for the proportionate sizes of issues within each group, but it will present a distorted view of the Second Period issues if these are compared with those of the other Periods, because it includes data from hoards buried after these coins seem no longer to have been in general circulation. Table G includes only hoards buried (and probably assembled) after Severus's debasement. It therefore gives a very distorted picture of the relative representation of issues

Table E   Size of denarius issues, Hoards 1-12

Issue	Number of coins	% of Total	% against largest issue
81.1	2	0.5	4.3
81.2a	-	-	-
2b	-	-	-
81.3a	2	0.5	4.3
3b	9	2.2	19.2
82.1	5	1.2	10.6
82.2	-	-	-
82-83	4	1.0	8.5
83.1	-	-	-
83.2	5	1.2	10.6
84.1	-	-	-
84.2	1	0.2	2.1
85.1	-	-	-
85.2	3	0.7	6.4
85.3	-	-	-
85.4	-	-	-
85.5	4	1.0	8.5
85.6	1	0.2	2.1
86.1	4	1.0	8.5
86.2	2	0.5	4.3
86.3	1	0.2	2.1
86.4	2	0.5	4.3
86.5	2	0.5	4.3
87.1	7	1.7	14.9
87.2	3	0.7	6.4
88.1	10	2.5	21.3
88.2	2	0.5	4.3
88.3	4	1.0	8.5
88-89A	2	0.5	4.3
88-89B1	-	-	-
B2	8	2.0	17.0
B3	1	0.2	2.1
B4	31	7.7	66.0
B5	-	-	-
89	6	1.5	12.8
90	37	9.1	78.7
90-91	39	9.6	83.0
91	15	3.7	31.9
92.1	47	11.6	100.0
92.2	-	-	-
92-93	45	11.1	95.7
93-94	37	9.1	78.7
94	5	1.2	10.6
95	24	5.9	51.1
95-96	31	7.7	66.0
95-96?	1	0.2	2.1
96	3	0.7	6.4
Total	405		

Table F Size of denarius issues, Hoards 1-43

Issue	Number of coins	% of Total	% against largest issue
81.1	14	0.9	7.6
81.2a	4	0.3	2.2
2b	-	-	-
81.3a	9	0.6	5.0
3b	66	4.3	35.9
82.1	27	1.7	14.7
82.2	1	0.1	0.5
82-83	5	0.3	2.7
83.1	-	-	-
83.2	6	0.4	3.3
84.1	1	0.1	0.5
84.2	1	0.1	0.5
85.1	1	0.1	0.5
85.2	4	0.3	2.2
85.3	-	-	-
85.4	2	0.1	1.1
85.5	5	0.3	2.7
85.6	4	0.3	2.2
86.1	15	1.0	8.2
86.2	10	0.7	5.4
86.3	3	0.2	1.6
86.4	3	0.2	1.6
86.5	5	0.3	2.7
87.1	28	1.8	15.2
87.2	16	1.0	8.7
88.1	79	5.1	42.9
88.2	6	0.4	3.3
88.3	25	1.6	13.6
88-89A	6	0.4	3.3
88-89B1	2	0.1	1.1
B2	21	1.4	11.4
B3	5	0.3	2.7
B4	145	9.4	78.8
B5	2	0.1	1.1
89	22	1.4	12.0
90	109	7.0	59.2
90-91	125	8.1	67.9
91	52	3.4	28.3
92.1	159	10.3	86.4
92.2	2	0.1	1.1
92-93	184	11.9	100.0
93-94	135	8.7	73.4
94	19	1.2	10.3
95	78	5.0	42.4
95-96	134	8.6	72.8
95-96?	2	0.1	1.1
96	8	0.5	4.4
Total	1550		

Table G Size of denarius issues, Hoards 44-51

Issue	Number of coins	% of Total	% against largest issue
81.1	10	2.4	10.3
81.2a	-	-	-
2b	5	1.2	5.2
81.3a	2	0.5	2.1
3b	97	23.2	100.0
82.1	21	5.0	21.7
82.2	-	-	-
82-83	1	0.2	1.0
83.1	-	-	-
83.2	-	-	-
84.1	-	-	-
84.2	-	-	-
85.1	-	-	-
85.2	-	-	-
85.3	-	-	-
85.4	-	-	-
85.5	-	-	-
85.6	-	-	-
86.1	4	1.0	4.1
86.2	2	0.5	2.1
86.3	1	0.2	1.0
86.4	1	0.2	1.0
86.5	-	-	-
87.1	3	0.7	3.1
87.2	3	0.7	3.1
88.1	19	4.6	19.5
88.2	-	-	-
88.3	1	0.2	1.0
88-89A	1	0.2	1.0
88-89B1	-	-	-
B2	4	1.0	4.1
B3	-	-	-
B4	21	5.0	21.7
B5	-	-	-
89	7	1.7	7.2
90	21	5.0	21.7
90-91	27	6.5	27.8
91	14	3.4	14.4
92.1	37	8.9	38.1
92.2	4	1.0	4.1
92-93	38	9.1	39.2
93-94	26	6.2	26.8
94	3	0.7	3.1
95	20	4.8	20.6
95-96	23	5.5	23.7
95-96?	-	-	-
96	1	0.2	1.0
Total	417		

between the three Periods, because of the drastic reduction in survival of all denarii outside the First Period. However, Table G is of some value in checking the relative size of issues from within the First Period.

To summarise, it can be said that Table E provides in theory the most reliable guide, but its usefulness is reduced because it is based on a small sample. Table F represents a reliable guide to the relative sizes of most issues, based on the largest available sample, but it has to be remembered that the issues of Domitian's Second Period will be under-represented, so comparisons between issues in the three separate Periods should be made with great care. On the other hand, within each of the three Periods the relative sizes of the separate issues in all three Tables should be reliable[23].

Die studies

One way of attempting to confirm the reliability of the figures in Tables E, F and G is to undertake die studies of the denarius issues. By comparing the designs on all available specimens it is possible to estimate the total number of dies which may have been used to produce an issue. There are, of course, several problems involved in such a study.

Firstly, there is the availability of examples for study; a large number of coins are required before any pattern of die-identity is likely to emerge (unless the issue is very small). Also, it can sometimes be difficult to compare the dies themselves. Most coins vary greatly in their condition, and it can be quite hopeless attempting to recognise the die which produced the design on a very worn or damaged piece, especially on small coins such as denarii. There are also major difficulties resulting from the processes of die production. Some coins have dies which appear virtually identical to each other, yet have certain minor features (eg. letter spacing) which differ slightly. Dies were obviously produced from recognised patterns which the die-engravers would copy as carefully as possible, thereby making it difficult to tell the dies apart. There is also evidence for widespread re-cutting of dies. A die which was getting old might require "touching up" in order to increase clarity of striking; or a change in imperial titles might require dies to be re-cut with altered legends. It is even possible that coins of one imperial personage could be struck from dies originally used for another, the portrait and legend having been altered (sometimes only slightly) to identify the new person.

Despite these many difficulties it can still be said that die-studies, laborious as they are, so far represent the only scientific method available for increasing our knowledge on the size of coin issues. Therefore, selected die studies of Domitian's denarii have been made. Two issues which the hoard survey clearly suggested were very different in size, and which would have been sufficiently large to be well represented in the trays of museum collections, were chosen for a detailed die-examination. It was hoped that such a study would confirm that the hoard survey gives a reliable indication of the relative size of denarius issues. The issues selected were 81.3b and 92.1. In addition, a number of "provisional" die-studies of a more restricted nature were undertaken on all the issues of the Second Period, so that additional evidence might be made available for understanding the coinage of this most interesting phase of mint activity. The results of these die studies are included in the following commentary on sizes of issues[24].

Commentary on size of denarius issues, AD 81-96

First Period : issues 81.1-82.1

All the coins of 81 issued after Domitian's accession were produced within a period of only three and a half months, from September 13th until the end of the year. The issues 81.1 to 81.3a were all very small; the dies which struck them were presumably replaced quite rapidly by new dies which included and rearranged more of the Emperor's newly acquired titles[25]. In contrast, issue 81.3b, which represents the culmination of the process of legend development in the early months of the reign, was undoubtedly and overwhelmingly the largest issue of the year. In fact, according to Tables E to G this was probably the largest issue of denarii minted in the first half of the reign. It has already been explained that it could not have begun production until November or December 81, so this issue represents a very heavy and sudden emission of new coinage.

The die study of issue 81.3b revealed the following results:-

178 denarii = 121 obverse dies (three types[26])
101 reverse dies (eight types)

Not many die links were counted in a large sample of coins, so there can be no doubt that many more dies would have been used than are indicated here. It is interesting that more obverse than reverse dies were noted. It is generall true that reverse dies are more numerous because, being the unfixed punch die that received the hammer blows, they more often needed to be replaced because of deterioration through wear. However, many of these dies would have been employed for issue 3a (obverse) and 2b (reverse), so the comparative condition and hence life expectancy of the dies of this issue should not be considered in isolation[27].

Issue 82.1, the last denarius issue of the First Period, was apparently larger than any produced before 81.3b, but it was very much smaller than that last issue of the preceding year. This is perhaps somewhat surprising because it was probably under production for a longer period, the only other issue of 82 being apparently very small, and therefore presumably of short duration (although we do not know for how long output may have been suspended between issues 82.1 and 82.2 while preparations were made to introduce the new standards of fineness). In any case, issue 82.1 is a very interesting issue for comparative purposes; it especially highlights the importance the issue which preceded it (81.3b).

Second Period : issues 82.2-85.3

Tables E and F indicate that, according to hoard evidence, only modest emissions of denarii appeared throughout this Period. Because of the unusually high fineness of these coins it is appreciated that they were not likely to survive in circulation for long, and therefore the hoard evidence is less reliable than usual. However, the scarcity of denarii from these issues in even the earliest hoards suggests that they could never have been very numerous. Indeed, the evidence of hoards buried as early as the later years of Domitian's reign, which would normally be expected to contain even the finest recently struck coins, seems to corroborate that of the hoards of Table E. Two hoards, from Otricoli (Italy) and Cirencester (England), with latest coins dated to 90 and 93-94, contained not one Second Period denarius out of a total of eleven coins dated to Domitian's reign[28].

The "provisional" die studies revealed the following results:-

82.2	:	14 denarii	= 14 obverse dies (one type) 12 reverse dies (one type)
82-83(a-b)	:	30 denarii	= 25 obverse dies (one type) 24 reverse dies (two types)
82-83(f-h)	:	68 denarii	= 27 obverse dies (one type) 28 reverse dies (three types)
82-83(i)	:	14 denarii[29]	= 5 obverse dies (one type) 9 reverse dies (one type)
83.1	:	2 denarii	= 2 obverse dies (one type) 1 reverse die (one type)
83.2	:	24 denarii	= 18 obverse dies (one type) 21 reverse dies (four types)
84.2a	:	14 denarii	= 9 obverse dies (three types) 12 reverse dies (four types)
85.1	:	15 denarii	= 11 obverse dies (two types) 12 reverse dies (five types)

These die studies have obviously not progressed far enough for any firm conclusions to be drawn, but from the die links so far counted it is clear that all the above issues were considerably smaller than the largest issue of the First Period (81.3b). The one issue for which there was sufficient readily available material for a detailed study, 82-83(f-h : Domitia), yielded far fewer dies than issue 81.3b had at the same stage of study. Also, even for issues where very few specimens were inspected it is noticeable that die links began to appear.

Therefore, all the evidence seems to confirm that although the hoard survey gives an exaggerated impression of the limited nature of these issues, because their almost total disappearance after the reign of Hadrian has caused them to be under-represented in the totals, the issues of the Second Period must be classed as amongst the smallest emissions of denarii in the reign. However, several of the coin types introduced in this Period seem to have had a special commemorative aspect, so it is perhaps unfair to compare their volume of emission with earlier and later issues which employ standard types. Also, the rapidly changing sequence of reverse types and the variations in portraiture and legend form indicate that this was a period of experimentation.

Third Period (I) : issues 85.4-87.2

In this first phase of Domitian's Third Period of coinage emission of denarii continues to be relatively low, although there are signs of a definite increase in comparison with the Second Period. The Third Period issues of 85 seem to have been very small. It is possible that coins from these issues (85.4-85.6) might have been confused with denarii of the same year belonging to the Second Period, and therefore removed from circulation as early as the finer coins[30]. Also, issues 85.5 and 85.6 were both produced in the short period between mid-September and December of that year; but we have already seen (in 81) that large denarius issues could be produced within brief time spans.

The five issues minted in 86 suggest that a steady, and slightly increased, output of denarii was continuing. The first two issues are the largest, but these span the period January to mid-September, whereas the three subsequent (smaller) issues have all to be accomodated within the months mid-September to end of December. The total output of denarii in 87 was contributed by only two issues, but a similar pattern to 86 emerges, with the first issue (January to mid-September) having apparently twice the volume of the second issue (mid-September to December). The closely dated issues of 85-87 clearly suggest that emission of denarii was spread throughout the year, and it appears that the volume of output is closely related to the duration of each issue[31].

Third Period (II) : issues 88.1-89

In 88 there was, according to Tables E-G, a substantial increase in emission of denarii. 88.1 appears to have been the largest issue of the reign so far; it contrasts sharply with the very small succeeding issue, 88.2, which presumably came into production shortly before mid-September 88. The third issue of 88 was minted after mid-September and was probably issued to coincide with the Secular Games (celebrated in the October) which provided the inspiration for the reverse legends and types. Although the designs have a special commemorative purpose this issue was struck in quite large quantities and was obviously a proper currency issue.

The denarius issues classified as 88-89A and 88-89B1-5 show considerable variations in size. Issue 88-89B1 was produced at some date between mid-September and early November 88, and as this period also included the Secular Games coins (88.3) it is no surprise that it appears to be such a small issue. Considerably larger is issue B2 which would have been produced mostly later in 88, presumably after the Secular Games issue. B3, B4 and B5 would all have been issued within the period January to mid-September 89. The exceptionally large issue B4, apparently much greater than the previous largest issue 88.1, might have been produced over a period of several months, and it is sandwiched between two much smaller issues. The irregular denarii which constitute the silver of issue 88-89A are rare finds in hoards and, in common with the variant denarii of 87 and 88, they could not have been an important element in the currency.

Issue 89 seems to have been the largest of the mid-September to December issues since 81.3b. It confirms the impression that there has been a general increase in denarius emission.

Third Period (III) : issues 90-91

The three issues of this period again vary in size according to the extent of time during which they could have been produced. Thus the largest issue (90-91) covers a full twelve month period, the second largest (90) an eight and a half month period, and the smallest (91) a three and a half month period. Altogether, these issues confirm the impression gained from the issues of 88 to 89, which is that much greater quantities of new denarii were being issued than earlier in the reign.

Third Period (IV) : issues 92.1-94

This period contains the largest denarius issues of the reign. At first the issues vary in size relative to the lengths of time during which they could have been minted. Thus, according to Table F (the most reliable guide for Third Period denarii), issue 92.1 (about eight months) is a little smaller than issue 92-93 (a full twelve months); whereas the tiny issue 92.2 must, like issue 88.2, have been squeezed into a very short space of time[32]. But more important is the fact that the two issues 92.1 and 92-93 seem undoubtedly to have been the largest issues of denarii in the reign. The die study of issue 92.1 revealed the following results:-

155 denarii = 140 obverse dies (one type)
142 reverse dies (four types)

Although a large number of coins was examined not many die links were observed. It is clear that many more dies than have so far been counted must have been employed to produce this issue. A brief comparison with the results of the die study of issue 81.3b, which yielded fewer dies from a larger number of coins examined, suggests that 92.1 must have been a much larger issue. The die study therefore confirms the impression given by the hoard survey, which is that at this time there was a massive output of denarii.

However, from a peak in 92 and 92-93 there then seems to have been a definite reduction in output, possibly later in 93, and certainly in 94. In Table F the twelve-months issue 93-94 registers a reduction of about 25% on the output of the previous issue (92-93); then in the mid-September to December issue of 94 there is a further drop of almost 50%.

Third Period (V) : issues 95-96

In the last two years of Domitian's reign the two main issues of denarii (issues 95 and 95-96) were, according to Tables E and F, not as large as the great issues from 92 and 93, but, on the other hand, they were large enough to indicate that large quantities of new coinage were still being produced towards the end of the reign. However, only two denarii of the "temple" issue (95-96?) were identified in the hoard survey; these unusual coins must therefore have been issued very sparingly. Also, issue 96, although it was a normal currency issue, with the usual reverse types, was produced and issued in perhaps less than a week so it is not surprising that it appears so small.

Calculations of issue sizes from die counts

The die studies have in general provided confirmation of the reliability of the denarius hoard survey. Although most of the studies were far from complete, the relationship between the numbers of dies counted for the separate issues examined tends to correspond in broad terms with the representation of the issues in the hoard survey. In the course of the die studies it was also observed that the patterns established early in the process of die counting were almost invariably maintained throughout the studies. Thus, the issues which yielded early die links usually provided many more links before long, confirming that they must have been very small issues, whereas the opposite was true of the larger issues (eg. 92.1, which did not yield a single obv or rev die link until more than forty coins had been examined). This general consistency in the progress of the die studies is significant; it suggests that even the most superficial die counts of coinage issues can be of some use. Die studies can also easily be shown to be a much more reliable guide to the commonness or rarity of individual issues than estimates based purely on numbers of examples observed in museum trays[33]. For instance, issue 81.3b is almost invariably better represented in museum collections than issue 92.1, simply because it contains twice as many reverse types. But the die studies confirm that issue 92.1 must have been a much larger issue (confirming the findings of the hoard survey).

In recent years attempts have been made to calculate the total number of dies which may have been used to produce an issue of coinage[34]. It was not the main intention of this survey to make estimations of mint output based on calculations of total die numbers. However, as an experiment the "Lyon" equation for calculating die numbers can be applied to the selected die studies of Domitian's denarii.

The "Lyon" equation[35]:-

$$\frac{Dk}{C} = \frac{1 - e^{-R}}{R}$$

Dk = number of dies identified
C = number of coins
D = total calculated number of dies
R = C/D
e = the natural logarithm base (2.71828)

Using this equation the die studies of Domitian's denarius issues revealed the following results[36] (observations of the first die links in the course of each die count are also included).

Issue	No. of coins examined		first die link noted	No. of dies identified	calculated total of dies
81.3b	178	obv	(18)	121	214 ± 18
		rev	(18)	101	141 ± 9
82.2	14	obv	(-)	14	-
		rev	(7)	12	44 ± 21
82-83(a-b)	30	obv	(13)	25	80 ± 24
		rev	(13)	24	65 ± 17

Issue	No. of coins examined		first die link noted	No. of dies identified	calculated total of dies
82-83(f-h)	68	obv	(12)	27	30 ± 2
		rev	(11)	28	32 ± 3
83.1	2	obv	(-)	2	-
		rev	(2)	1	-
83.2	24	obv	(9)	18	40 ± 10
		rev	(18)	21	88 ± 34
84.2	14	obv	(5)	9	15 ± 4
		rev	(18)	12	44 ± 21
85.1	15	obv	(7)	11	23 ± 7
		rev	(8)	12	32 ± 12
92.1	155	obv	(43)	140	741 ± 130
		rev	(45)	142	862 ± 163

These estimated die-totals must be treated with caution. It is especially important to note the standard deviations in the final column. In the more comprehensive die studies (81.3b, 82-83(f-h), and 92.1) the standard deviation is small, apart from issue 92.1 for which the shortage of die links after as many as 155 coins had been examined suggests that the issue was so massive that many more coins would have to be inspected before the study could be expected to yield satisfactory results. Similarly, most of the die studies of the Second Period issues have relatively large standard deviations. These die counts were mostly no more than experimental, so accurate results were not anticipated; but they still provide useful figures. For instance, according to the hoard survey (Tables E, F) issue 83.2 was probably the most substantial of these generally very small issues. The die study was not very complete, but it can be said that after only 24 coins had been examined there were enough die links to suggest that the issue was only small, comprising about forty obverse dies. Thus the die study and the projected die-total calculations have provided confirmation that even one of the largest of the Second Period issues was probably a quite limited issue by most standards. The early appearances of first die links throughout the Second Period are also worth noting.

It must be stressed that the calculated die-totals are only broad estimates. The equation adopted took no account of the number of coins in each sample which were struck from the same single die. Thus no recognition was given to the fact that one die may have yielded five links whereas many dies connected only two coins; and of course there were many coins for which no die links were observed. Obviously, some dies would have produced far more coins than others. But what the calculations do provide are figures for die-totals which give a more dramatic impression of issue sizes than the basic numbers of identified dies, and these figures also provide an opportunity for calculating estimates for total output.

Annual output of denarii and rate of production

When the information provided by the hoard survey and the die-studies is combined it becomes possible to make estimates from the calculated die-totals of the annual rate of denarius emission from the mint of Rome throughout the reign of Domitian. Such estimates, of course, depend on the reliability of the "Lyon" equation for calculating the die-totals, and also on the reliability of any guess on coinage output per die. For the purposes of this experiment I have decided to adopt M.H. Crawford's suggestion for die output of 30,000 coins per die, which he estimated for production of denarii in the Roman Republic[37]. The method I am using for estimating total output is quite simple. It is based on establishing a relationship between calculated die-total estimates for issues included in the die study and numbers of examples recorded in the hoard survey (Tables E, F). If this relationship is, firstly, accepted as reliable, and secondly, used by extrapolation for establishing die-totals for all other issues included in the hoard survey though not in the die study, an estimate of die-totals for the entire reign can be made. If these figures are then multiplied by 30,000 and arranged into annual production periods an estimate for total denarius output and rate of production can be calculated. These results take no account of the fact that many issues were probably produced in fits and starts, perhaps with instances of heavy emission interspersed with long blank periods[38]. Nevertheless, the estimates provide an interesting, though extremely tentative, suggestion of the annual rate of denarius production, based on statistical evidence.

The calculations of die-totals and output per issue are set out in Tables H and J, dealing separately with the data from hoards 1-12 and hoards 1-43. For the First and Third Periods of Domitian's denarii the calculations were made as follows.-

Issue	die-calculation		Hoards 1-12	Hoards 1-43
81.3b	214 obv / 141 rev	(ave. 177.5 dies)	9 coins	66 coins
92.1	741 obv / 862 rev	(ave. 801.5 dies)	47 coins	159 coins

From hoards 1-12 (Table E) the ratio of recorded coins to die-totals is:-

First Period : $177.5 \div 9 = 19.72$ (issue 81.3b) = approx. 20

Third Period : $801.5 \div 47 = 17.05$ (issue 92.1) = approx. 17

From hoards 1-43 (Table F) the ratio of recorded coins to die-totals is:-

First Period : $177.5 \div 66 = 2.69$ (issue 81.3b) = approx. 2.7

Third Period : $801.5 \div 159 = 5.04$ (issue 92.1) = approx. 5.0

Thus, to establish die-totals, for Table H the numbers of coins recorded in Table E are multiplied by 20 for each First Period issue, and by 17 for each Third Period issue. For Table J the numbers recorded in Table F are multiplied by 2.7 for each First Period issue, and by 5.0 for

Tables H, J Numbers of denarii per issue

Issue[39]	H : Hoards 1-12 dies	H : Hoards 1-12 coins	J : Hoards 1-43 dies	J : Hoards 1-43 coins
81.1	40	1,200,000	37.8	1,134,000
81.2a	-	-	10.8	324,000
2b	-	-	-	-
81.3a	40	1,200,000	24.3	729,000
3b	177.5 av.	5,325,000	177.5 av.	5,325,000
82.1	100	3,000,000	72.9	2,187,000
82.2	44	1,320,000	44	1,320,000
82-83	103.5 av.	3,105,000	103.5 av.	3,105,000
83.1	-	-	-	-
83.2	64	1,920,000	64	1,920,000
*84.1	-	-	15.6 av.	469,500
84.2	29.5 av.	885,000	29.5 av.	885,000
85.1	27.5 av.	825,000	27.5 av.	825,000
*85.2	56.25 av.	1,687,500	62.6 av.	1,878,000
85.3	-	-	-	-
85.4	-	-	10	300,000
85.5	68	2,040,000	25	750,000
85.6	17	510,000	20	600,000
86.1	68	2,040,000	75	2,250,000
86.2	34	1,020,000	50	1,500,000
86.3	17	510,000	15	450,000
86.4	34	1,020,000	15	450,000
86.5	34	1,020,000	25	750,000
87.1	119	3,570,000	140	4,200,000
87.2	51	1,530,000	80	2,400,000
88.1	170	5,100,000	395	11,850,000
88.2	34	1,020,000	30	900,000
88.3	68	2,040,000	125	3,750,000
88-89A	34	1,020,000	30	900,000
88-89B1	-	-	10	300,000
B2	136	4,110,000	105	3,150,000
B3	17	510,000	25	750,000
B4	527	15,810,000	725	21,750,000
B5	-	-	10	300,000
89	102	3,060,000	110	3,300,000
90	629	18,870,000	545	16,350,000
90-91	663	19,890,000	625	18,750,000
91	255	7,650,000	260	7,800,000
92.1	801.5 av.	24,045,000	801.5 av.	24,045,000
92.2	-	-	10	300,000
92-93	765	22,950,000	920	27,600,000
93-94	629	18,870,000	675	20,250,000
94	85	2,550,000	95	2,850,000
95	408	12,240,000	390	11,700,000
95-96	527	15,810,000	670	20,100,000
95-96?	17	510,000	10	300,000
96	51	1,530,000	40	1,200,000
Total		211,312,500		231,946,500

each Third Period issue. For the Second Period there was no need to extrapolate the figures from the major die studies for use on the hoard survey coin numbers, because "provisional" die study figures exist for almost all the issues of this Period and, however inadequate these may be, they are surely better than a calculation based on the meagre totals for Second Period coins recorded in Tables E and F.

For the estimates of output in Tables H and J the calculated die totals have simply been multiplied by 30,000. The output figures for each issue can now be arranged into years of production and added together to provide estimates of annual output (together with monthly rate of production). These calculations are set out in two separate tables. Table K lists the output estimated from the figures of Table H, and Table L lists the output estimated from Table J. Although both tables use data calculated from the same die studies and the same survey of hoards there are notable, though not very great, differences in the estimated totals. These differences are caused by the changes in the survival pattern of denarii of Domitian resulting from the withdrawal of finer coins in the second century. It might be assumed that Table K presents the more accurate estimates, because they were calculated from data which should have been least affected by the withdrawal of finer coins. However, the sample for Table K was very much smaller than that for Table L and therefore it could have been distorted in the multiplication. It also appears that, according to the estimates of issue sizes in Tables H and J, some issues produced no coins, because no examples were found in the hoard survey. This is obviously impossible because we know that such issues of coinage exist. I had considered giving an arbitrary minimum figure for the output of these issues but, if the calculations for the issues that were represented in the hoard survey are to be accepted at all, it is necessary to leave the data as it stands. These figures of nil output in Tables H and J are obviously false, but it is hoped that the totals for the other issues of the same years will, in their fluctuations, neutralise any such discrepancies when the output is considered over each full year (in Tables K and L).

Throughout these Tables there will inevitably be distortions, resulting largely from the multiplication of sometimes very small numbers (based on chance appearances in hoards of perhaps uncommon coins) by quite large factors. There are particular difficulties in the Second Period. There is obviously an imbalance in the representation of, for example, issues 82-83 and 83.2 according to estimates of their totals based on ("provisional") die studies. The size of issue 85.2, which has been estimated on an extrapolation from these issues, is therefore suspect. Further distortions, in First and Third Period output, occur because the representation numbers have been multiplied by factors which have been rounded up or down, according to how exactly the results of the die studies of issues 81.3b and 92.1 were divisible by the numbers of examples of these issues in the hoard survey. This causes issues 81.3b and 92.1 to be very slightly under- or over-estimated relative to the other issues in their Periods. However, it has to be remembered that the purpose of these calculations is to make only a very tentative and approximate estimate of denarius output, so these relatively minor inaccuracies are unimportant. The Second Period estimates present the greatest problem. A more detailed study of these issues would be needed in order to confirm reliability; but at least these calculations offer a clear indication of output in

Table K Output of denarii (from Hoards 1-12 - Tables E, H)

	Annual	Monthly rate
AD 81	7,725,000	2,207,143 (3½ months)
AD 82	5,872,500 (1,552,500 from 82-83)	489,000
AD 83	3,472,500 (1,552,500 from 82-83	289,375
AD 84	885,000	73,750
AD 85	5,062,500	421,875
AD 86	5,610,000	467,500
AD 87	5,100,000	425,000
AD 88	12,780,000 (4,620,000 from 88-89)	1,065,000
AD 89	19,890,000 (16,830,000 from 88-89)	1,657,500
AD 90	24,671,250 (5,801,250 from 90-91)	2,055,937
AD 91	21,738,750 (14,088,750 from 90-91)	1,811,562
AD 92	30,738,750 (6,693,750 from 92-93)	2,561,562
AD 93	21,760,000 (16,256,250 from 92-93; 5,503,750 from 93-94)	1,813,333
AD 94	15,916,250 (13,366,250 from 93-94)	1,326,354
AD 95	17,000,000 (4,760,000 from 95-96)	1,416,666
AD 96	13,090,000 (11,560,000 from 95-96)	1,540,000 (8½ months)
Total	211,312,500 denarii = 14,087,500 per annum (average output)	

Table L   Output of denarii (from Hoards 1-43 - Tables F, J)

	Annual	Monthly rate
AD 81	7,512,000	2,146,286 (3½ months)
AD 82	5,059,500 (1.552,500 from 82-83)	421,625
AD 83	3,472,500 (1,552,500 from 82-83)	289,375
AD 84	1,354,500	112,875
AD 85	4,353,000	362,750
AD 86	5,400,000	450,000
AD 87	6,600,000	550,000
AD 88	20,400,000 (3,900,000 from 88-89)	1,700,000
AD 89	26,550,000 (23,250,000 from 88-89)	2,212,500
AD 90	21,818,750 (5,468,750 from 90-91)	1,818,229
AD 91	21,081,250 (13,281,250 from 90-91)	1,756,771
AD 92	32,395,000 (8,050,000 from 92-93)	2,699,583
AD 93	25,456,250 (19,550,000 from 92-93; 5,906,250 from 93-94)	2,121,354
AD 94	17,193,750 (14,343,750 from 93-94)	1,432,812
AD 95	17,650,000 (5,950,000 from 95-96)	1,470,833
AD 96	15,650,000 (14,450,000 from 95-96)	1,841,176 (8½ months)

Total   231,946,500 denarii = 15,463,100 per annum (average output) this period relative to the rest of the reign.

The figures from Tables K and L can be illustrated most effectively in the form of histograms (Figures 3 and 4). In these histograms output is measured according to the monthly rate of production, so that the volume of new denarii produced for each year of Domitian's reign is represented by the area within each column in the histograms, the width of which varies when a period of less than twelve months is involved[40].

These Figures provide quite dramatic pictures of the pattern of denarius output in Domitian's reign. The heavy emission in the first few months of the reign can be seen in stark contrast to the meagre output of the next six years (82 to 87), and this in turn can be contrasted with the sustained high levels of output operating between the years 88 and 96. This outline pattern of denarius output, and the historical background behind it, will be discussed in more detail later in this work, in conjunction with the output of the gold aureus and major bronze issues from Rome, which now have to be investigated.

Figure 3 Output of denarii (from Table K)

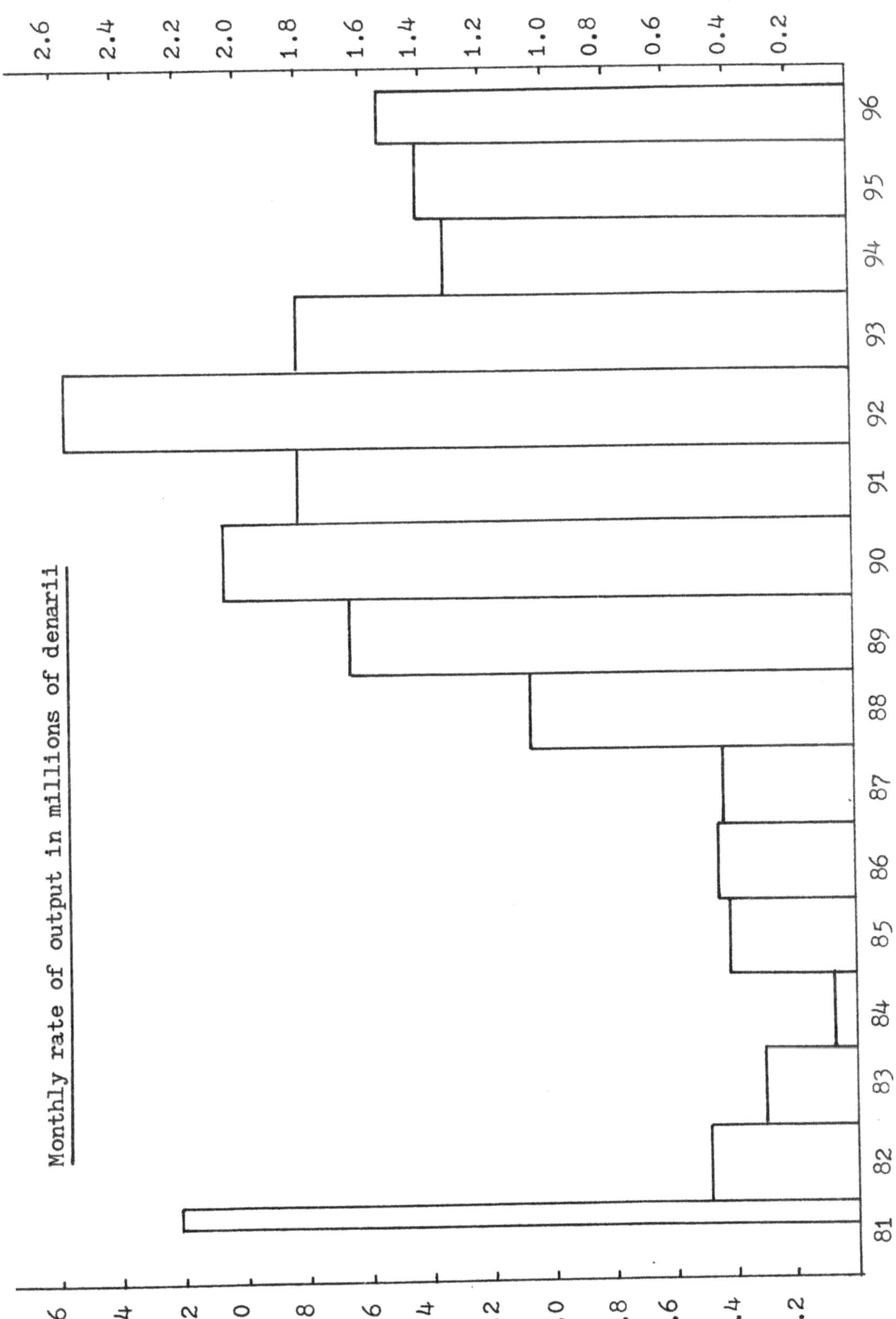

Figure 4 Output of denarii (from Table L)

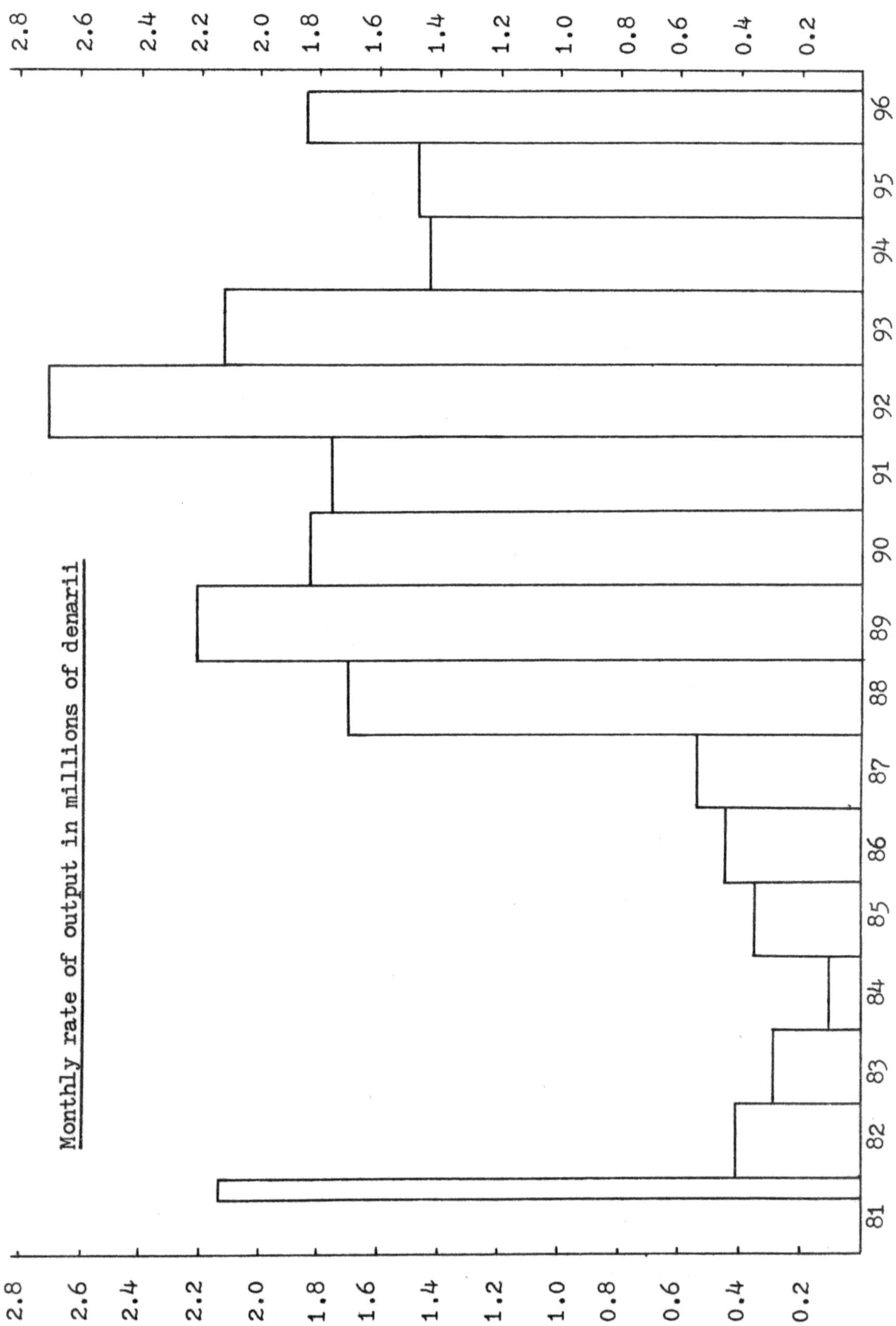

NOTES

1. Most of the principles discussed here also apply to the aureus survey. For the importance of the denarius (and aureus) for finances see below, p.158.

2. However, from what I have observed, the scattered evidence from loose finds tends to corroborate the hoard figures.

3. See P. Grierson's Presidential address in NC 1965, i-xii, NC 1966, i-xv.

4. For a discussion of hoards as concealed savings see A.S. Robertson, in Coins and the Archaeologist, 13-15.

5. cf. A.S. Robertson, op. cit., 28-34.

6. cf. K. Hopkins, JRS 1980, 113.

7. The most impressive examples have come from Scandinavia. The Lohe hoard from Sweden (B. Thordeman, NC 1948, 188-204) illustrated a remarkable similarity in composition when compared to the output of the Swedish mint in the 17th and 18th centuries (pp. 197-200), and the author found that this phenomenon was not just restricted to this one large hoard, but was confirmed by a sample of 30 other finds (pp. 200-1). It has also recently been noted that numbers of Swedish coins found in hoards in Finland show a remarkably close correlation with numbers issued (M.H. Crawford, NC 1979, 272 - reviewing P. Sarvas, "De finska myntskatterna fran 1700-talet", NNÅ 1967, 23-146). In this study it was also observed that the pattern in a single hoard was the same as the overall pattern from all the hoards together.

8. The name "Gresham's Law" was first used by the economist H.D. Macleod in 1857. He believed that the principle that "bad money drives out good" was first explained by Sir Thomas Gresham, financial agent of the English court, 1551-1567. The principle was, in fact, known well before Gresham's time.

9. For the effect of "Gresham's Law" on the Roman imperial coinage, see S. Bolin, State and Currency.., (esp. pp. 58-62).

10. D.R. Walker, Metrology III, 121-138.

11. S. Bolin, State and Currency.., 227-8.

12. Bolin's assessment of the survival of Domitian's denarii was based on the assumption that there were no extremely fine pieces (above 92.5% silver); but he was aware of the likelihood that coins from the start of the reign survived into the third century because of their low fineness (p.231).

13. H. Mattingly, BMCRE III, lxxxvi-xciii. D.R. Walker has discovered that Trajan actually began dropping the silver standard of the denarius earlier, in 104 (Metrology II, 56).

14. See R.E.M. Wheeler, Rome Beyond the Imperial Frontiers (London, 1954), 83-8, 164-71.

15. See Appendix 1 for information on the composition and intactness of hoards in the denarius survey (in cases where such information was available). Aureus hoards are listed more briefly in Appendix 2.

16. See A.S. Robertson in Coins and the Archaeologist, 17-21, for a discussion of the composition of Romano-British hoards, including the apparent selection of unusual coins.

17. See Appendix 1. In the Castagnaro hoard (no. 7, marked * in Table B) the coins were listed in groups according to consular title and reverse type, without indications of the numbers of each separate variety involved (eg. "5 examples of Cohen nos. 119 and 120"). In these cases (which were confined to the later issues - all within the Third Period) I have divided the totals as equally as possible between the separate coins involved.

18. See D.R. Walker, Metrology III, 130 (also figs. 14-15, p.141-2).

19. In Figure 2 under Antoninus Pius Group C has been omitted because the sample (6 coins from one hoard) was too small to be relevant.

20. cf. K. Hopkins, JRS 1980, 112.

21. Note that the large Castagnaro hoard (Po valley, Italy) has the same pattern of distribution as contemporary hoards from the frontiers.

22. The Tables appear to confirm that the disappearance of Domitian's finest denarii would have begun in earnest with Trajan's debasement (104-7) and his calling-in of old, worn denarii (107).

23. The remarkable consistency in the metrological composition of Domitian's denarii from issues 82.2-85.3 and 85.4-96 greatly facilitates the making of comparisons; note the extremely low standard deviations revealed by the analyses in D.R. Walker, Metrology I, 96-99.

24. The two major die studies were based on a selection of material from sale catalogues and in trade, plus all the available examples from the museums of the following cities (see Appendix 3):- Bacau, Basel, Belfast, Berlin, Brussels, Bucharest, Cambridge, Copenhagen, Edinburgh, Glasgow, The Hague, Krakow, Liverpool, London, Milan, Munich, New York, Oslo, Oxford, Paris, Rome, Stockholm, Varna, Vienna, Winterthur, Zurich. The "provisional" die studies made use of the collections in Berlin, Cambridge, Glasgow, Livorno, London, Milan, New York, Oxford, Paris and Vienna, plus a sample of sale catalogue material.

25. See above, p. 13.

26. Including the two varieties with legend ..DIVI VESP F DOMITIAN.., head left and right.

27. Die links exist between coins of issues 81.2a and 3a, and issues 81.2b and 3b.

28. Otricoli: S.L. Cesano, Notizie degli Scavi di Antichita 1935, 366-380; Cirencester: R.A.G. Carson and A.M. Burnett, Recent Coin Hoards from Roman Britain (Brit. Mus. occ. paper no. 5, London 1979), 7-8.

29. This type was originally omitted from the die studies because it has only recently been attributed to Domitian's reign. The sample is therefore based only on sale catalogues, plus the London specimen (BMC Titus 137).

30. Note the aegis, which was one of the notable features on many obverses of denarii in the latter part of the Second Period, was still used for issue 85.4, though this was the last occasion on which it appeared on denarii of Domitian (regular issues).

31. This argues against Mattingly's proposal (BMCRE II, lxxxiv) that most coinage seemed to be issued in the first half of each year.

32. See I. Carradice, ZPE 1978, 159-60.

33. eg. as RIC II provides for "rarity" values.

34. eg. C.S.S. Lyon, Num Circ 1965, 180-1; G.F. Carter, "A graphical method for calculating the approximate total number of dies from die-link statistics of Ancient coins", in W.A. Oddy (ed.), Scientific Studies in Numismatics (Brit. Mus. occ. paper no. 18, London 1980), 17-29.

35. This equation was discussed in the 1979 Archaeometry Conference at the British Museum. A modified equation, taking into consideration underproduction by a small number of dies, was also discussed and it was suggested that the modified equation would probably be more suitable for estimating total sizes of issues (G.F. Carter, op. cit.). However, for the purpose of this study the initial equation, which avoids making subjective estimations of underproduction, is considered adequate.

36. Mr. M. Cowell of the British Museum Research Laboratory made these calculations on the British Museum's computer.

37. RRC, 694; see the comments of K. Hopkins, JRS 1980, 106-7.

38. eg. no denarii appear to have been produced in 84 after mid-September.

39. In Tables H and J the die totals for issues 84.1 (Table J only) and 85.2 were calculated by extrapolating the average ratic from comparisons of die and hoard totals of issues 82-83 and 83.2 (the only reasonably well represented issues of the Second Period).

40. Years 81 and 96.

CHAPTER 4

SURVEY OF AUREI

The Hoards

The large hoard of aurei from Zemun in Yugoslavia has already been mentioned. This hoard was used in the Catalogue of Domitian's precious metal issues as the basis for measuring changes in the weight of Domitian's aureus. In addition to Zemun, a further fourteen hoards containing aurei of Domitian have been included in this survey. Four of these hoards (Nos. 9,11,14,15) did not contain any coins dated to Domitian's reign, but they contained a number of Flavian gold coins, including aurei of Domitian Caesar minted in the reigns of Vespasian and Titus. These four hoards have been included in the survey because they help to illustrate the overall pattern of survival of gold coinage from this period. The hoards are listed below in chronological order, according to the date of the last coins in each hoard. The regional divisions used for the denarius hoard survey have not been included this time, although the country of origin is indicated.

	Hoard	Country	Aurei of Dom. pre-81	Aurei of Dom. 81-96	Reign when buried	Date of last coin
1	Zirkowitz	Austria	10	10	Domitian	92-94
2	Clunia	Spain	1	3	Nerva	98
3	Zemun	Yugoslavia	10	187	Trajan	98-99
4	Fins d'Annecy	France	3	12	Trajan	104-110
5	Emona	Yugoslavia	-	4	Trajan	107-111
6	Castagnaro	Italy	1	1	Hadrian	126
7	Erla	Austria	5	1	Hadrian	134-138
8	Vidy	Switzerland	-	2	Ant.Pius	140-144
9	Corbridge	Britain	5	-	Ant.Pius	159-160
10	Liberchies	Belgium	15	2	M.Aurelius	166
11	Braga(?)	Portugal	9	-	M.Aurelius	167-168
12	Diarbekir	Turkey	8	2	M.Aurelius	177-178
13	Villach	Austria	8	1	Sept.Sev.	194-197
14	Szőny	Hungary	4	-	Sept.Sev.	196-211
15	Cannet	France	3	-	Geta	211

There is an insufficient number of coins in each of these hoards to merit a tabulation of the frequency figures in the manner employed for the denarius survey. Instead, in Table M, recording the frequency of Domitian's aurei surviving in the hoards, the issues represented in

Table M   Frequency of aurei of Domitian in hoards

Issue	Zirk.*	Clu.	Zemun	Hoards 4-5	6-8	9-12	13-15	Total
Domitian Caesar	10	1	10	3	6	37	15	82
81.3a	-	-	-	-	-	-	-	-
81.3b	-	-	2	-	-	3	1	6
82.1	-	-	-	-	-	1	-	1
82.2	1	-	17	-	-	-	-	18
82-83	1	1	25	2	-	-	-	29
83.2	-	-	10	-	-	-	-	10
83.3	-	-	-	-	-	-	-	-
84.1	1	-	1	-	-	-	-	2
84.2	1	-	3	-	-	-	-	4
84.3	-	-	2	-	-	-	-	2
85.1	-	-	2	-	-	-	-	2
85.2	-	-	-	1	-	-	-	1
85.3	-	-	-	-	-	-	-	-
85.4	-	-	-	-	-	-	-	-
85.5	-	-	2	-	-	-	-	2
85.6	-	-	1	-	-	-	-	1
86.1	1	-	5	-	-	-	-	6
86.2	-	-	5	-	-	-	-	5
86.3	-	-	2	-	-	-	-	2
86.4	-	-	2	-	-	-	-	2
86.5	-	-	1	-	-	-	-	1
87.1	2	-	7	1	-	-	-	10
87.2	-	-	-	1	-	-	-	1
88.1	-	-	3	-	-	-	-	3
88.3	-	-	2	-	-	-	-	2
88-89A	-	1	18	4	1	-	-	24
88-89?	-	-	6	1	-	-	-	7
90-91	-	1	59	2	3	-	-	65
90-91?	-	-	1	-	-	-	-	1
92-94	1	-	9	4	-	-	-	14
95-96	-	-	2	-	-	-	-	2
Total (81-96)	8	3	187	16	4	4	1	223

* The Zirkowitz hoard also included a hybrid aureus with obv issue 84.2, rev issue 82.2; also an aureus with rev issue 84.2, obv legend IMP CAES DOMIT AVG GERM P M , which is otherwise unrecorded and must be regarded as an error, or a description of a contemporary forgery.

the first three hoards, from Zirkowitz (buried late in Domitian's reign), Clunia and Zemun (both buried circa 98-99), are all listed separately, but the coins from the later hoards are listed together in four groups. In the first group are the two hoards (Fins d'Annecy and Emona) dated to the later period of Trajan's reign, some years after his reform of gold standards in 98-99 [1]. The second group comprises hoards 6,7 and 8, from Castagnaro, Erla and Vidy, which date from the reign of Hadrian and the early years of Antoninus Pius. The third group contains hoards 9 to 12 (Corbridge, Liberchies, Braga(?) and Diarbekir), spanning the period from about the death of Pius to the last years of Marcus Aurelius. Finally, group four comprises three hoards (Villach, Szöny and Cannet) all buried in the Severan period, about 197-211. The main purpose of Table M is to present the distribution of coins within the reign of Domitian, but also the quantity of coins of Domitian Caesar (pre-81) in each hoard or group of hoards has been included in order to illustrate the pattern of survival of these coins in comparison with the aurei struck during the Three Periods (issues 81-82.1, 82.2-85.3, 85.4-96) of precious metal coinage production in Domitian's reign.

The survival rate of Domitian's aurei

Table M records the changing pattern of survival of Domitian's gold coinage. The Zemun hoard, of course, dominates the Table. Over 80% of all the coins from Domitian's reign in the survey are from this hoard, so that a distribution pattern calculated from the "Total" column in Table M would in reality be little more than a reflection of the Zemun pattern. On the other hand, in some of the columns in Table M the sample of coins is perhaps individually too small for any serious stastical conclusions to be drawn. However, a close scrutiny of the Table does reveal that if the different periods of burial are taken into account there is a definite consistency in the representation of issues between the separate hoards, or groups of hoards, no matter how small the samples might be.

The first three hoards all have a large representation (between $\frac{1}{3}$ and $\frac{1}{2}$ of the total number of coins struck within the reign) of Second Period aurei, contrasting with an almost total absence of First Period coins. Hoards 4 to 5 record a shift in emphasis towards the Third Period, which now supplies four-fifths of all the coins from Domitian's reign (as opposed to one-half to two-thirds in hoards 1 to 3). Coins of Domitian's First Period are still absent, and aurei of Domitian Caesar are still greatly outnumbered (as in hoards 1 to 3). However, the next group of hoards (Nos. 6 to 8) reveals a different pattern. The Second Period aurei (Domitian's heaviest) seem to have disappeared altogether, and although the issues of the First Period still fail to be represented, there is a noticeable increase in coins of Domitian Caesar, which now outnumber those of Domitian's Third Period. It appears that all of Domitian's heavier aurei, struck between 82 and 96, must have been driven out of circulation in the course of the early- to mid-second century because the next group of hoards (Nos. 9 to 12) illustrates an even more dramatic change in the overall pattern of survival. The only aurei of Domitian's reign which now survive are those of the First Period; those same issues which were so poorly represented in the early hoards. These in turn are greatly outnumbered by the aurei of Domitian Caesar, and as the proportional representation of these two groups of coins is approximately the same in the final column (hoards 13 to 15), it can be assumed that this ratio reflects the relative volume of emission of these coins.

The changing pattern of survival of Domitian's aurei, as recorded in Table M, seems to have been profoundly affected by the weight of gold in the original issues. This is made clear by the division of the Table according to Domitian's Three Periods of precious metal coinage, and by a comparison of the representation of Domitian Caesar and Domitian Imperator issues. Thus, the seven latest hoards examined (hoards 9-15) contained a total of 52 coins of Domitian Caesar and 5 coins from Domitian's First Period (struck to the same standards as the pre-81 coins), but not a single specimen of Domitian's heavier aurei from Periods 2 and 3 of the reign. Contrast the findings of the earlier hoards. Even if the rather exceptional Zemun hoard is excluded the remaining seven hoards yielded a total of 20 coins of Domitian Caesar against 31 coins of Domitian as emperor, all from Periods 2 and 3 of the reign. Zemun of course, being essentially a sample of heavy aurei, contained only 10 Domitian Caesars and 2 coins from Domitian's First Period, against a total of 185 Second and Third Period pieces.

In order to clarify the relationship between survival of aurei and weight standards we can extend this study into a consideration of the distribution of all the coins in these same fifteen hoards. In the upper part of Table N the hoards are again arranged in chronological order, and the number of examples from ten periods of aureus production, defined largely on the basis of weight, are listed[2]. The ten periods of production are as follows :-

1.	before the reform of Nero in AD 64	ave.	weight	7.64g.
2.	Nero - Vitellius, AD 64-69	"	"	7.31g.
3.	Vespasian - Titus, AD 69-81	"	"	7.23-7.27g.
4.	Domitian, First Period, issues AD 81-82.1	"	"	7.18g.
5.	Domitian, Second Period, issues AD 82.2-85.3	"	"	7.65g.
6.	Domitian, Third Period, issues AD 85.4-96	"	"	7.54g.
7.	Nerva - Trajan (pre-reform), AD 96-98/99	"	"	7.56-7.59g.
8.	Trajan (post-reform), AD 98/99-117	"	"	7.22-7.25g.
9.	Hadrian, AD 117-138	"	"	7.25g.
10.	Antoninus Pius and later, AD 138-	"	"	7.21g.

In the lower part of Table N the hoards are grouped together in the same divisions used for Table M, and the number of coins from the ten periods in each group is listed, together with the proportion of this figure to the total, expressed as a percentage. These percentage figures are then illustrated in the form of histograms (Figure 5).

Table N Survival of aurei, 1st to 2nd centuries AD

Hoard	1	2	3	4	5	6	7	8	9	10	Total
1	15	22	32	-	4	4	-	-	-	-	77
2	-	10	6	-	1	2	1	-	-	-	20
3	-	6	28	2	60	125	6	3	-	-	230
4	-	-	12	-	1	11	6	6	-	-	36
5	-	-	2	-	2	2	3	7	-	-	16
6	-	1	2	-	-	1	-	7	9	-	20
7	-	16	15	-	-	1	1	33	37	-	103
8	-	-	1	-	-	2	-	12	34	23	72
9	-	17	31	-	-	-	-	48	40	24	160
10	1	82	90	2	-	-	1	65	76	51	368
11	-	5	26	-	-	-	-	28	25	86	170
12	-	77	45	2	-	-	1	39	39	99	302
13	-	19	35	1	-	-	-	17	9	19	100
14	-	16	27	-	-	-	-	16	12	43	114
15	-	-	10	-	-	-	-	10	24	85	129

(Periods: columns 1–10)

Hoards	1	2	3	4	5	6	7	8	9	10	Total
1	15	22	32	-	4	4	-	-	-	-	77
%	19	29	42	-	5	5	-	-	-	-	
2-3	-	16	34	2	61	127	7	3	-	-	250
%	-	6	14	1	24	51	3	1	-	-	
4-5	-	-	14	-	3	13	9	13	-	-	52
%	-	-	27	-	6	25	17	25	-	-	
6-8	-	17	18	-	-	4	1	52	80	23	195
%	-	9	9	-	-	2	1	27	41	12	
9-12	1	181	192	4	-	-	2	180	180	260	1000
%	-	18	19	-	-	-	-	18	18	26	
13-15	-	35	72	1	-	-	-	43	45	147	343
%	-	10	21	-	-	-	-	13	13	43	
											1917

(Periods: columns 1–10)

Figure 5 Survival of aurei, 1st to 2nd centuries AD

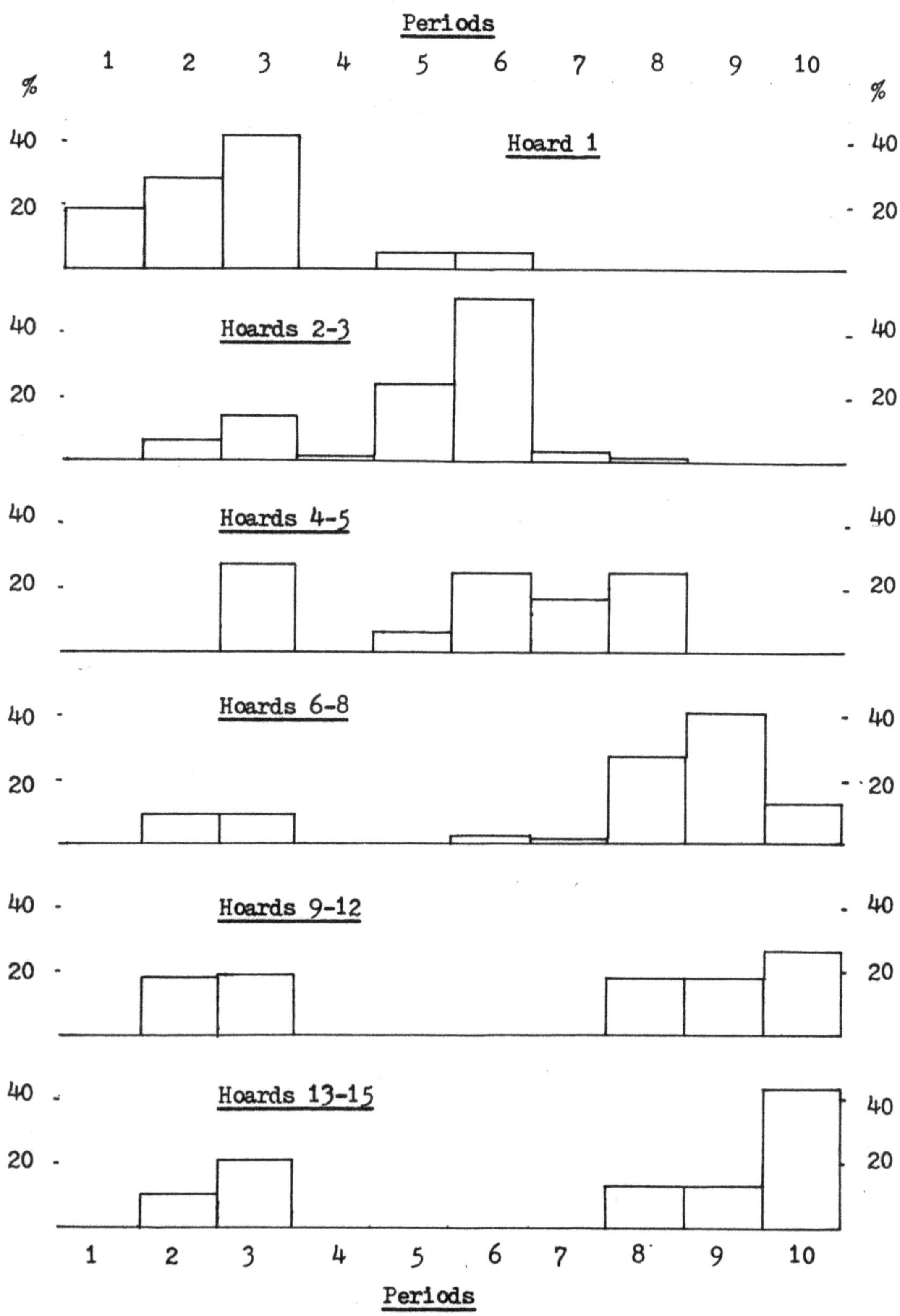

The first noticeable feature of Table N is the absence of aurei minted before Nero's reform of AD 64 (period 1). Apart from one solitary example in the large hoard from Liberchies, all the examples recorded were found in the Zirkowitz hoard, which was also the only hoard buried before the end of Domitian's reign. A more detailed study of these pre-Neronian reform issues would be required before we can be sure of when they disappeared from circulation. Their absence from the Clunia and Zemun hoards is probably significant, but Clunia provides too small a sample and Zemun has an untypically strong late-Flavian bias. Zirkowitz proves that Julio-Claudian aurei dating from before Nero's reform were still in circulation late in Domitian's reign, but so far there is no evidence to confirm that they survived any later[3].

The hoards from Clunia and Zemun appear to have been buried about AD 99, at the time of Trajan's reform of the gold coinage, when he reduced the weight of the aureus by about half a gramme below the standard of Domitian (post-85) and Nerva. The Zemun hoard shows a quite remarkable concentration of high weight aurei. 191 of the 230 coins in the hoard were minted between AD 82 and 98/99 when the heavier standards introduced by Domitian were operating, whereas coins from the period Nero - Titus are relatively few in number, as also are aurei of the first issues of Domitian before he increased the weight of the coin. This contrasts sharply with the distribution pattern of later hoards. It suggests that the Zemun hoard represents a stock of heavy aurei deliberately removed from circulation at the time when the lighter coins first started appearing. This of course means that the Zemun hoard contains an excellent, indeed unique, large sample of Domitian's aurei from the period 82 to 96. Table M has shown that these heavy coins were rapidly withdrawn from circulation from the reign of Trajan onwards, until they had apparently disappeared altogether by the mid-second century.

The light weight aurei from periods 2,3 and 4 which are so noticeably outnumbered in the Zemun hoard become, according to Table N, relatively more common in the course of the second century. Despite the increasingly large number of new second century aurei, struck to the same standards, which entered circulation, because of the disappearance of the heavier aurei struck between 82 and 98/99 these light coins are able to occupy a larger share of the total pool of coinage in circulation.

The disappearance of aurei from period 5, Domitian's heaviest gold coins, has already been discussed. The survey suggests that these coins were no longer available for hoarding by the time of Hadrian's reign. The slightly lighter aurei struck between Domitian's reform of 85 and Trajan's reform of 98/99 (periods 6 and 7) remained in circulation a little later, with occasional examples surviving as late as the 190's. However, these coins had effectively disappeared during the reign of Antoninus Pius; the data in Table N on the post-Domitianic issues (period 7) confirms the information from within Domitian's reign in Table M.

Aurei issued after Trajan's reform quite naturally tend to dominate the distribution pattern of the later hoards. Figure 5 clearly shows a drift in the position of the highest columns in the histograms from left to right, illustrating the greater survival rate of recently minted coins. However, it can also be seen, as has already been noted, that the light aurei from the period AD 64-82, which must by now have become considerably worn, apparently survived in plenty.

The overall impression gained from Table N and Figure 5 is that the survival pattern of Domitian's aurei is consistent with the general pattern of precious metal coin survival, as represented in hoards. In the course of time older issues tend to become less prominent as a proportion of the total pool of coinage in circulation except when different weight standards have been introduced. When coins of the same denomination are struck at different weights the heavier coins inevitably disappear from circulation, unless the reductions in weight are so gradual that the increased wear of the earlier issues neutralises this effect. In the case of Domitian's aurei the heaviest coins of his Second Period were doomed as soon as Trajan reduced the gold standard in 98/99. Also, the aurei of Domitian's Third Period, which were only a little lighter, were bound to disappear soon afterwards, although it is understandable that these issues, covering a ten year period, should be represented in later hoards by a small number of survivors whose weight was presumably reduced sufficiently by wear to enable them to continue in circulation. By the same principle, the light issues of Domitian's First Period were able to survive in circulation the longest, so that in the later second century they were still widely available to hoarders who could no longer have expected to obtain any other aurei of Domitian.

It has to be concluded that most of the hoards in the survey cannot provide a reliable indication of the overall pattern of aureus emission under Domitian, either individually or grouped together. However, the hoards can be assumed to give a reliable impression of the relative size of issues within each of the Three Periods of Domitian's coinage. The earliest hoards, buried before the full impact of Trajan's reform of 98/99 had been felt, should provide the most workable data, because these hoards are the only ones which contained Second Period aurei. The Zemun hoard, of course, dominates the survey, and although it is a somewhat unusual hoard, in that it seems to have been restricted largely to heavy aurei of the late first century, it was buried quite soon after Domitian's death and its sheer size (for an aureus hoard) makes it overwhelmingly the most important hoard for providing information on the gold coinage from Domitian's reign.

Size of issues according to the Zemun hoard

Using the Zemun figures it is possible to estimate the relative size of each issue of aurei in the manner employed to gauge the denarius issue sizes in Tables E,F and G[4]. The results, set out in Table P, are obviously conditioned by the particular characteristics of the Zemun hoard, and they have to be discussed in the context of the Three Periods of fineness operating during Domitian's reign.

First Period : issues 81.3a - 82.1

This is the only Period of Domitian's coinage that is not well represented in the Zemun hoard. The hoarder of these coins seems to have descriminated against lighter pieces, so that only the least worn aurei from Domitian's First Period issues could have qualified for

Table P   Size of aureus issues according to the Zemun hoard

Issue	Number of coins	% of Total	% against largest issue
81.3a	-	-	-
3b	2	1.1	3.4
82.1	-	-	-
82.2	17	9.1	28.8
82-83	25	13.4	42.4
83.2	10	5.4	17.0
83.3	-	-	-
84.1	1	0.5	1.7
84.2	3	1.6	5.1
84.3	2	1.1	3.4
85.1	2	1.1	3.4
85.2	-	-	-
85.3	-	-	-
85.4	-	-	-
85.5	2	1.1	3.4
85.6	1	0.5	1.7
86.1	5	2.7	8.5
86.2	5	2.7	8.5
86.3	2	1.1	3.4
86.4	2	1.1	3.4
86.5	1	0.5	1.7
87.1	7	3.7	11.9
87.2	-	-	-
88.1	3	1.6	5.1
88.3	2	1.1	3.4
88-89A	18	9.6	30.5
88-89?	6	3.2	10.2
90-91	59	31.6	100.0
90-91?	1	0.5	1.7
92-94	9	4.8	15.3
95-96	2	1.1	3.4
Total	187		

inclusion in the hoard. However, aurei of these early issues are also absent from all the other hoards in the survey that were buried before the middle of the second century, so perhaps these coins were not issued originally in very large numbers. When, in the later hoards, First Period coins do begin to appear, it seems clear that the largest of these issues must have been 81.3b; but there is insufficient evidence available to make any serious comments on the volume of emission from any of these issues compared with that of the issues in the later Periods.

Second Period : issues 82.2 - 85.3

The Zemun hoard is crucial for our understanding of aureus emission in this Period. A third of all the aurei of Domitian's reign in the Zemun hoard belong to these issues. This contrasts sharply with the pattern established for denarii, as a comparison of Tables E,F and P clearly shows.

In issues 82.2, 82-83 and 83.2 aureus production appears to have been, at least in relative terms, far more substantial than denarius production. These issues of aurei are larger than most of the other gold issues in Domitian's reign. According to the Zemun hoard, only the exceptionally well represented issue 90-91 was substantially larger. In the undated issue, 82-83, it is noticeable that reverse type (a) accounted for 17 of the 25 examples recorded from Zemun. The coins of the Flavian _divi_ (types c and d) are rare (only two examples), but six "Domitia" pieces were included, suggesting that these "family" aurei as a whole were by no means an insignificant element in the gold currency.

From the Zemun hoard it would appear that in 84 and the early part of 85 production of new aurei was considerably reduced in comparison with the years 82 and 83. Nevertheless, relative to the overall pattern of aureus emission, these issues seem, in common with the other issues of the Second Period, to have been more important than the corresponding issues of denarii.

Third Period (I) : issues 85.4 - 87.2

Although in 85 the weight of the aureus was decreased slightly, in line with the corresponding reduction in the fineness of the denarius, it was still a heavier coin than at any other time since AD 64, and it would therefore not have been avoided by the Zemun hoarder, as the very large number of examples from the years 85-96 in the hoard clearly shows. Thus the Zemun hoard continues to provide the most useful evidence for emission of aurei throughout Domitian's Third Period.

Between the reform of 85 and the end of 87 it appears that no issues of aurei on the scale of the largest issues of the Second Period were produced. Instead, emission continued in general at the lower levels operating since 84. In the latter part of 85 production of new aurei was apparently very low, but in 86 and 87 there seems to have been an increase. The most substantial issues are 86.1, 86.2, and 87.1, which are also three of the four largest denarius issues for these years. It seems that production of both denominations at this time was running parallel, and the rate of emission was closely related to the length of time during which these issues could have been minted. The

Zemun hoard contained no coins of issue 87.2 (mid-September to December 87) so this appears to have been a very small issue, although one example did appear in the Fins d'Annecy hoard.

Third Period (II) : issues 88.1 - 88-89(?)

The two aureus issues dated securely to 88 were, according to the Zemun figures, not very large. Production of denarii (especially in issue 88.1) appears to have been far more important. However, there was a large emission of aurei dated only by the emperor's consular title (issue 88-89A). Because these coins cannot be more closely dated they are less useful for tracing the pattern of coinage emission, and for the rest of the reign the main aureus issues all share this same drawback. The presence of six examples of the later coins of Domitia and Julia assigned to this period (issue 88-89?) suggests that again these "family" aurei were produced and issued in not insignificant quantities. Overall, emission of aurei in 88 and 89 shows a slight increase compared with the preceding two years.

Third Period (III) : issues 90-91

According to the Zemun hoard, the issue dated to the years 90-91 must have been the largest aureus issue of Domitian's reign. A total of 59 coins of this issue were found in Zemun, representing a quarter of the entire hoard. It is always possible that this figure might be misleadingly large. The Zemun hoard was buried only eight years or so after these coins were minted, and the hoarder may have obtained a cache of them virtually straight from the mint (eg. because they were used for a particular payment at that time). However, we have no evidence to prove that this was not the largest aureus issue of the reign; a further six examples were recorded in the other hoards. The corresponding issue of denarii was also large, but in relative terms not so dominant as the aureus issue. The Diva Julia issue of 90-91(?) was represented by only one coin in Zemun. These coins are exceedingly rare in collections, the reverse type suggests a largely commemorative purpose and perhaps not many pieces were issued.

Third Period (IV) and (V) : issues 92-94 and 95-96

The aureus issues of 92-94 and 95-96 can be contrasted with the denarius issues of these years which were huge (Tables E and F). The Zemun hoard yielded only nine coins dated 92-94, a very small number for an issue spanning three whole years. However, aurei of this issue were relatively well represented in other hoards, so the Zemun figure may be somewhat misleading. Meanwhile, from issue 95-96 Zemun contained only two aurei, and no examples from this issue were recorded in any of the other hoards in the survey.

It may be significant that of the post- 90-91 issues in Zemun, not only the coins of Domitian are scarce, but also those of Nerva and Trajan. It is not easy to find an explanation for this phenomenon. It may be argued that the hoarder was most active in 90/91 and thereafter added only the occasional coin to his hoard. It is not at all unusual for hoards of gold or silver to "tail off" towards the end. However, the fact that this hoarder apparently took particular pains to select the heavier aurei of Domitian in preference to the coins of his predecessors and his own First Period suggests that the hoard should have been gathered together, as well as buried, in 98-99 when Trajan re-introduced the lighter weight standard[5]. The possibility of a definite reduction in output of aurei in 92-94 and 95-96 cannot therefore be discounted. It can also be noted that, according to their scarcity in collections and in the Zemun hoard, the aurei from these issues with bare-headed obverse types were the most rare.

Output of aurei, AD 81-96

Because many of the aureus issues cannot be dated closely, and because the evidence is based effectively on only one hoard, it is unlikely that a very meaningful pattern of annual output, on the lines of that attempted for denarii, could be constructed. Instead, it would be more useful to see how the pattern of aureus emission from the Zemun hoard compares with that of denarii from the earliest hoards in the denarius survey (cf. Table C and Figure 1). If the reign is divided into the same seven phases of minting as were used for illustrating the survival of denarius issues the emission of aurei can be set out in a similar table (Table Q) and illustrated on a histogram (Figure 6).

Table Q

	Phases of minting							
Zemun	1	2	3	4	5	6	7	Total
coins	2	60	25	29	60	9	2	187
%	1.1	32.1	13.4	15.5	32.1	4.8	1.1	

Figure 6

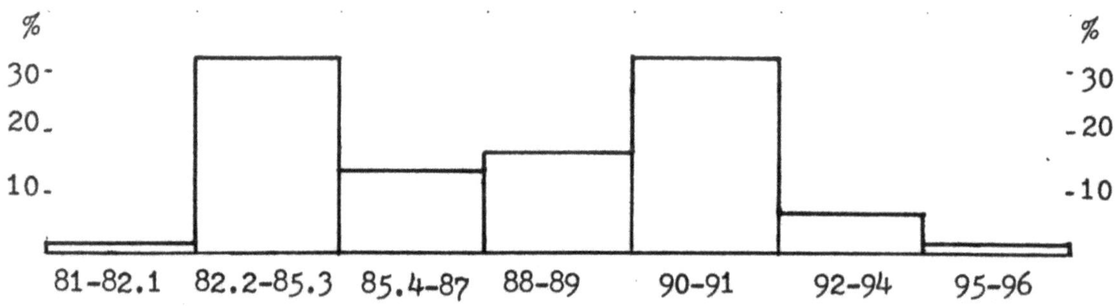

It has already been suggested that the Zemun hoard might not give a fair picture of aureus output in the First Period (81-82.1), so the first column in Figure 6 should not be subjected to comparison with the other columns. Also, it is possible that the last three columns may have been distorted by special factors related more to the activity of the hoarder in these years than to the availability of coins. Nevertheless, the results are still important. Most significant is that they illustrate an important increase in output of the heaviest aurei, which were minted in the Second Period at exactly the time when the correspondingly very fine denarii were apparently being issued so sparingly.

NOTES

1. H. Mattingly, BMCRE III, xv, lvii.

2. The weights of aurei listed here for all periods except the reign of Domitian are averages calculated from British Museum specimens, as recorded in the Introductions to BMCRE I-IV. The weight for period 2 is that recorded for Nero; aurei of the Civil Wars and the emperors Galba, Otho and Vitellius vary considerably in weight, but still retain a similar average to Nero. For Domitian's reign (periods 4 to 6) the weights have been calculated not only from the British Museum, but from a larger sample described above in the Introduction to Chapter 2. In Period 10 the figure quoted is the average for Antoninus Pius; weights after his reign vary, but they never exceed significantly the average of Pius.

3. Hoards from earlier in the Flavian period confirm that Zirkowitz is not unusual in containing pre-Neronian reform aurei. The Boscoreale hoard (latest coin AD 78) contained over 200 examples (C. Canessa, Le Trésor Monétaire de Boscoreale", le Musée 1909, 259-265). Pre-Neronian reform aurei were also noted in the Howe hoard (latest coin AD 87) recently examined in the British Museum.

4. Unfortunately it was not possible to undertake a die study of the aurei from the Zemun hoard. Although the Zagreb museum retained one example of every type and variant from each issue represented, the remainder of the coins were dispersed in the last century.

5. The only drawback to this argument is finding an explanation for the huge number of coins of 90-91, but it has been suggested that this may have been caused by special circumstances.

CHAPTER 5

THE BRONZE COINAGE OF ROME, AD 81-96

Catalogue of issues

The standard catalogues of Roman imperial coins refer to two series of *aes* coinages of Domitian. By far the largest series has always, not surprisingly, been attributed to the mint of Rome. The second, much smaller, series, which was produced only in the early years of the reign, has traditionally been attributed to a mint in Lugdunum in Gaul, but no sound evidence has ever been cited to justify this attribution. More recently it has been suggested that these coins should be re-attributed to an eastern mint, mainly on the evidence of type analogies with Greek imperial issues from Bithynian mints and the fact that, while the occasional specimen has appeared in trade in the East, these coins are virtually unknown from western provenances[1].

The following outline catalogue of issues is not intended to constitute a comprehensive revision of Domitian's bronze coinage. Only the main developments in legend structure and types will be listed so that an overall impression of the progressive organisation and development of *aes* production might be gained. The list will also serve to identify the issues of bronze coins arranged in the survey of finds below. The regular issues of the mint of Rome will be listed first, followed by the "irregular" issues (including "Restorations" and the so-called "Lugdunum" group).

Mint of Rome : Sestertius, Dupondius and As

Standard portrait types throughout the reign :-

Sestertius	:	head laureate (pl.XII,6,7,12,18)
Dupondius	:	head radiate (pl.XII,13)
As	:	head laureate (pl.XII,14)

AD 81 *obv* IMP CAES DIVI VESP F DOMITIAN AVG P M
rev TR P COS VII DES VIII P P ; S C
RIC 232-238 (pl.VI,1-2,4)

AD 82 *obv* IMP CAES DIVI VESP F DOMITIAN AVG P M
rev TR P COS VIII DES VIIII P P ; S C
RIC 239-242 (pl.VI,5-8)

AD 81-82 Types : obv characteristics: head right; head left (pl.VI,5 - rare); no aegis

rev[2] S : Minerva 1; Minerva 4; Domitian standing l., holding palladium.
Dp: Minerva 3; Pax[3] standing l., leaning on column, holding branch and caduceus.
As: Minerva 1; Minerva 3.

AD 84.1 obv IMP CAES DIVI VESP F DOMITIAN AVG GER COS X
rev S C (various rev legends according to types)[4]
RIC 242 (pl.VII,9)

AD 84.2 obv IMP CAES DOMITIAN AVG GERM COS X (variants with ..DOMIT and ..GERMAN)
rev S C
RIC 243-251 (pl.VII,10-11)

AD 84 Types : obv characteristics: head right; head left (rare); aegis; no aegis (rare, and unrecorded for issue 84.1)

rev S : -
Dp: (84.2 only): ANNONA AVG, Annona std. r.; FIDEI PVBLICAE, Fides stg. l.; VIRTVTI AVGVSTI, Virtus stg. l.; Mars adv. l.
As: IOVI CONSERV(AT(ORI) (IVPPITER CONSERV), Jupiter stg. l.; MONETA AVGVST, Moneta stg. l.; SALVTI AVGVST(I), Altar; Victory adv. r., holding legionary eagle; Victory adv. l., holding shield.

AD 85.1 obv IMP CAES DOMITIAN AVG GERM COS XI
rev S C
RIC 252-272 (pl.VIII,1-4,8-9)

AD 85.2 obv IMP CAES DOMIT AVG GERM COS XI CENS POT P P
rev S C
RIC 277-304 (BMC 323-359A) (pl.VIII,10-13)

AD 85.3 obv IMP CAES DOMIT AVG GERM COS XI CENS PER P P
rev S C
RIC 277-305 (BMC 360-367) (pl.IX,1-3)

AD 85 Types : obv characteristics: head right; head left (rare); aegis (pl.XII,12-14); no aegis (rare)

rev S : ANNONA AVGVST, Annona stg. r., Ceres std. l.; GERMANIA CAPTA, German stg. r., German woman std. l., trophy; IOVI VICTORI, Jupiter std. l., holding Victory and sceptre; PACI AVGVST, Pax stg. l., setting fire to arms; Pax (no legend) stg. l., setting fire to arms; Domitian stg. r., with 2-3 soldiers; Domitian riding down German; Domitian stg. l., sacrificing; Domitian stg. l., with Rhenus; Domitian stg. l., with German captive; Domitian stg. l., crowned by Victory; Victory stg. r., inscribing shield DE GER.

Dp: AETERNITATI AVGVST, Aeternitas stg. l.; ANNONA AVG; FIDEI PVBLICAE, Fides stg. r. or l.; FORTVNAE AVGVSTI, Fortuna stg. l.; VICTORIAE AVGVSTI, Victory stg. l., inscribing shield; VIRTVTI AVGVSTI, Virtus stg. l. or r.; Mars adv. l.; Trophy with two German captives; Two German shields, crossed.

As: AETERNITATI AVGVST; ANNONA AVG; FIDEI PVBLICAE, Fides stg. l. or r.; FORTVNAE AVGVSTI; IOVI CONSERVAT(ORI) (IVPPITER CONSERV); MONETA AVGVST(I); SALVTI AVGVST(I); VICTORIAE AVGVSTI; VIRTVTI AVGVSTI, Virtus r.(standard type from now); Mars adv. l.; Victory adv. l., holding shield; German shields, crossed.

AD 86 obv IMP CAES DOMIT AVG GERM COS XII CENS PER P P
rev S C
RIC 311-340 (pl.IX,4-6)

Types : obv characteristics: head right; head left (rare); aegis; no aegis (rare)

rev S : ANNONA AVGVST; GERMANIA CAPTA; IOVI VICTORI; IVPPITER CVSTOS, Jupiter std. l., holding thunderbolt and sceptre; 6 Domitian types as in AD 85; Victory inscribing shield DE GER

Dp: ANNONA AVG; FIDEI PVBLICAE, Fides r.; FORTVNAE AVGVSTI; MONETA AVGVSTI (?)[5]; VICTORIAE AVGVSTI; VIRTVTI AVGVSTI; Mars adv. l.; German shields, crossed.

As: ANNONA AVG; FIDEI PVBLICAE, Fides r.(standard type from now); FORTVNAE AVGVSTI; IOVI CONSERVAT(ORI); MONETA AVGVSTI; Pacis, Altar (?); SALVTI AVGVSTI; VICTORIAE AVGVSTI; VIRTVTI AVGVSTI; Mars adv. l.; German shields, crossed.

variants : S : obv IMP CAES DOMITIAN AVG GERM COS XII
rev S C; types: Domitian with two soldiers (RIC 306);
Domitian with German captive;
Domitian sacrificing.

As: obv IMP CAESAR DOMIT AVG GER COS XII CENS PER P P
rev S C; German shields, crossed (RIC 337A)

AD 87 obv IMP CAES DOMIT AVG GERM COS XIII CENS PER P P
rev S C
RIC 341-356 (pl.IX,7-9)

Types : obv characteristics: head right; head left (rare); aegis; no aegis.

rev S : GERMANIA CAPTA; IOVI VICTORI; Domitian with soldiers; Domitian riding down German; Domitian sacrificing; Domitian with Rhenus; Domitian crowned by Victory.

Dp: FIDEI PVBLICAE; FORTVNAE AVGVSTI; MONETA AVGVSTI; VIRTVTI AVGVSTI.

As: FIDEI PVBLICAE; FORTVNAE AVGVSTI; MONETA AVGVSTI; VIRTVTI AVGVSTI

variant : Dp : obv IMP CAES DOMIT AVG GERM P M TR P VI (aegis)
rev IMP XIIII COS XIII CENSOR PERPETVVS P P,
S C large, in centre
RIC 357 (wrongly recorded as TR P VII), BMC 398

AD 88 obv IMP CAES DOMIT AVG GERM P M TR P VIII CENS PER P P
rev COS XIIII LVD SAEC (A POP FRVG AC)
RIC 375-387 (pl.IX,10; pl.X,1-3)

Types : obv characteristics: head right; head left (rare); aegis (rare); no aegis.

rev S, Dp, As : various types relating to the celebration of the Secular Games

---

AD 88-89 obv IMP CAES DOMIT AVG GERM COS XIIII CENS PER P P
rev S C
RIC 358-373 (pl.X,4-5)

Types : obv characteristics: head right; head left (rare); aegis (rare); no aegis.

rev S : IOVI VICTORI (variants with this type and legends IOVIS VIRTVTI and IVPPITER CVSTOS have also been recorded); Domitian riding down German; Domitian sacrificing; Domitian with Rhenus; Domitian crowned by Victory.
Dp: ANNONA AVG (?)[5]; FIDEI PVBLICAE; FORTVNAE AVGVSTI; VIRTVTI AVGVSTI.
As: ANNONA AVG; FIDEI PVBLICAE; FORTVNAE AVGVSTI; MONETA AVGVSTI; VIRTVTI AVGVSTI.

AD 90-91 obv IMP CAES DOMIT AVG GERM COS XV CENS PER P P
rev S C
RIC 388-397 (pl.X,8-9)

Types : obv characteristics: head right; head left (?); aegis (v. rare); no aegis.

rev S : IOVI VICTORI; Domitian with Rhenus; Domitian crowned by Victory.
Dp: FORTVNAE AVGVSTI; VIRTVTI AVGVSTI.
As: FORTVNAE AVGVSTI; MONETA AVGVSTI; VIRTVTI AVGVSTI

AD 92-94 obv IMP CAES DOMIT AVG GERM COS XVI CENS PER P P
rev S C
RIC 401-409 (pl.X,11)

Types : obv characteristics: head right; head left (v.rare); no aegis.

rev S : IOVI VICTORI; Domitian with soldiers; Domitian crowned by Victory (a variant of this type also includes Minerva in the group)
Dp: FORTVNAE AVGVSTI; VIRTVTI AVGVSTI;
As: FORTVNAE AVGVSTI; MONETA AVGVSTI; VIRTVTI AVGVSTI

AD 95-96 obv IMP CAES DOMIT AVG GERM COS XVII CENS PER P P
rev S C
RIC 412-424A (pl.X,12; pl.XI,1-7)

Types : obv characteristics: head right; draped, head right (pl.XII,18 - rare); aegis (? genuine); no aegis.

rev S : IOVI VICTORI[6]; Domitian crowned by Victory; Triumphal Arch; Equestrian Statue; Three-storey building; Temple or Shrine (? genuine).
Dp: FORTVNAE AVGVSTI; VIRTVTI AVGVSTI; Victory stg. l. on globe; Eagle on palm; Helmet and shield.
As: FORTVNAE AVGVSTI; MONETA AVGVSTI; VIRTVTI AVGVSTI; Eagle on palm; Owl on branch.

Additional variants[7], AD 81-96

AD 82: S : obv IMP CAES DIVI VESP F DOMITIAN AVG P M; head laur. r.
rev TR POT COS VIII P P; S C, Minerva 4
H.A. Cahn, NC 1946, 24

AD 84: S : obv IMP CAES DIVI VESP F DOMIT AVG GERM COS X; draped, head laur. l.
rev P M TRIB P III IMP VII P P; S C, horseman riding down enemy, decapitated corpse.
C.M. Kraay, ANS Museum Notes 1960, 109-114

AD 84: S : obv IMP CAES DIVI VESP F DOMIT AVG GERM COS X; head laur. r., with aegis
rev STIP IMP DOMITIAN AVG; S C, Domitian stg. l., before group including 3 soldiers
C.M. Kraay, ANS Museum Notes 1960, 114-116

AD 85: S : obv IMP CAES DOMITIAN AVG GERM COS XI CENSORIA POT P P; head laur. r., with aegis
rev S C; IOVI VICTORI
British Museum 1981 acquisition

AD 85: As: obv IMP CAES DOMITIAN VAG(sic) GERM COS XI; head laur. r., with aegis
rev S C; Victory adv. l., with wreath and palm
H.A. Cahn, NC 1946, 24-25

AD 92-94: Dp(?): obv DOMITIANVS AVGVSTVS; draped, head laur. r.
rev GERMANICVS COS XVI; Germania std. r.
Oxford

AD 93-94: As: obv IMP CAES DOMIT AVG GERM P M TR P XIII..; head laur. r.
rev S C; VIRTVTI AVGVSTI
H.A. Cahn, NC 1946, 25

Mint of Rome : Semis and Quadrans[8]

AD 81-82 [9] Semis: obv IMP DOMITIANVS AVG; head laur. r.
rev S C; cornucopiae
RIC 425 (pl.VI,7)

Quadrans: obv IMP DOM(IT) AVG; Minerva bust r.
rev S C in wreath
RIC 436, 436A,B (pl.VII,8)

AD 85 Semis: obv IMP DOMIT AVG GERM COS XI; Apollo bust r.
rev S C; Types: Lyre; Tripod; Raven on branch
RIC 273-275 (pl.VIII,5-6)

Quadrans: obv IMP DOMIT AVG GERM COS XI; Ceres bust r. or l.
rev S C; Modius with corn ears
RIC 276 (pl.VIII,7)

AD 86 Semis: obv IMP DOMIT AVG GERM COS XII; Minerva bust r.
rev S C; Owl
RIC 308

Quadrans: obv IMP DOMIT(IAN) AVG GERM COS XII; Ceres bust r.
rev S C; Corn ears and poppies in bundle
RIC 309-310

AD 88-89 Semis: obv IMP DOMIT AVG GERM COS XIIII; Minerva bust r.
rev S C; Owl
RIC 374 (pl.X,5)

AD 90-91 Semis: obv IMP DOMIT AVG GERM COS XV; Apollo bust r. or l.
rev S C; Raven on branch
RIC 398-399 (pl.X,6)

Quadrans: obv and rev as above; RIC - (pl.X,7)

AD 92-94 Semis: obv IMP DOMIT AVG GERM COS XVI; Apollo bust r.
rev S C; Raven on branch
RIC 410

AD 95-96 Semis: obv IMP DOMIT AVG GERM COS XVII; Apollo bust r.
rev S C; Raven on branch
RIC 424B

Undated Quadrantes : obv IMP DOMIT(IAN) AVG GERM; various types
rev S C; various types
RIC 426-435 (pl.XI,8-13)

obv and rev type combinations:-
Minerva bust r. / S C; Minerva bust r. / Owl; Minerva bust r. / Olive branch; Minerva bust r. / S C in wreath; Ceres bust l. / Corn ears and poppies; Ceres bust l. / Ship; Ceres bust l. / Modius with corn ears; Trophy / Olive branch; S C / Rhinoceros r. or l.[10].

"Family" and "Irregular" issues : Mint of Rome and "Lugdunum"[11]

"Family" 1 (AD 81-82)

S[12] obv Colosseum; (no legend)
rev DIVO AVG T DIVI VESP F VESPASIAN; Titus std. l. on pile of arms, S C in exergue. (Copenhagen)

S obv T DIVO AVG (or DIVO T AVG) DIVI VESP F VESPASIANO; Titus seated l. on throne
rev IMP CAES DIVI VESP F DOMIT AVG P M TR P P P; S C, large, in centre. RIC 437-438 (pl.VII,1)

S obv DOMITIA(E) AVG IMP CAES DIVI F DOMITIAN AVG; bust of Domitia r., hair piled on back of head (pl.XII,23) or in long plait.
rev DIVI CAESAR MATRI (or DIVI CAESARIS MATER); Domitia std. l., facing a standing child, S C.
RIC 440-441 (pl.VII,2)

Dp obv DOMITIA AVG IMP CAES DIVI F DOMITIAN AVG; bust of Domitia r., hair in long plait (pl.XII,22)
rev DIVI CAESARIS MATER; Domitia stg. l. sacrificing.
RIC 442 [13] (pl.VII,3)

"Restorations" (AD 81-82)

S[14] obv TI CLAVDIVS CAESAR AVG P M TR P IMP P P; Claudius head laur. r.
rev IMP D CAES AVG REST; Spes adv. l., S C

Dp[15] obv DIVVS AVGVSTVS PATER; Augustus head rad. l.
rev IMP D CAES AVG REST; Victory adv. l., S C

As obv DIVVS AVGVSTVS PATER; Augustus head rad. l.
rev IMP D AVG REST, PROVIDENT (in exergue); Altar, S C

As obv DIVVS AVGVSTVS PATER; Augustus head rad. l.
rev IMP D CAES AVG RESTITVIT; Eagle on globe, S C (pl.VII,4)

As obv TI CAESAR DIVI AVG F AVGVST IMP VIII; Tiberius head bare l.
rev IMP D CAES DIVI VESP F AVG REST; S C, large, in centre (pl.VII,5)

As obv M AGRIPPA L F COS III; Agrippa head, with rostral crown, l.
rev IMP D AVG REST; Neptune stg. l., S C (pl.VII,6)

As obv DRVSVS CAESAR TI AVG F DIVI AVG N; Drusus head bare l.
rev IMP D CAES DIVI VESP F AVG REST; S C, large, in centre

As obv GERMANICVS CAESAR TI AVG F DIVI AVG N; Germanicus head bare l.
rev IMP D CAES DIVI VESP F AVG REST; S C, large, in centre

As[16] obv TI CLAVDIVS CAESAR AVG P M TR P IMP P P; Claudius head bare l. or r. (Riv.It 1897, 149)
rev IMP D AVG REST; Minerva adv. r.
RIC 454-463 (pl.VII,4-6)

"Lugdunum" (AD 81-82)

Sestertius, Dupondius and As : standard portrait types, as Rome, but different style (pl.VI,3,9-11; pl.XII,7)

AD 81 obv IMP D(OMITIAN) CAES DIVI VESP F AVG P M TR P P P COS VII
rev S C (various rev legends according to types)
RIC 444-447 (pl.VI,3)

AD 82 obv IMP D(OMITIAN) CAES DIVI VESP F AVG P M TR P P P COS VIII
rev S C
RIC 448-451 (pl.VI,9-11)

AD 81-82 Types : obv characteristics: head right; no aegis

rev S : PAX AVGVST, Pax stg. l., holding branch and cornucopiae; Mars adv. r., holding spear and trophy over shoulder
Dp: ROMA, Roma std. l.
As: CERES AVGVST, Ceres stg. l.

"Family" 2, (Diva Julia, AD 90-94)

AD 90-91 S obv IMP CAES DOMIT AVG GERM COS XV CENS PER P P; S C, large, in centre
rev DIVAE IVLIAE AVG DIVI TITI F, SPQR; Carpentum drawn r. by two mules
RIC 400 (pl.X,10)

AD 92-94 S obv IMP CAES DOMIT AVG GERM COS XVI CENS P P; S C, large, in centre
rev DIVAE IVLIAE AVG DIVI TITI F, SPQR; Carpentum, as above
RIC 411

Mint attribution

The issues listed under the heading "Mint of Rome", in sestertii, dupondii and asses (including a small number of coins with the same style, but with variant legends or types, listed as "additional variants"), together with all the semisses and quadrantes, constitute the normal, regular issues of bronze coinage produced in Domitian's reign. Although there are variations in portrait types, legends and reverse typology, all these coins share essentially the same style and fabric. But the other issues, listed under the rather unsatisfactory heading of " 'Family' and 'Irregular' issues : Mint of Rome and 'Lugdunum' ", do not have all the same characteristics as the "Roman" issues. These therefore merit a closer examination.

The group which differs most from the "Roman" series is composed of the coins described above under the heading "Lugdunum". C.M. Kraay, in his unpublished doctoral thesis, identified three principal features by which the coins of this "mint" can be distinguished from the regular "Roman" aes :-

a) style : massive, intense portraits, and ample, well-marked reverse figures[17].
b) lettering : "crowded, uneven and fussy, composed of lines of

varying thickness and encumbered with a quantity of serifs and terminal flourishes..." ("Roman" lettering is described as "evenly spaced, neat in appearance, and composed of strokes of uniform thickness throughout").

c) fabric : the field of the reverse is flat, or even slightly convex. ("Roman" coins have concave reverses).

Kraay listed the following issues as the product of this "mint" :-

1. (Some issues of) Titus and Domitian, AD 80-81
2. (Some issues of ?) Julia, AD 80-81
3. Some of the "restored" issues of Titus, AD 80-81
4. (Some issues of) Domitian, AD 81-82
5. All the "restored" issues of Domitian, AD 81-82

It will be interesting to investigate all the issues listed above under the heading " 'Family' and 'Irregular' issues : Mint of Rome and 'Lugdunum' " (which include Kraay's nos. 4 and 5), in order to see to what extent Kraay's "Lugdunum" characteristics are present. For this purpose all the examples in the British Museum were examined.

Of the "Family" coins issued in 81-82, the sestertii of the deified Titus (BMC 284-5) have a large "reverse" figure[18] (feature a), their lettering is somewhat crowded and includes many serifs (feature b), and they have a flat reverse fabric (feature c). On the other hand, the sestertii and dupondii of Domitia (BMC 501-3) have entirely "Roman" style, lettering and fabric. Most of the "Restoration" coins (BMC 505-512) have all the features described by Kraay ; the one example which appears to have a "Roman" style and lettering, and which has a noticeably concave reverse fabric, is the tooled coin (BMC 504) whose attribution to Domitian is uncertain[19]. The "Lugdunum" aes of Domitian in the British Museum (BMC 513-520) all have features (a), (b) and (c). Finally, the second group of "Family issues", the sestertii of the deified Julia (BMC 458-63, 471-3), includes some of Kraay's features. All the coins have a flat fabric as (c), and the legend on the face with the Carpentum type is invariably crowded and includes serifs, although the legend on the other side appears to be "Roman". These coins were struck in 90-91 and 92-94, many years after the "mint" responsible for the "Lugdunum" issues is supposed to have ceased production (in 82). How then can the appearance of the unusual features be explained ?

Firstly, it has to be noted that these two issues have a special, commemorative purpose. They revive a design, the Carpentum drawn by mules, that was used only in association with important female members of the imperial family, in commemoration of their death or deification[20]. It had last been used for the Memoriae Domitillae coins of Titus, and details on the designs of these coins and on those of Julia are so close as to suggest that the same dies may have been re-cut and used again (cf. the coins illustrated in BMCRE II, pl.51,8 (Domitilla) and pl.80,3 (Julia)). It is therefore not surprising that apparently anachronistic features appear on these particular coins. However, it can also be observed that serifs on the lettering on later issues of Domitian are not confined to these deified Julia coins. Although not so marked as on the "Lugdunum" coins of 81-82, they are nevertheless present on "Roman" aes issues, from the resumption of production in 84 through to the end of the reign[21].

The flat fabric is also more common than it might at first appear. In Domitian's reign it is a feature of the bronze coins struck for the deified Julia and the deified Titus, all the "Lugdunum" aes, and possibly all the "Restoration" coins. In the reign of Titus it characterises, as Kraay observed, all the "Lugdunum" aes[22] and some of the "Restoration" and the Julia coins, but it is also used for all the Titus and deified Vespasian (BMC Titus 221-5) and Titus and Domitilla (BMC Titus 226-9) sestertii. In fact it is invariably, though not exclusively, associated with the coins of this period which have a large "S C" as the central element of the design. These same coins have types that suggest a commemorative, almost "medallic" purpose. It is also worth noting that the majority of imperial aes coins (from the mint of Rome) dating from the period Augustus to Claudius have these same flat flans (and large "S C" types are common too). Only after Nero's monetary reforn in 64, when a whole new series of aes coinage was introduced, does the concave reverse fabric become common.

In the light of all these observations a new theory on the attribution of Domitian's "irregular" issues of bronze coinage can be proposed :-

All of the coins listed above were produced by the mint of Rome. The "Lugdunum" or "eastern" mint of Titus and Domitian (AD 80-82) is, instead, just another section or officina of the Roman mint. This mint had always been capable of producing coins with a flat fabric, but usually in the Flavian period such flans were reserved for special "medallic" issues, including deification, memorial and "Restoration" types, all of which had designs copying coins from the Julio-Claudian period when the flat fabric had been standard. The dies for these "irregular" Flavian bronzes were also cut in an unusual, but fine, elaborate style (with many serifs on the lettering). The officina producing these pieces would then have completed its capacity with additional issues which employ non-commemorative types, but which can be distinguished from the product of the other officinae by their style, legends and fabric (ie. the "Lugdunum" coins). The simple continuation on Domitian's early "Lugdunum" aes of "unusual" types and legend format carried over from the series struck by Titus is cited by Kraay as one of the reasons why these coins should be attributed to a separate mint distant from Rome, on the basis that this practise indicates an absence of new instructions following the accession[23]. However, an alternative interpretation is that this officina simply continued to produce coins with the same designs and legend forms that it had employed under Titus in the way that the other officinae of the mint of Rome continued to churn out theirs. Lack of change does not necessarily denote absence of instruction due to remoteness. The earliest coinage of Domitian in all metals is entirely conservative, until the full-scale overhaul of mint operations in 82.

The Bithynian type analogies brought into the argument in support of the reattribution of the "Lugdunum" coins to an eastern mint deserve consideration. It is certainly true that some "Greek imperial" coins of domitian struck for the Κοινον of Bithynia and for the cities of Nicaea and Nicomedia do share similarities of portraiture and reverse typology with "Lugdunum" coins. However, the Greek issues all date after 83, and it could be argued that these coins are simply using the earlier "Lugdunum" issues of the Roman mint as their prototype. The Bithynian moneyers were either copying existing coins from the Roman issues or they selected these particular designs from the available "patterns"; or perhaps they even might have acquired the services of the die engraver, or one of his followers, who had been responsible for the earlier "Lugdunum" issues.

This reconstruction of the mintage of Domitian's "Lugdunum" and associated *aes* issues must be regarded for the time being as only tentative. However, the location of the "Lugdunum" style within the mint of Rome is the only satisfactory, and perhaps the only possible, explanation for the presence of its characteristic features on so many separate issues in the Flavian period, and particularly for its presence on coins which also have marked "Roman" features[24]. Although the style of the "Lugdunum" coins is so distinct as to suggest that a completely separate establishment might have produced them, there is no evidence that any such "mint" existed at this time. And what would have been the purpose of another separate mint striking small groups of Latin-inscribed *aes* coins? If it is accepted that the Lugdunum *aes* mint of Nero produced its last issues under Vespasian, it seems illogical that another new branch mint producing fine style bronzes with a "western" appearance should be opened by Titus, perhaps in the East, in 80 [25]. In the absence of any definite evidence for an alternative, these "Lugdunum" issues must be considered together with all other "regular" *aes* coinage of Domitian as the product of the mint of Rome.

Production and Types

The above outline catalogue of Domitian's bronze issues indicates when the most significant developments in production took place. The most noteworthy feature is the absence of any bronze coinage dated to 83. As far as *aes* was concerned the mint seems to have closed altogether in 82, and it did not resume production until 84.

In the period 81-82 the bronze coinage, not surprisingly, bears a strong resemblance to the coinage of the previous reign. The "regular" portraiture (pl.XII,6) follows that of Domitian as Caesar under Titus; and the "Lugdunum" portraits (pl.XII,7) are stylistically identical to those produced by the same branch of the mint in 80-81 under Titus. The reverse types in both the "Rome" and "Lugdunum" styles are similarly non-progressive. They are mostly ones which were in use during the previous reign either for Titus or, more especially, for Domitian as Caesar. Most prominent is Domitian's favourite deity, Minerva (pl.VI, 1,6-8). One new type which refers directly to Domitian's accession has the emperor holding palladium (pl.VI,4). The type recording Titus's deification (pl.VII,1) is a simple copy from types on sestertii of Titus for the deified Vespasian and "Restorations" of the deified Augustus; and Domitian's "Restoration" types (pl.VII,4-6) also amount to nothing more than a straightforward, though reduced, continuation of the series issued under Titus. The most novel coins in Domitian's first bronze issues are the sestertii and dupondii struck for Domitia (pl.VII,2-3). Of the two portraits used, one (pl.XII,22) is the same as that employed on the early gold and silver issues of Domitia (pl.XII, 21); the other portrait has a more elaborate hair style (pl.XII,23). The reverse types for Domitia represent the empress as Vesta sacrificing (pl.VII,3 : complementing the type with Domitian holding palladium), and as the mother of the deified baby Caesar (pl.VII,2 : cf. the similar type on silver, pl.I,22). Finally, the remaining *aes* issues of 81-82, the undated semisses and quadrantes (pl.VII,7-8), use types already familiar to these denominations.

In 84, when the mint again resumed production of bronze following its temporary cessation, the forerunners of a whole new series of reverse types were introduced (pl.VII,9-11), and at the same time the aegis was added to Domitian's portrait (pl.XII,12-14). The issues of 85 saw the full production of the new series of reverse types, the most numerous and diverse since the reign of Nero.

The sestertii are dominated by types illustrating Domitian's first and greatest military success, the victory against the Chatti, which had resulted in his acquisition of the title *Germanicus*. The most direct references to the victory are provided by the *Germania Capta* design (pl.VIII,1) and the type depicting Victory inscribing the words *DE GER* on a shield, adjacent to a trophy and a German captive (pl.IX,5). Domitian himself appears in various scenes alluding to the campaign. He is seen in combat against the enemy (pl.VIII,10), receiving submission (pl.IX,6), standing over the personification of the Rhine (pl.IX,7), sacrificing in thanks for the victory (pl.VIII,3), and finally standing with his partners in the success, the Roman army officers and soldiers (pl.VIII,4). Victory again appears crowning the emperor (pl.X,4), and Pax symbolically marks the termination of hostilities by setting fire to a pile of arms (pl.VIII,2). The chief god of Rome, Jupiter, appears as Jupiter Victor (pl.X,8,12), and finally, the only non-martial sestertius type depicts Annona and Ceres (pl.IX,4), representing the bountiful nature of the emperor.

Further war and victory reverse types are included on the dupondii and asses (pl.VIII,12-13;IX,2), but these denominations are mostly given over to a varied range of personifications. The personifications seem to complement the more directly personal types of Domitian, his family, and his favourite deities, which appear on the sestertii and on gold and silver issues. Together all these types would, if we can assume that they were selected intentionally, represent and illustrate the ideology that the Emperor wished to project. The specific relevance of the personification is not always clear to us, although the types would presumably have been more intelligible to the Roman people of the time[26]. It is sometimes impossible for us to tell whether or not a coin design was consciously introduced for a particular purpose and, even if it was, whether the people who used the coins would have understood the reason; so care must be taken in the interpretation of these designs. This applies especially to personifications. However, we can briefly consider possible interpretations of Domitian's personifications. Aeternitas should have a dynastic significance (pl.IX,3), linked also to Fortuna (pl.X,9), which has a more specific attachment to Domitian as the ruling emperor. Virtus is a military type (pl.IX,9), symbolic of the courage of Domitian and the mutual devotion between the army and emperor. Its civilian counterpart should be Fides (pl.IX,1), the expression of trust between the emperor and his people. This trust is guaranteed by Annona (pl.VIII,8) and, perhaps even more so, by the personification on the new type, Moneta (pl.VII,11). Both the troops, who had been awarded a pay rise, and the people, who not infrequently received *congiaria* and other expressions of the emperor's liberality, might have considered Moneta an appropriate and welcome symbol. Domitian had, of course, also undertaken some major reforms in order to improve the quality and appearance of his *moneta*. Other types on dupondii and asses include a Mars (pl.VII,10), and an altar type which refers to the preservation (Salus) of the emperor (pl.VII,9).

On the dated semisses and quadrantes new types were introduced when production of these denominations was resumed in 85. Apollo (pl.VIII,5-6; X,6-7) and the ubiquitous Minerva (pl.X,5) dominate the obverses of the semis, with their various attributes occupying the reverses. The quadrans uses types of Ceres, the corn goddess (pl.VIII, 7).

From the main series of types used on the large denomination aes coinage the number of designs employed in each issue was gradually reduced in the years following 85, and a core of principal reverse types was then retained for the rest of the reign:-

sestertius : IOVI VICTORI; Domitian crowned by Victory
dupondius : FORTVNAE AVGVSTI; VIRTVTI AVGVSTI
as : FORTVNAE AVGVSTI; MONETA AVGVSTI; VIRTVTI AVGVSTI

But in 88 a major interruption to the regular pattern of types on the main aes denominations occurred. This was caused by the Secular Games. In order to commemorate this rare occasion all the Roman coinage, including the bronze, was given over to a detailed display of the various ceremonies enacted in the course of the Games (pl.IX,10; X,1-3). At the same time, incidentally, the aegis suddenly becomes much rarer on the obverse portraits, and in subsequent issues it virtually disappears.

After the special circumstances of 88 the reverse typology returned to its former pattern. The only coins which interrupt the regular series in the early 90s are the two special commemorative issues honouring the deified Julia, dated 90-91 (pl.X,10) and 92-94. These sestertii follow a long tradition of such issues with memorial types, struck probably in limited numbers, but as part of the normal currency. Then, towards the very end of the reign, one further change occurred, with the introduction of another new group of designs on the aes coinage. These coins, dated by Domitian's seventeenth consulship to 95-96, all have new reverse types: for sestertii a group of monuments (pl.XI,1-3), and for dupondii and asses a series of attributes belonging to the deities Jupiter and Minerva (pl.XI,4,6-7). All the coins of this special series lack reverse legends (they include only the S C), and the sestertii are further distinguished by two exceptional portraits of Domitian, one with drapery representing a military cloak (pl.XII,18), and one in which the aegis reappears[27]. The nature of the types, their style and their great rarity all suggest that these coins perhaps formed a special commemorative issue. Domitian's assassination in September 96 brought to a sudden end his coinage; we therefore cannot tell whether or not this extraordinary group of types (or elements thereof) might have become incorporated into the regular aes series.

Finally, mention must be made of Domitian's undated quadrantes (pl.XI,8-13). These form a large group, and they display a variety of types related mainly to the goddesses Minerva and Ceres[28]. The semis and quadrans were of little economic significance, but the large number of dated issues of these coins, and the quantity and diversity of undated quadrantes, testifies to the systematic and organised nature of aes output in all denominations under Domitian.

NOTES

1. The possible re-attribution of the "Lugdunum" aes of Domitian and Titus to the East was mentioned by M. Grant, "The Pattern of Official Coinage in the early Principate", ERCHM 96-112 (p.107, n.8). C.M. Kraay examined these issues in his D. Phil. thesis, The aes coinage of Rome and its subsidiary mints in the West AD 68-81. He concluded that an eastern attribution is most likely, and his theory has recently received support from H.A. Cahn, who presented a paper at the Greek Imperials Convention in Jerusalem, January 1983, arguing for the re-attribution of these coins to Bithynia.

2. Minerva reverse types as for AU and AR.

3. Felicitas, according to RIC (235).

4. This applies to all subsequent issues of regular sestertii, dupondii and asses from the mint of Rome.

5. Requires confirmation.

6. An unusual variant of this type from this issue with two figures on Jupiter's outstreched arm has been recorded (A.A. Boyce, "A New Sestertius of Domitian", ANS Museum Notes 2 (1947), 21-33).

7. The following unusual pieces have been noted here because of their interesting types or titulature.

8. For a discussion of these denominations in detail, see J. van Heesch, Studie over de Semis en de Quadrans van Domitianus tot en met Antoninus Pius (unpublished Ph. D. thesis).

9. These coins can be dated to the years 81-82 because of the absence of the name Germanicus in Domitian's titles. They were probably minted in 82 - see J. van Heesch, Studie, 33, 40.

10. It has also been argued that the "Anonymous" quadrantes with types Rhinoceros/S C, Olive branch; Rhinoceros/S C, Owl (RIC p.219, 36-37) were also produced under Domitian (J. van Heesch, Studie, 229-230).

11. These coins have been separated from the "regular" issues of the mint of Rome because of their irregular issue, their "commemorative" types, the absence of Domitian's portrait, or their unusual style. C.M. Kraay, The aes coinage of Rome, 205-6, attributed the "Restoration" issues and the "Lugdunum" issues to an uncertain eastern (probably Bithynian) mint. The remainder have always been attributed to Rome.

12. This coin may be a hybrid, combining an obv of Titus and rev of Domitian.

13. The as of Domitia *RIC* 443 (=*Cohen* 5) has been omitted. The Cohen reference requires confirmation and the cast noted in the British Museum (*BMCRE* II p.414 n*) has an unconvincing style.

14. The sestertius (*RIC* 453) in Vienna with *obv* DIVVS AVGVSTVS PATER, *rev* DOM CAES DIVI VESP F AVG P M TR P P P COS VIII, was thought by Kraay to have been a sestertius of Titus (as *BMC* Titus 261-4) from the mint of Rome on which the IMP T of the *rev* legend has been altered to DOM.

15. The only example of this coin I have seen (*BMC* 504) has been tooled, and the D for Domitian is, in any case, not clearly visible, so the piece may have originated from the issue struck under Titus (*BMC* Titus 265-7).

16. The "Spes" restored as of Claudius (*RIC* 464) known only from *Cohen* (Claudius 109), is suspected of having a mis-described *obv*; and the restored "Spes" sestertius (*Cohen*, Claudius 108 = A. Banti and L. Simonetti, *Corpus Nummorum Romanorum* vol. XV (Florence 1977), p.210-211) may also be un-verifiable.

17. This description is based on Mattingly in *BMCRE* II, lxx.

18. In this particular case the "reverse" figure appears on the *obv* of the coin because this issue does not have a portrait type. There seems no reason for this side to be considered the *rev* and the "S C" side the *obv* (as *BMCRE* II and *RIC* II).

19. See n.15 above.

20. The design first appears on sestertii of Tiberius for Livia (*BMCRE* I, pl.23,18-19); cf. also *Memoriae Agrippinae* under Caligula (*BMCRE* I, pl.30,4-6).

21. In the plates of *BMCRE* II many of the less worn bronze coins of Domitian appear to have letters with serifs. See, eg. pl.70,5 (*rev*); pl.70,6 (*obv*); pl.70,7 (*rev*).

22. It should be noted that many of the *aes* of Titus attributed to "Lugdunum" by Mattingly in *BMCRE* II are in fact from Rome (C.M. Kraay, *The aes coinage of Rome*, 193-9); but a small number with the characteristically unusual style (eg. *BMCRE* pl.57,5-6) were undoubtedly produced by the same "mint" as Domitian's "Lugdunum" issues.

23. Kraay rightly noted that Domitian's "Lugdunum" dupondii and asses have an *obv* legend: IMP D CAES DIVI VESP F AVG P M TR P P P COS VII (VIII) borrowed directly from Titus's "Lugdunum" *obv*: IMP T CAES DIVI VESP F AVG P M TR P P P COS VIII. The T of Titus has simply been changed to a D for Domitian.

24. eg. the serifs on the lettering of *aes* of Domitian minted after 84; the flat fabric but apparently inconsistent lettering ("Rome" and "Lugdunum" styles on different faces ?) of many "S C" sestertii of Titus (BMC Titus 321-9, 261-4) and bronzes of Julia (eg. *BMC* Titus 255 - pl.53,6).

25. On the cessation of bronze production at Lugdunum see C.M. Kraay, _The aes coinage of Rome_, 213. Two recent articles have now added more weight to the theory of eastern branch mint production of "western" style coinage under the Flavians. W.E. Metcalf, "The Flavians in the East", in _Proc. 9th Int. Congress of Numismatics_ (I.A.P.N. publication no. 7, Louvain and Luxembourg 1982), 321-339, has managed to sort out the previously confused issues of eastern-attributed denarii of the early years of Vespasian into a small and mainly coherent group of branch mints whose establishment was probably based on monetary policy, not military necessity. However, the minting of denarii in the East early in Vespasian's reign does not, in itself, provide any proof for the later existence of eastern "Roman _aes_" mints. C.M. Kraay, "An unattributed Flavian issue, AD 77-78", in _Studia Paulo Naster Oblata I, Numismatica Antiqua_ (Louvain 1982), 175-186, has proposed another Asia Minor "mint" as the source of a group of Flavian bronzes, struck in 77-78, which are included with the issues attributed to "Commagene" in _BMCRE_ II. If a mint in Asia Minor was producing Latin-inscribed "Roman-style" bronzes in the late 70s, then it is highly plausible that a mint in the same area could produce a not dissimilar group of issues in 80-82, but more evidence is still required before the existence of these mints can be accepted. I believe that the attributions will only finally be settled when more information on the distribution of finds is available, and when a complete study has been made of all the known eastern Flavian issues of every category, so that an overall pattern of production can be established and placed in comparison with the output of Rome.

26. On the interpretation of personifications see J.M.C. Toynbee, "Picture Language in Roman Art and Coinage", in _ERCHM_, 205-226.

27. For a detailed discussion of this series, including reasons for the rejection of all earlier-dated examples (eg. _BMCRE_ II p.364† = pl.71,6 = _Cohen_ 350; _BMCRE_ II p.388 n* = pl.77,9; _BMCRE_ II p.399* = Cohen 672), see I. Carradice, "Coins, monuments.."

28. The rhinoceros reverse type is also worth a special mention. Domitian was reputedly the first emperor to exhibit this particular beast in Rome (_BMCRE_ II, xcv).

CHAPTER 6

SURVEY OF BRONZE COINAGE

Introduction : Survey of finds

This study of Domitian's bronze coinage had to be conducted by different methods from those employed for the surveys of the silver and gold issues. Most of the material for the quantitative survey of aes is provided not by hoards, but by loose finds. Aes hoards (especially of sestertii) are known, and many are included in this survey; also, many so-called loose finds may in fact represent the remains of disturbed hoards. However, most of the bronze coins for which provenances have been recorded were discovered either casually or in the course of archaeological excavations as loose finds.

For the purpose of this survey a large sample of coin finds was required. Fortunately, the recent compilation of the series Die Fundmünzen der römischen Zeit in Deutschland (FMRD), and its smaller companions, Monnaies antiques découvertes au Grand-Duché de Luxembourg (FMRL) and Die Fundmünzen der römischen Zeit in Österreich (FMRÖ), has greatly facilitated the undertaking of such a survey. These volumes provide, in a compact and accessible form, carefully recorded lists of finds gathered from a truly massive amount of material. Obviously, this material is confined to Germany, Austria and Luxembourg, and most of it therefore derives from just one area of the Roman world, or, more precisely, one part on the edge of the western half of the Roman Empire. However, as the requirements for bronze coinage in the East were apparently satisfied largely by local production it was the western areas of the Empire which absorbed most of the aes produced in the central mint of Rome. Furthermore, Germany was a frontier region, and the presence of large numbers of troops ensured a relatively high concentration of bronze coinage in circulation in the area.

The following volumes of FMRD, FMRL anf FMRO have been included in the survey:-

FMRD	I,1	Oberbayern	FMRL	I	
	I,2	Niederbayern		II	
	I,3,4	Oberpfalz, Oberfranken		III	
	I,5	Mittelfranken			
	I,6	Unterfranken			
	I,7	Schwaben	FMRO	III,1	Carnuntum
	II,1	Nordbaden			
	II,2	Südbaden			
	II,3	Südwürttemberg Hohenzollern			
	II,4	Nordwürttemberg			
	III	Saarland			

FMRD	IV,1	Rheinhessen
	IV,2	Pfalz
	IV,3/1	Stadt Trier
	VI,4	Münster
	VI,5	Arnsberg
	VI,6	Detmold

For comparative purposes, and in order to utilise as much material as possible in a necessarily brief study, in addition to the *FMRD*, *FMRL* and *FMRÖ* coins, the finds from a small number of additional archaeological sites which yielded relatively large quantities of bronze coinage of the Flavian period have also been included in the survey. The sites are Avenches and Vindonissa in Switzerland, Neuss (*Novaesium*) in West Germany, and the River Liri in Italy[1].

The results of the survey are set out below in a chronological table (Table R), with the coins identified by *RIC* numbers and reverse types so that indications of substantive types as well as relative sizes of issues may be gained. Any coin types and varieties not appearing in Table R have been omitted because they were not represented by any identified examples in the survey.

Table R Frequency of aes in loose finds and hoards

RIC	Denom	Type	FMRD/L/O	Av	Vin	N	R.L	Total
AD 81								
232a	S	Minerva 1	1					1
233a	S	Minerva 4	2		2			4
233b	S	Minerva 4	2					2
236	Dp	Minerva 3	3	1				4
237	As	Minerva 1	25		3		1	29
238a	As	Minerva 3	3					3
238b	As	Minerva 3	1					1
AD 82								
239a	S	Minerva 1	4					4
240a	S	Minerva 4	6		4		2	12
240b	S	Minerva 4			1			1
241a	Dp	Minerva 3	3					3
241b	Dp	Minerva 3	3					3
242a	As	Minerva 1	44	6	8	5		63
242b	As	Minerva 1	15		5	2		22
242*a	As	Minerva 3	3					3
448	S	Pax august	2					2
AD 81-82								
454	Dp	Augustus rest.	1					1
457	As	Agrippa rest.	1					1
463	As	Claudius rest.			1			1
AD 84.1								
242A	As	Moneta	7					7
242D	As	Saluti Augusti	1					1

Table R (continued)

RIC	Denom	Type	FMRD/L/O	Av	Vin	N	R.L	Total
AD 84.2								
244	Dp	Fides	1					1
245a	Dp	Mars	1					1
246	Dp	Virtus (left)	2					2
248	As	Moneta	5					5
250a	As	Saluti August	1					1
251	As	Saluti Augusti	2		1			3
AD 85.1								
256	S	Dom. sacrificing	1					1
257	S	Dom. riding	1					1
258	S	Dom., captive	2					2
262	Dp	Annona Aug	1					1
263	Dp	Fides (left)	1	1				2
264	Dp	Fortuna	2					2
265a	As	Mars	3					3
267	Dp	Crossed shields	2					2
268	Dp	Vict. Augusti	3					3
269	As	Iovi Conservat	2					2
270	As	Moneta	8	1			1	10
271	As	Saluti August			3			3
272	As	Saluti Augusti	7					7
AD 85.2								
284	S	Dom. riding	1					1
286	S	Dom., Rhenus		1	1			2
288	S	Dom., soldiers	1		1			2
288B	S	Dom., soldiers	1					1
291a	Dp	Fides (right)	2					2
292	Dp	Fides (left)	2					2
293	Dp	Fortuna	3		1		1	5
295	Dp	Crossed shields	1					1
296n	As	Vict. Augusti	1					1
298	As	Fides (left)	1					1
299a	As	Fortuna	4	1				5
300	As	Iuppiter Cons.	1					1
301a	As	Moneta	4					4
302a	As	Victory left	5	1				6
303	As	Crossed shields	1					1
304a	As	Saluti Augusti	2					2
AD 85.3								
278b	S	Germania Capta	1					1
287	S	Dom., Victory	1					1
299b	As	Fortuna	2					2
300A	As	Iovi Conservat	1					1
301b	As	Moneta	4					4
301A	As	Moneta	2					2
302b	As	Victory left	2					2
304b	As	Saluti Augusti	1					1

Table R (continued)

RIC	Denom	Type	FMRD/L/O	Av	Vin	N	R.L	Total
305	As	Vict. Augusti	1					1
305A	As	Virtus	5					5
AD 86								
311	S	Annona Augusti			1			1
313	S	Iovi Victori	2	1			1	4
314	S	Iuppiter Custos	1					1
316	S	Dom. sacrificing	1					1
322	S	Dom., Victory	1					1
325	Dp	Fides (right)	3					3
326a	Dp	Fortuna	2	1				3
326b	Dp	Fortuna	1					1
331	Dp	Virtus	10				1	11
332	As	Fides (right)	3					3
333	As	Fortuna	10	1	3		1	15
334	As	Iovi Conservat	3					3
334a	As	Io. Conservatori	1					1
335	As	Moneta	8		1			9
337	As	Crossed shields	1					1
337A	As	Crossed shields	1					1
339	As	Vict. Augusti	1					1
340	As	Virtus	15	2	1			18
AD 87								
342a	S	Iovi Victori	1	2	3			6
342b	S	Iovi Victori	5					5
345	S	Dom., Rhenus	1					1
346	S	Dom., soldiers	1					1
347	S	Dom., Victory	1					1
349	Dp	Fortuna	5			2		7
349A	Dp	Fortuna	1					1
350	Dp	Moneta	3					3
351	Dp	Virtus	2					2
351	As	Virtus	3					3
352	As	Fides (right)	3		1			4
353a	As	Fortuna	7	1	1			9
353b	As	Fortuna	19		3		3	25
354a	As	Moneta	1					1
354b	As	Moneta	6		2		1	9
356a	As	Virtus	8					8
356b	As	Virtus	16		2		1	19
357	Dp	S C Censor Perpetuus	1		1			2
AD 88								
376	S	Secular Games	2					2
382	Dp	Secular Games	1					1
385a	As	Secular Games	8		1		1	10
385b	As	Secular Games	1					1
386	As	Secular Games	1					1
387	As	Secular Games	2					2

Table R (continued)

RIC	Denom	Type	FMRD/L/O	Av	Vin	N	R.L	Total
AD 88-89								
358	S	Iovi Victori	3		1			4
363	S	Dom., Victory	2					2
366	Dp	Fides (right)	3	1				4
367	Dp	Fortuna	6		1			7
368a	Dp	Virtus	1	2	1			4
371	As	Fortuna	9	2	1			12
372	As	Moneta	5	1				6
373	As	Virtus	13	2	1			16
AD 90-91								
388	S	Iovi Victori	27	3	6			36
389	S	Dom., Rhenus	1					1
390	S	Dom., Victory	9		1			10
392	Dp	Fortuna	11	1	1	1	1	15
393	Dp	Virtus	29	4	8		1	42
394	As	Fortuna	21		2	1		24
395	As	Moneta	32	2	5			39
397	As	Virtus	36	3	6	2	1	48
399	Semis	Apollo/Raven					1	1
400	S	Diva Julia	2	1				3
AD 92-94								
401	S	Iovi Victori	10	2	4		2	18
402	S	Dom., soldiers	1				1	2
403	S	Dom., Victory	2	2	1			5
404	S	Dom., Minerva, Victory					1	1
405	Dp	Fortuna	6					6
406	Dp	Virtus	6		2			8
407	As	Fortuna	11		1	2		14
408	As	Moneta	30	1	1	1		33
409	As	Virtus	9	1	1			11
410	Semis	Apollo/Raven	1					1
411	S	Diva Julia	1					1
AD 95-96								
412	S	Iovi Victori	7					7
415	S	Dom., Victory		1				1
417	Dp	Fortuna	2	2				4
420	Dp	Vict. on globe	1					1
421	Dp	Virtus	7	2				9
422	As	Fortuna	2	1				3
423	As	Moneta		1				1
424A	As	Virtus	2					2
Undated								
429	Quad	Minerva/Owl					1	1
432	Quad	Ceres/Modius	1					1

Table R (continued)

RIC	Denom	Type	FMRD/L/O	Av	Vin	N	R.L	Total
434	Quad	S C/Rhino (r.)	1	1	2		1	5
435	Quad	S C/Rhino (l.)	1					1
436	Quad	Minerva/S C	2		1	1	3	7
Total			698	56	98	17	27	896

Table S Totals for each aes denomination

Issue	Sestertii		Dupondii		Asses		Sem.	Quad.	Totals	
	No.	%	No.	%	No.	%			No.	%
81	7	4.6	4	2.4	33	5.9			44	4.9
82	19	12.4	6	3.6	88	15.8			113	12.6
81-82	-	-	1	0.6	2	0.4	-	-	3	0.3
84.1					8	1.4			8	0.9
84.2			4	2.4	9	1.6			13	1.5
85.1	4	2.6	10	5.9	25	4.5			39	4.4
85.2	6	3.9	10	5.9	21	3.8	-	-	37	4.1
85.3	2	1.3	-	-	18	3.2			20	2.2
86	8	5.2	18	10.7	52	9.3	-	-	78	8.7
87	14	9.2	15	8.9	78	14.0			107	11.9
88	2	1.3	1	0.6	14	2.5			17	1.9
88-89	6	3.9	15	8.9	34	6.1	-		55	6.1
90-91	50	32.7	57	33.7	111	19.9	1		219	24.4
92-94	27	17.6	14	8.3	58	10.4	1		100	11.2
95-96	8	5.2	14	8.3	6	1.1	-		28	3.1
Undated								15	15	1.7
Totals	153		169		557		2	15	896	

Bronze denominations : incidence of loss and recovery

Tables R and S illustrate the discovery rate of finds of the separate issues of Domitian's bronze coinage in the areas and sites included in the survey. This discovery rate is bound to be influenced by certain factors which might affect our interpretation of the results. The most important influences on the distribution of bronze coins as finds are the circumstances of arrival of these coins in the areas of the survey and the circumstances of their loss or deposition. It will be easier first to consider the latter of these influences.

Bronze coins would have been lost much more frequently than precious metal coins because they would have been carried around much less carefully, and, once dropped or mislaid, much less time would have been spent in searching for them. For the separate denominations of aes the same principle applies. The loss of a quadrans would have been shrugged off more easily than the loss of an as, and in turn the loss of an as would have been borne more easily than the loss of a sestertius. Thus, of the bronze coin finds which represent accidental losses of ancient money, we should expect to see a greater proportion of the smaller denominations. But not all bronze coins now being found were lost accidently. Some represent ancient votive deposits, and many more pieces, especially of the higher denominations, were hoarded, and these hoards, or at least their remains, make up a not insignificant portion of the total number of finds. Obviously, the chance discovery of a large hoard of, for instance, sestertii, can distort the distribution pattern of bronze denominations found in any particular area. All the larger aes denominations from the as upwards were hoarded, but the emphasis would have been on the most valuable coins. Thus ancient hoarding activity should result in a proportionately greater representation of higher value pieces. To some extent this factor should provide a counterbalance to the increased casual loss of lower denomination coins.

These proportionate differences in incidence of finds of separate denominations obviously relate to the volume of coinage originally available in the areas considered. This volume would be greatly influenced by the needs of the particular area for bronze coins. In the survey the largest number of coins, and therefore the best stastical sample from which to gauge the rate of survival of each issue, is provided by the as. Because the as is invariably the commonest coin found in military sites it has been suggested that it might have had a special importance related to army pay[2]. If this was true it would be over-represented in military sites compared with the sestertius and dupondius. The data in the survey was drawn predominantly from military areas so the as should therefore dominate the sample. However, although the as does outnumber all other denominations in Table R, it does not dominate the results sufficiently to suggest that they have been distorted by reason of the intrusion of one denomination having a special military role. There are over $3\frac{1}{2}$ times as many asses as sestertii in the survey, but as each sestertius was worth four asses the total value of lost sestertii is in fact greater than that of lost asses. There are over three times as many asses as dupondii in the survey and, because the dupondius was worth two asses, this does mean that a greater total value of asses than dupondii was lost. However, the difference is not at all dramatic. Whatever the significance of the role of the separate denominations from the as to the sestertius might have been, they are all quite well represented in the survey.

The regional bias of the survey is a much more important factor, especially as regards the survival of the two smallest denominations of aes, the semis and the quadrans. Only two closely identifiable semisses are present, and one of these was found in the River Liri. Fourteen quadrantes are listed, of which five come from the Liri. It is obvious that these denominations are grossly under-represented in the survey (apart from in the River Liri where they constitute over 20% of the closely identifiable coins of Domitian). It is known, on the other hand, that these fractional pieces are extremely common as finds in urban sites in Italy[3]. It is therefore clear that the shortage of semisses and quadrantes in the survey is due to the fact that the material comes mainly from military areas outside Italy, and at this time such areas obviously must have had little use for these particular coins.

Because the smallest denominations have virtually no relevance to the financial policy of the Empire, the inadequacy of the survey in their respect is not so serious. The information required of these coins, namely their place in the coinage of the reign, has already been provided by the definition of their chronology in the list of aes issues The following commentary on the emission of bronze coinage under Domitian will therefore be confined to the three larger denominations.

Size of bronze coinage issues, AD 81-96

AD 81-82

In the first months of Domitian's reign there was, according to the survey, heavy production of aes coinage, especially in 82. For each denomination the issue dated to 82 is considerably better represented than the issue dated to 81. This perhaps suggests that the mint for aes was operating in 82 for longer than the three-and-a-half months in 81 for which it issued coins for Domitian as emperor, following his accession on September 13. Table R shows clearly that the coins with Minerva types in all three denominations are overwhelmingly dominant. The principal type for each denomination is : sestertius - Minerva type 4; dupondius - Minerva type 3; as - Minerva type 1.

The so-called "Lugdunum" issues are represented by only two sestertii, both of which have the PAX AVGVST type. Such a feeble yield would appear to provide additional evidence against the attribution of this series to a mint at Lugdunum, because surely the product of a Gallic mint would have been better represented in the particular areas covered by this survey. If the source for these coins was an eastern mint it is perhaps equally surprising that two pieces did appear in the survey, although as these coins abviously have Roman denominations they might be expected to have circulated in the West even if they were issued in the East. However, the appearance of two examples can be argued to be perfectly consistent with an attribution of this series of coins to the mint of Rome. Some types from the "regular" Roman issues (the sestertius type with Domitian holding the palladium, and the dupondius with type of Pax) are entirely absent from the survey. Other types which may have had a special commemorative significance, but whose Roman origin has never in the past been questioned (eg. the

Domitia types and the deified Titus sestertii) are also absent. Meanwhile, the "Restoration" types are represented by only three examples. It seems logical to conclude from these distribution figures that all these coins, including the "Lugdunum" types, have a similar status and background. They can, according to these findings, be classified as subsidiary or secondary types of the issues of the mint of Rome.

AD 84-96

In 82 the minting of aes coinage ceased, and production did not recommence until two years later. After the resumption of production in 84 output appears at first to have been low and confined to just one denomination, the as, although later in the year (issue 84.2) dupondii were also issued. In issue 84.1 the dominant reverse type on the as is the new Moneta design; in issue 84.2 another new type with Altar (SALVTI) shares prominence with Moneta. The substantive types on the dupondii of 84 cannot be identified from the survey.

The introduction of the full series of new reverse types for aes in 85 coincides with an increase in production in all denominations with the exception of the dupondius in issue 85.3. The sestertius resumes regular minting for the first time since 82[4]. Production seems to have been spread quite evenly between the many sestertius types in each separate issue of 85. For the dupondius and as the following substantive types can be suggested:-

85.1 : as - Moneta, Altar (SALVTI)
85.2 : dupondius - Fortuna; as - Fortuna, Moneta, Victory
85.3 : as - Moneta, Virtus

However, there are insufficient coins of these issues in the survey for this to be considered more than just a tentative reconstruction.

In 86 production of aes seems to have continued at a similar level to that which was operating in 85. The substantive types are now clearly identifiable. For sestertii the Jupiter (IOVI VICTORI), for dupondii the Virtus, and for asses the Fortuna, the Moneta and the Virtus types are now dominant. In 87 there was apparently another increase in output of sestertii and asses, although the survey records a slight drop in dupondius production. Jupiter is still the principal sestertius type, but Fortuna has replaced Virtus as the dominant type for dupondii[5]. Fortuna and Virtus, and to a lesser extent Moneta, are again the major types on asses.

In the years 88-89 there was, according to Table R, a considerable drop in aes output. The substantive types now appear to be :- sestertius - Jupiter, Domitian and Victory; dupondius - Fides, Fortuna, Virtus[6]; as - Fortuna, Virtus and, again to a lesser extent, Moneta. The Secular Games coins (issue 88) are not very common finds in the survey, but they are sufficiently well represented to be classified as part of the normal currency issue, rather than as solely commemorative pieces.

According to the survey the largest single issue of aes in the reign is the issue dated 90-91. However, as production of these coins could have been spread over a full two year period, the average rate of output is by no means exceptional. Once again, Jupiter is the principal type on sestertii, with the design illustrating Domitian being crowned by Victory coming a clear, though distant, second. These two types, in this relationship, virtually monopolise the sestertius from now until the end of the reign. A similar concentration of production on a reduced number of reverse types occurs also on the dupondius and as. Until the arrival of the coins dated 95-96 the only types now being employed are the substantive types Fortuna and Virtus for dupondii, and Fortuna, Moneta and Virtus for asses.

After 90-91 there seems to have been a decline in production of all aes denominations. Considering that it spans a three year period the issue dated 92-94 is represented in Table R in limited numbers, suggesting a low average output; and this output was apparently further reduced in 95-96. The new types introduced in 95-96 are almost entirely absent from the survey. The sestertii of this series appear to have a commemorative, perhaps medallic, nature, which might explain their great rarity[7]. The dupondii and asses can at best be classified as no more then subsidiary types.

Summary : Output of bronze coinage, AD 81-96

Because the duration of the separate issues of aes coinage is so varied it would be useful, using the results of the survey, to estimate the average annual rate of output for each denomination. Problems of dating tend to reduce the usefulness of any attempts to illustrate the emission of a coinage series, and with Domitian's aes there are certain issues which cannot be dated within exact time limits. The most important of these are the issues of 82 and 84, the exact dates of which depend on the length of time during which minting of aes ceased between these years. We cannot date the end of issue 82, nor the beginning of issue 84.1, so for these two years the coinage has been given in each case an entirely arbitrary six months time span. There are also instances when, within a single year (eg. 84 and 85), there were fluctuations in production of each denomination between separate issues. The following table (Table T) and histogram (Figure 7) should therefore be studied in conjunction with Table S, which lists the total number of recorded coins of each denomination in every issue encountered in the survey.

Figure 7 illustrates the volume of aes coinage of Domitian included in the survey. As with the corresponding estimates for the annual emission of denarii (Tables K,L; Figures 3,4) the separate columns in the histogram vary in width according to the length of time during which the coinage could have been issued. The height of each column records the monthly rate of production estimated from the total volume of coinage for each issue. Obviously it is not suggested that production was evenly spread throughout each year. The mint was presumably mobilised for production of bronze coinage whenever this was considered necessary, so the real pattern of emission would probably have looked very different. However, this Figure does provide an illustration of the relative volume of emission of the coins from the survey in the various periods within Domitian's reign.

The first observation worth making concerns the relationship between each denomination. It has to be stressed that the as provided the largest statistical sample for the survey, and it should therefore yield the most reliable results . The difference between the pattern for asses and the pattern for dupondii and sestertii may to some extent reflect this disparity in the reliability of the samples. However, Figure 7 shows a sufficient consistency between the separate denominations to allow at least a tentative interpretation of the emission of each denomination of bronze coinage.

Table T Output of bronze coinage

	Sestertius		Dupondius		As		
Year	coins	monthly rate	coins	monthly rate	coins	monthly rate	
81*	7	2.0	5	1.4	35	10.0	(3½ months)
82	19	3.2	6	1.0	88	14.7	(6 months)
83	-	-	-	-	-	-	
84	-	-	4	0.7	17	2.8	(6 months)
85	12	1.0	20	1.7	64	5.3	
86	8	0.7	18	1.5	52	4.3	
87	14	1.2	15	1.25	78	6.5	
88-89	8	0.3	16	0.7	48	2.0	(24 months)
90-91	50	2.1	57	2.4	111	4.6	(24 months)
92-94	27	0.75	14	0.4	58	1.6	(36 months)
95-96	8	0.4	14	0.5	6	0.3	(20½ months)
	153		169		557		

* The "Restoration" coins of 81-82 have been included in 81.

In the opening months of the reign the very high overall rate of *aes* production is caused by a massive emission of asses. Sestertii were also issued at a greater rate than usual, but not, apparently, dupondii. Later in the reign, after the resumption of full production of *aes* in 84-85, the three denominations retain a relatively consistent relationship. The as remains the most plentiful coin, revealing an estimated emission rate approximately double that of either the dupondius or sestertius. An exception to this general rule is provided by the issue dated 95-96, for which very few asses were recorded in the survey, but the sample for this issue is unusually small and therefore it may be unreliable. From 84 to 96 the dupondius seems usually to have been issued in slightly larger quantities than the sestertius, except for the issues dated 87 and 92-94.

It has to be remembered that the material in this survey was

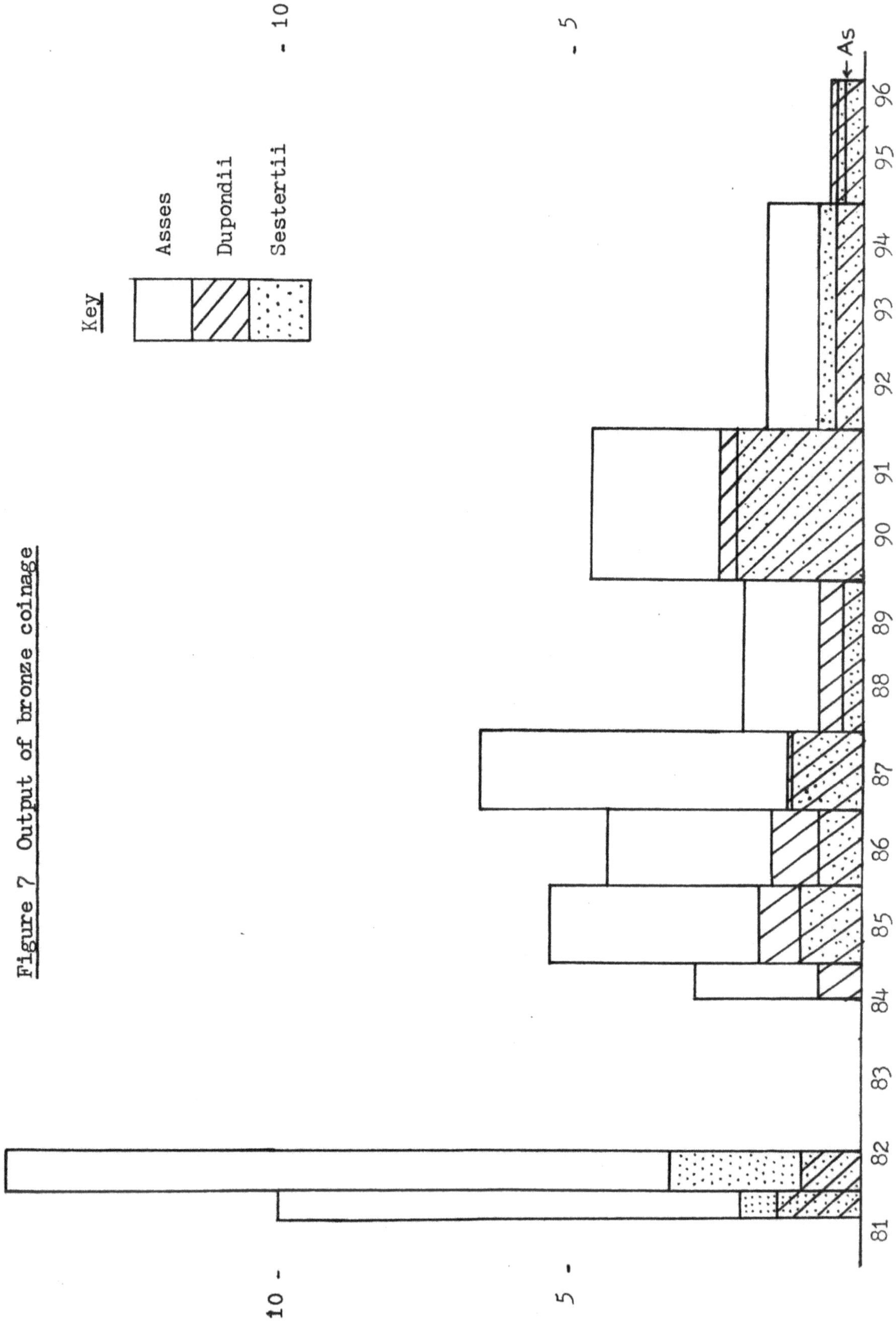

Figure 7 Output of bronze coinage

restricted largely to one area[8]. Only if these results could be compared with the evidence of studies based on other areas would the reliability of this emission pattern be confirmed. Nevertheless, this survey has provided an outline picture of aes emission that can be taken into account in a consideration of mint output and policy for the reign as a whole.

NOTES

1. Avenches : A. von Vietinghoff, SNR 1975, 97-163; Vindonissa : C.M. Kraay, Die Münzfunde von Vindonissa (bis Trajan); Neuss : H. Chantraine, Novaesium III. Die antiken Fundmünzen der Ausgrabungen in Neuss; River Liri : B.W. Frier, A. Parker, NC 1970, 89-109; W.E. Metcalf, NC 1974, 42-52.

2. cf. A.S. Robertson, "Two groups of Roman Asses from North Britain", NC 7.8 (1968), 61-6.

3. M.H. Crawford, JRS 1970, 42-4.

4. No examples of the "irregular" sestertii dated to 84 appeared in the survey.

5. It is worth noting that two dupondii of the variant type with reverse legend ending CENSOR PERPETVVS P P were identified in the survey.

6. The Annona type recorded in the list of issues for the dupondius with a query: (?) did not appear in the survey.

7. One sestertius of this issue with "monumental" reverse type (three-storey building) discovered in a grave in Bonn, West Germany, was mounted in a frame. It had probably been issued in this state as a "medallised" coin - see I. Carradice, "Coins, monuments.."

8. The pattern of finds from British sites, for example, seems to be somewhat different. I have recently been informed that the bronze coins of Domitian from Bath (information, D.R. Walker) show an overwhelmingly high concentration in the years 85-86, and I have heard that this pattern can be confirmed at other sites in Britain.

CHAPTER 7

THE CHARACTER OF DOMITIAN'S ROMAN COINAGE

Bringing together the information supplied by the revised catalogues of issues and the surveys of gold, silver and bronze coinages, it is now possible to summarise the history of the mint of Rome in Domitian's reign[1]. Factors such as use of denominations, organisation of production, intrinsic quality and external appearance (fabric, legends, types etc.) will be considered. The rate of output from the mint will also be mentioned, but possible explanations for the patterns of output revealed will not be discussed until after Domitian's finances have also been outlined (in the next Chapter). Comments on the effectiveness of the numismatic studies will also be made, together with suggestions for further areas of research.

The First Period, AD 81-82

The single most striking feature of Domitian's earliest coinage is its similarity to the coinage of his predecessor, Titus. After Domitian's accession there were virtually no immediate changes. The same standards of weight and fineness in gold and silver coinage continued. The appearance of the coinage was also very similar to that of Titus. The fabric and dimensions of all denominations remained unchanged; legend forms and directions were copied from earlier issues; the portrait of Domitian as Emperor was no different from the head on coins of Domitian Caesar; and in all metals the same reverse designs were carried over from the previous reign, supplemented only by a few new additions relating directly to the accession (eg. Domitian holding palladium, deified Titus, and Domitia types on sestertii). Perhaps the only novelty worth mentioning is the re-appearance of the semis, which was now re-introduced for the first time since the reign of Nero. Otherwise, all the denominations in use were also carried over from Titus's issues.

Regarding levels of coinage output, it is difficult to make a reasoned judgement because details on production under Titus, which might have been useful for purposes of comparison, are lacking. However, comparing output from this Period with estimates for the rest of the reign, a few comments can be made on the results of the surveys. For gold little can be said; the Zemun hoard does not provide sufficient evidence for these issues. For denarii the survey clearly reveals that this Period included one very large issue, of short duration, struck towards the end of 81. For the minting of this issue an unusually high rate of production would probably have been required at the mint (see Figures 3 and 4); but afterwards, production of denarii apparently fell away again. Meanwhile, the rate of production for *aes* coinage was, according to the survey of finds, slightly different. Moderate, even low, emissions of dupondii were accompanied by larger than usual (compared with the rest of Domitian's reign) issues of sestertii, and very large issues of asses, which reach a peak in 82. This high rate of output for asses was never, according to the evidence from the area of the survey, surpassed, or even approached, again during the reign.

The Second Period, AD 82-85

In 82, probably less than a year after the accession, dramatic changes occurred throughout the entire coinage:-

1) The standards of the precious metal coinage were improved to the levels of Augustus. The fineness of silver in the denarius (and quinarius) was increased by approximately 10%, and the weight of the aureus rose accordingly.
2) The long-serving secretary *a rationibus* (the man in over-all charge of coinage production) was removed from office and sent into exile[2].
3) All but one of the reverse types employed on the First Period gold and silver coinage were abandoned, to be replaced by a succession of new designs.
4) Minting of *aes* coinage in all denominations ceased completely, and all the old reverse types were dropped. When production resumed in 84 an entirely new series of reverse types appeared (together with a new obverse portrait of the Emperor).

These changes amount to what must have been a complete overhaul of the Roman mint[3]. For the precious metal coinage the period between issues 82.2 and 85.3, during which the new, very high standards were maintained, has been given the label "Second Period". In this Period the gold and silver issues adhered very carefully to the new standards of fineness, but in the organisation of production and in typology they show definite signs of experimentation. The denarius usually has a broader flan than in the First Period, and this perhaps facilitated the flexibility of production (ie. shared dies) between denarius and aureus which seems to have been applied at least for some issues in the Second Period. The types and legends on the coinage also suggest that these issues were produced in an atmosphere of experimentation and change. A new, more imposing portrait of Domitian, frequently adorned with an aegis, was introduced, and at the same time various new reverse types appeared, and then often disappeared. One particularly noteworthy group of designs was a short-lived series celebrating most of the members (living and dead) of the Emperor's family. However, in 83 four standard Minerva reverse types (including two hitherto unrecorded types) were issued together as a series, and as other reverse designs were abandoned this series came to dominate typology on both denarii and aurei by the end of the Period. Finally, the legend direction on the obverse of the coins was changed to a new, standard form, and at the same time the titulature was reorganised to include all of Domitian's titles, including the newly-acquired *Germanicus*. The aforementioned introduction of the aegis on Domitian's portrait may be connected with Domitian's victories in Germany. It makes its first appearance on the gold and silver coins of the second issue of 84, at the same time as the change in legend direction and not long after the first appearance of the title Germanicus (late 83).

Meanwhile, the aes coinage, after a total intermission in 83, resumed production in 84. It is possible that the major change in standards of precious metal coinage also affected the bronze issues, although this could only be tested by scientific analyses[4]. The new bronze coins, in line with the gold and silver, show a changed titulature and typology. The new portrait of Domitian, again usually with aegis, was used, and a completely new series of reverse types, appearing in full for the first time in 85, took the place of the old types of 81-82. The most interesting new type to appear in 84 was the personification Moneta, whose introduction seems particularly appropriate considering all the recent changes at the mint. The full range of new reverse designs was introduced early in 85 (issue 85.1 : before Domitian became Censor in April), so the mobilisation of the mint for production of this series did not coincide with Domitian's second reform (debasement) of the precious metal coinage. The most novel aspect of these new reverse types is the prominence (on sestertii) given to the Emperor himself, taking part in various scenes representing his victories in Germany against the Chatti.

Regarding output, the difficulties in estimating production of Second Period denarii and aurei have already been discussed at some length. There remain doubts concerning the accuracy of the estimates, but the evidence suggests that throughout this Period output of denarii was unusually low (see Figures 3 and 4), whereas the Zemun hoard suggests that output of aurei was higher than usual (Figure 6). For bronze coinage production resumed in 84 with apparently quite modest output of just dupondii and asses, but then in 85 there was a definite increase in production, with all three large bronze denominations issued in considerable quantities.

The Third Period, AD 85-96

Domitian's second "reform" of the precious metal coinage, in 85, was as sudden, but not as drastic, as the first. The fineness of silver in the denarius and quinarius was reduced by about 5%, returning it to the level introduced by Nero in 64 (still noticeably higher than the standard operating at Domitian's accession). At the same time there was also a slight reduction in the weight of the aureus. These new standards were retained until the end of the reign, and they were adhered to with a quite astounding degree of care (Table A). This is perhaps one of the most important features of the coinage as a whole. Although Domitian apparently felt compelled to reduce the fineness of his coinage from the heights to which he had raised it, it seems he obviously insisted that at least there would be no slackening from the new level[5]. This accords well with Domitian's attitude to the quality of imperial statues[6]:-

> "He suffered no statues to be set up in his honour
> in the Capitol, except of gold and silver and of
> a fixed weight."

From 85 to 96 the uniformity of Domitian's coinage is undoubtedly its most noticeable characteristic. The consistency of standards is almost equalled by the regularity of legend forms and typology and the methodical cycle of production in all denominations. For the legends on the coinage different standard formulae were used on aurei, denarii (and quinarii), large bronzes (sestertii, dupondii and asses) and small bronzes (semisses and quadrantes); but for each of these groups the same formula was repeated without change for virtually every issue, and variant legends are rarely seen. Another feature of Domitian's coin legends is the inclusion and careful numeration of all the Emperor's titles. This is exactly what we would expect of Domitian. His obsession for the recognition and correct observance of form and custom was typified by such deeds as the expulsion of the general public from the knights' seats at theatres[7], and the execution of his own cousin, T. Flavius Sabinus, for having been announced on the day of the consular elections as emperor elect instead of consul[8]. The relentless numeration on denarii of all the titles also provides an illustration of that megalomaniac aspect of his character, which can be seen on the omission of his fellow consuls' names from inscriptions and of the names of the original builders on dedications of buildings he restored[9].

The types used for each denomination of coinage were repeated year after year. There seems to have been a definite purpose, both for organisation and for propoganda, in the usage of particular groups of types. The principal types would probably have identified the product of separate officinae, whose output and standards could therefore be checked. At the same time the groups of designs for each class of coinage tend to complement each other. The silver coinage was almost entirely devoted to Domitian's patron deity, Minerva[10]. The gold coinage joined in the indulgence of Minerva, and also celebrated Domitian's German victories with two types, the Germania and the triumphal quadriga, symbolising the Emperor's most enduring military success. The more graphic illustrations of Domitian's German campaign on sestertii have already been noted, but the sestertius type which was clearly issued in the largest quantities was the design inscribed IOVI VICTORI, depicting a seated Jupiter, the king of the gods and the deity with whom Domitian was most often compared in contemporary poetry[11]. The second most common sestertius reverse, and the only other type which appeared in every issue from 85 onwards, also deserves special mention. This was the type showing Domitian holding a thunderbolt (an attribute of Jupiter) and being crowned by Victory. The design has been interpreted as an indication either of Domitian's desire for deification or of his claim to have been divinely elected as Jupiter's vice-gerent[12]. The fact that the type was issued year after year in company with the IOVI VICTORI type does suggest that it was meant to illustrate Domitian as Jupiter on earth, and that he qualified for this position partly, at least, through his victories in war[13]. Some of the designs used on dupondii and asses also relate to Domitian's victories, but the most regularly employed types, the personifications Fortuna, Virtus and Moneta, are not so clearly identifiable with the personality of the Emperor himself[14]. Finally, the composition of coinage typology is completed by the designs on the semisses and quadrantes, which are dominated by types relating to Minerva, Apollo and Ceres, presumably in connection with the Emperor's care for the entertainment and well-being of his subjects.

Between the years 85 and 96 there were very few interruptions to the regular pattern of reverse typology. In 88 a series of new designs appeared on all denominations from the as to the aureus commemorating the Secular Games. Another commemorative type was used, on sestertii only, to honour the memory of the deified Julia in the early 90s, and special (very rare) issues of gold aurei also depicted Domitia and Julia. Finally, towards the end of the reign new types, for both obverses and reverses, were introduced on most denominations; some of the reverse types again seem to be commemorative, but others may have represented the beginnings of a more general change in typology. However, all these irregular types were invariably confined to the rarest coins (as is clearly shown by the surveys), so they do not alter the overriding impression of standardisation and repetition that Domitian's coinage from 85 to 96 in general presents.

The regularity of issue of virtually every denomination is yet another symptom of the peculiarly rigid uniformity and organisation of Domitian's coinage, especially in the Third Period. It may be that the closely dated nature of Domitian's coins tends to exaggerate the impression that the coinage was so systematic. Nevertheless, the regular striking of all denominations, with the sole exception of the gold quinarius, is a notable feature. The silver quinarius, for instance, was issued with impressive regularity, although it is probable that the rate of emission was never very high[15]. Similarly, semisses and quadrantes, surely the least important coins in the mint master's programme of production, appeared with unusual frequency under Domitian, whereas in other periods they were often neglected. One is left with the impression that the mint was organised in a strictly regimented manner, so that each denomination could be, and indeed usually was, produced at any time.

However, although there was this continual capability for producing all denominations, the volume of production varied, suggesting that output was regulated according, presumably, to needs and resources. In the first phase of the Third Period, from 85 to 87, output of denarii remained quite low (Figures 3 and 4), but in 88 there was a sharp increase, and for the remainder of the reign there seems to have been a quite consistently high average level of production, with noticeable peaks in 90 and, more especially, 92. The picture provided for aurei by the Zemun hoard is somewhat different (Figure 6). The relatively high output of the Second Period fell away between mid-85 and 87, and it did not increase again significantly until the years 90-91, when it regained the peak reached in 82 to 85. After 90-91 output of aurei apparently dropped dramatically, in complete contrast to denarius production at this time. However, there remain doubts concerning the accuracy of the estimates for aureus output from the last years of the reign derived from the Zemun material. Output of aes, meanwhile, as estimated from the bronze coinage survey (Figure 7), followed a pattern quite similar to that of gold between the years 88 and 96, with a noticeable peak in 90-91; but in the years 85 to 87, when output of aurei (and denarii) was relatively low, there seems to have been quite a high level of emission in sestertii, dupondii and asses.

Organisation of coin production

It was not the intention of this work to attempt a detailed elucidation of the internal organisation of Domitian's mint. However, some observations on methods of production can be made, based on information gained from the die-inspections and the surveys.

It was noted in the course of the revised catalogue of precious metal issues that in the Second Period obverse dies were shared between denarii with different reverse types. This applied to coins from the same issue and from successive issues. On the other hand, in the die studies of issues 81.3b and 92.1 not a single obverse die was observed to connect coins with different reverse types. This suggests that at the start of the reign production of denarii was controlled within separate *officinae* which drew on separate stocks of obverse dies, as well as reverse dies. Incidentally, it was noted that in issue 81.3b aurei and denarii with the same reverse types sometimes shared the same dies, so aurei were produced within the same workshops. Then, from issue 82.2 (the first issue of the Second Period) the separate *officinae* apparently shared obverse dies, presumably stored in a central pool. For some issues in the Second Period aurei and denarii employed different reverse types, so for these particular issues the separate workshops were presumably producing different denominations, although they might still be sharing the same obverse dies. Then, according to the findings of the die-examination of issue 92.1, it appears that later in the reign (possibly throughout the Third Period) there was again a stricter division of *officinae*, so that they were once more using their own obverse as well as reverse dies. Aurei and denarii again frequently employed the same reverse types, but differences in both obverse and reverse legends ensured that the same dies could not be used for both denominations.

It has been mentioned that recognition of substantive reverse types (and greater general knowledge of the status of individual types or their issues, and their output) can provide the basis for a reconstruction of the mint's system of *officinae*. From the revised catalogues of issues it can be seen that many coins with unusual or anomalous designs or inscriptions, which were noted without firm dispositions in *RIC* II or *BMCRE* II, have been omitted. The quantitative surveys have supported the elimination of irregular pieces, and they have also helped to confirm the substantive types . For example, the following denarii with standard Minerva reverse designs do not appear in the latest edition of *BMCRE* II (in the catalogue, notes or addenda), but they were all represented in the denarius hoard survey:-

Issue	Type	Hoards	Minerva types now substantiated
83.2	Minerva 2	Egypt	4
85.3	Minerva 3	Swaby	4
86.4	Minerva 1	Tiszanagyrev, Volubilis, Réka Devnia	2
86.5	Minerva 3	Osiek, Magura	4
	Minerva 4	Egypt, Osiek	
87.2	Minerva 2	Castagnaro, Eleutheropolis, Osiek	4
88.2	Minerva 2	Swaby	4
88-89B3	Minerva 4	Osiek, Magura	4

92.2	Minerva 1	Szombathely	3
	Minerva 2	Middels Osterloog, Réka Devnia	
94	Minerva 1	Vyskovce, Szombathely, Réka Devnia	4
	Minerva 3	Osiek, Sotin	

This list helps to confirm that probably all issues of denarii from 83 to 96, apart from special commemorative issues, employed the full range of four standard Minerva reverse types[16]. It is reasonable to presume that any remaining gaps in the series will be filled by future discoveries. At the same time the denarius hoard survey recorded very few "variant" coins. From a total of almost 2,000 closely identifiable denarii the only "variants" noted were a small group from issue 81.3b with obverse legend ..DIVI VESP F.., and a total of just seven examples from the well established "variant" issue (for denarii) 88-89A.

Thus the revised catalogue of denarius issues and the hoard survey together present a picture of a coinage of quite simple and well regulated composition, and the use of the same four Minerva types on all "regular" denarius issues from 83 to 96 clearly suggests an internal division of production between four _officinae_. These workshops seem to have been operating almost continuously because it was observed in the survey of denarius hoards that all four Minerva types were represented in approximately equal numbers. Any further investigation of this _officina_ system would have to concentrate on the details of usage between these and the other substantive types (in all metals) to see how they might knit together. Production of gold coinage was apparently less systematic. The regular appearance of the same four Minerva types from the denarius issues suggests that these particular aurei might have been struck in the same _officinae_ as the corresponding silver coins, but the frequently issued Germania and quadriga types are less easy to place in the system. For Domitian's _aes_ coinage the substantive reverse types for many issues were clearly revealed by the survey of finds. The Jupiter sestertii, Fortuna and Virtus dupondii, and Fortuna, Moneta and Virtus asses make up the bulk of the bronze coinage struck between 85 and 96. Further, more detailed studies will be needed before the definitive relationship which must have existed between these and other types can be explained, but these types reveal the framework around which the cycle of _aes_ production would have been organised.

A more comprehensive study of dies, encompassing all issues and denominations, would provide more information on the usage of dies and the relationship of dies to _officinae_ in the cycle of coinage production, but there would be obvious difficulties in undertaking such a massive task. Another, perhaps more realistic, contribution could be made by a detailed examination of style in die-manufacture. Little is known of the organisation of die engraving, but in the course of the die studies of Domitian's denarii it became apparent that certain distinct styles could be recognised. A more detailed study of style, for example on portraiture, on all denominations would reveal a pattern for the style of engraving for the whole coinage. Such an investigation would also have to include issues of coinage from the Provinces, because in the imperial period there are occasions when a distinctly "Roman" style can be detected on coins minted for circulation in the East[17]. Within the mint of Rome the pattern of style might reveal whether the same engravers cut different metals or if the same _imago_ was being copied by different engravers. It might also reveal whether or not an artist or "style" or imago "travelled" within the mint or outside the mint of Rome to the Provinces, and when any such movements occurred. A comparison of styles between Rome and the eastern provinces would also show how closely the provincial mints attempted to copy the style of Rome, or to what extent this "style" was imposed on them by government control or efficiency of supervision[18].

Conclusions

Two fundamental conclusions can be drawn from this re-examination of Domitian's coinage. Firstly, there are clear signs that the development of the coinage was heavily influenced by "policy" decisions; and secondly, the resulting coinage in many ways reflects the character of Domitian. These two points are clearly inter-related; the policies brought into operation on the coinage obviously represent, to some extent, the interests of the Emperor.

The most important event in the history of Domitian's coinage was the reform of 82. Not only did this reform mark the end of the coinage inherited from Titus and therefore the true beginning of Domitian's own coinage, but also the changes were so comprehensive that they signify a definite "policy" shift. Perhaps the most important element in the reform was the improvement of standards for gold and silver. D.R. Walker has argued that this can best be explained as part of Domitian's more general policy to "restore a higher standard of morality and return to earlier ideals"[19]. Any alternative, including economic, explanations for this reform, and the subsequent debasement of 85, will be discussed in more detail later, after the finances of Domitian have been considered.

Domitian's coinage, however, has many other features that can be related to his own character. The strict adherence to standards of fineness, and the regulated organisation of issue in all denominations, with standard groups of types, suggest that firm control was being exercised at the mint, and it is impossible not to see in this the severe and systematic attitude to administration of the Emperor himself. The Roman Imperial coinage was, after all, produced in Rome, and it is unlikely to have been overlooked by Domitian's watchful eye.

The designs on the coinage also have close connections with the Emperor. There is nothing particularly unusual in this; but what is extraordinary is the extent to which Domitian, or his influence, dominates typology. Not only does Domitian himself appear on an unprecedented quantity of designs, but the deities which appear most commonly also had, in contemporary legend, the most intimate associations with him. Domitian even appears on one reverse type holding a divine attribute (the thunderbolt of Jupiter) and the regular use of the aegis on his obverse portrait adds to the impression that the coinage was being employed to project an ideological message related to the Emperor's aspirations to divinity. Mention should also be made of the high artistic quality and the imaginative composition of many of Domitian's coin designs, notably the "Domitian" and the Secular Games types on sestertii, which are fine examples of narrative art in miniature. It is not surprising that a number of coin designs first introduced under Domitian were revived by later emperors[20].

The output of coinage during Domitian's reign would have been regulated, one presumes, according to needs and to the dictates of policy. We have seen that there were shifts in the concentration of output between different metals. Some of this might have been caused by organisational adjustments in the working of the mint, but it is highly likely that the greatest influences on output would have been financial or economic. This subject will therefore be discussed after Domitian's financial history has been outlined. However, it might be useful here to make a few comments on the surveys which have provided the means to discuss output.

Regarding individual coin types and issues the surveys have obviously helped in confirming degrees of rarity or commonness. For example, coins of Domitian with "commemorative" types in all denominations have generally been confirmed as belonging to very limited issues, whereas the commonness of a small number of standard types has provided the basis for reconstructing the *officina* system within which the main currency production was organised. The surveys have also confirmed that realistic estimates of output can only be made as a result of detailed quantitative studies and/or die studies, rather than from mere observations on regularity of issue or numbers of types employed. One of the most encouraging features of the study of denarii was the general agreement between the findings of the hoard survey and the die studies. These together proved that it is possible to gauge the relative volume of emission of separate issues of coinage as long as certain critical rules are followed. Limitations to the potential usage of similar studies are imposed by the availability of reasonably well dated issues, and by the need to consider such factors as coinage distribution and circulation and (especially) the survival rate of coins of differing standards. Nevertheless, the possibilities suggested in the publication of the Lohe hoard for the successful extension of hoard surveys to the ancient world have, at least to some extent, been realised[21].

The chronological tabulation of the findings in the denarius hoard survey (Table B, with summary in Tables C,D, and Figures 1,2) illustrates the remarkable consistency with which silver coins of Domitian of certain standards apparently disappeared from circulation at the same time throughout the Empire. This phenomenom provides dramatic proof of the effectiveness of the so-called "Gresham's Law". The systematic removal of coins of a higher quality whenever current standards dropped sufficiently to render these earlier pieces of greater value (in spite of the wear they must have incurred) than most current coins, shows that there was an acute awareness of standards. Even when the finer coins have no obvious external features, such as typology, by which one assumes they would have been recognised, they still disappeared. Thus it is imperative to take account of changes in standards when investigating survival patterns and when making calculations on output from these patterns that might then be used as evidence for financial or economic history[22].

The survey of gold hoards showed a similar pattern to that of the silver. The remarkable Zemun hoard apparently represents a sample of high-standard aurei removed from circulation at a time when the government was reducing the weight of new gold coins, which again demonstrates how aware of standards the people were. The other hoards in the aureus survey contained very few coins, but their evidence was entirely consistent with the basic principles of survival of coinage, in that pieces struck at the lowest weight remained in circulation longest.

The investigation of finds of bronze coinage provided only a tentative exploration of the size of issues, based on the survival of coins from a more limited area. Even so there was sufficient consistency within the survey to suggest that the line of approach would be worth pursuing further. However, it would be necessary to extend any future investigation of Domitian's _aes_ issues to include finds from a wider area of the Roman world. Similarly, the principles involved in this study could be applied to virtually any period of ancient coinage, but for Roman imperial bronzes as many regions as possible should be explored so that the results can be assessed on an Empire-wide scale. This would ensure that any differences in the survival rate of coins that might have been caused by the distribution of coinage to particular areas and for particular purposes would be noted, because it is well known that bronze coins, unlike the actively re-circulating silver and gold, did not usually travel far from their original place of issue or distribution[23].

Above all, the separate quantitative surveys of Domitian's coinage have shown that it is of primary importance to obtain the largest possible samples. This reduces the likelihood of distortion from anomalous material, and it also ensures that the most satisfactory statistical results are obtained.

For Domitian's coinage it has been possible to make estimations of the rate of emission from the survival rate of coins in finds. For denarii the hoards together provided an acceptably large sample of coins, and these coins can usually be divided, because of their numbered titles, into issues of known duration. Whether or not the estimates, based on calculations of die output from the die studies, are accepted as accurate, a much clearer picture of the likely pattern of output for denarii has emerged (Figures 3 and 4). Similar estimations have also been made for the rates of emission for gold and _aes_ coinage, but in both of these studies the samples were much smaller, and perhaps less reliable, than for denarii. Nevertheless, enough material was available to produce results which can be compared so that an overall view of coinage output in all denominations for the whole reign may be presented. Of course, it would be desirable to compare the picture of Roman output with that from the Provinces when the evidence from the East can be put together; but perhaps even more important would be a comparison with output in other reigns. The ultimate goal should be a comprehensive picture of coinage emission for the entire imperial period. When this is achieved it will be possible to discuss coinage output in the context of the economic history of the Empire as a whole.

NOTES

1. It is here assumed that all the "Roman Imperial" issues of Domitian were struck at Rome, including the so-called "Lugdunum" bronzes (whose attribution is discussed in Chapter 5).

2. See I. Carradice, LCM 1979, 101-3.

3. It should be mentioned that H. Mattingly introduced a practical consideration into the discussion on the mint reorganisation at this time. In BMCRE II, p. lxxxiii-iv, he suggested that the intermission of aes production in 83 was part of the process of rehabilitation at the mint following possible serious damage in the fire in Rome in 80.

4. An increase in the weight of the semis at this time has been noted by J. van Heesch (Studie.., 34,41), who suggests that the aes coinage was perhaps not excluded from the reforms of quality.

5. D.R. Walker, Metrology I, 115. The careful adherence to standards in all Domitian's denarius issues from 82 to 96 contrasts sharply with the wildly fluctuating levels revealed by the coins of Vespasian and Titus (Walker, Metrology I, 88-94).

6. Suetonius, Dom 13,2.

7. Suetonius, Dom 8,3.

8. Suetonius, Dom 10,4.

9. Omission of consuls' names: eg. CIL VI,449, XIV,3530, XII,2602, III,37. Builders' names omitted: Suetonius, Dom 5,1.

10. Thus taking over from the aes coinage, which had been dominated by Minerva types in 81-82. On the propaganda of Domitian and Minerva, see K. Scott, The Imperial Cult under the Flavians (Stuttgart 1936), 166-188.

11. eg. Martial, IX,28,10, XIV,1; Statius, Silvae I,6,25-7, III,4,12ff. See K. Scott, op. cit., 133-40.

12. See J. Rufus Fears, Princeps a diis electus: The divine election of the emperor as a political concept at Rome (American Academy in Rome 1977), 223-6; cf. review by P.A. Brunt, JRS 1979, 173.

13. For the "theology of victory" see J.R. Fears, op. cit., 47-64, 90-111.

14. See above, p. 122.

15. See above, p.26. A. Kunisz (WN 1979, 5) has proposed that emission of quinarii was both very systematic and abundant; but the evidence does not suggest that this was true - systematic yes,

but not abundant.

16. All the regular issues of denarii from 83 to 96 (with the exception of issue 96) not listed here were already known to include the full complement of Minerva types.

17. A "Roman" style is particularly noticeable on silver coins of Caesarea in Cappadocia and on "cistophoric" issues of Asia. The issues of Domitian from these two series (see D.R. Walker, Metrology III, 120 - Caesarea) and also certain other pieces from Alexandria and Syria (eg. BMC Galatia etc. pl. XXII,8) have a distinctly "Roman" style. On the "Roman" connections of eastern imperial issues see I. Carradice and M. Price, "Greek Coinage under the Roman Empire" in A Survey of Numismatic Research 1972-1977 (I.A.P.N pub. no. 5, Berne 1979), 118-9; H.R. Baldus, Mon(eta) Urb(is) Antioxia (Frankfurt 1969).

18. However, on the subject of style it should be noted that any comparison is bound to be subjective, and great care has to be taken when drawing conclusions based on such evidence.

19. Metrology III, 118.

20. eg. Emperor holding thunderbolt, crowned by Victory (Trajan, BMCRE III, pl.30,4); Emperor riding over barbarian (Trajan, BMCRE III, pl.31,2); Moneta (Antoninus Pius, BMCRE IV, pl.29,3).

21. B. Thordeman, NC 1948, 204.

22. cf. K. Hopkins, JRS 1980, 112-4.

23. Phenomena such as the abundance of "Britannia" asses of Antoninus Pius in Britain (these coins seemingly are not found elsewhere - see M. Todd, "Romano British mintages of Antoninus Pius", NC 7.6 (1966), 147-52) have to be recognised and taken into consideration before too much can be made of the pattern of survival of aes from data restricted to any particular area.

CHAPTER 8

THE FINANCES OF DOMITIAN

The literary evidence and the problem of Domitian's finances

The finances of Domitian have presented historians with a problem which has provoked much discussion, but which remains so far unsolved. The principal difficulty lies in reconciling Domitian's reputation as a conscientious and efficient administrator with the claims that his mismanagement of finances caused bankruptcy.

S. Gsell, in his major work on the Emperor, Essai sur le Règne de l'Empereur Domitien, considered that, despite his being a careful and thorough administrator, Domitian failed to relieve a treasury which had become depleted during the brief, but disaster ridden, reign of Titus[1]. R. Syme argued against this theory, proposing that Domitian could not have left an empty treasury because his successors, Nerva and Trajan, spent lavishly and yet made no worthy economies[2]. C.H.V. Sutherland later defended Nerva against Syme's accusations, and he concluded that although Domitian was not bankrupt he had, as Gsell had said, failed to improve the financial position he inherited[3]. More recently A. Garzetti has joined Syme in doubting the ancient writers' assertions that Domitian's actions caused a financial crisis. He concluded that Domitian was able to spend freely because his efficient and rigorous collection of revenue provided him with the means to do so[4].

All these interpretations are based largely on analysis of information and opinion from ancient literary sources. Difficulties have resulted not from an absence of information. On the contrary, although matters of finance did not usually provide much inspiration for those ancient writers whose works have survived, they do seem to have taken notice of Domitian's finances. However, the ancient writers make frequent assertions of financial problems without providing much detailed information.

The literary authority generally considered to be the most reliable for Domitian is Suetonius. His Domitian is disappointingly brief in comparison with some of the other Lives, but it does include a number of references, both direct and indirect, to financial matters. According to Suetonius Domitian is said to have been generous and considerate in his early years as emperor[5]. Numerous benevolent actions are listed, including his refusal to accept inheritances from testators who had children, and his cancellation of law suits against certain debtors to the public treasury (aerarium). Also, his integrity is unquestioned : "He checked false accusations designed for the profit of the privy purse (fiscus) and inflicted severe penalties on offenders". But Domitian did not maintain this attitude for long. Suetonius says that he became rapax because of inopia[6]. This inopia was the result of enormously heavy expenditure, and numerous references to particular expenses are provided. Domitian frequently staged elaborate and expensive games, shows and banquets, and on three occasions he gave congiaria ("doles") to the public[7]. He also restored and constructed many fine buildings, he spent large sums on wars, and he gave the army a major pay rise[8]. Suetonius concludes that Domitian was "reduced to financial straits by the cost of his buildings and shows, as well as by the additions which he had made to the pay of the soldiers"[9]. He then goes on to say that Domitian attempted to alleviate the situation by "..resorting to every sort of robbery". He claims that "the property of the living and the dead was seized everywhere on any charge brought by any accuser"[10]. Thus Suetonius's description of the actions of the older Domitian exposes a character whose qualities are exactly the opposite to those of the earlier generous and sincere ruler.

Cassius Dio's history of Domitian's reign, as preserved by the epitomators of Book 67 of his Roman History, reproduces in general terms the tradition recorded in Suetonius. He reaffirms that Domitian was extravagant in providing entertainments for the public, and that he spared no expense in covering the Empire with statues of himself. He mentions the soldiers' pay increase, stating that it was financially ruinous, and he notes that further expenses were incurred as a result of the peace terms agreed with the Dacians following the wars of 88-89[11]. Following Suetonius, Dio also claims that Domitian's consequent lack of funds caused him to persecute the powerful in order to appropriate their wealth. He adds that the methods employed in extracting tribute from client-nations were sufficiently excessive to provoke revolts, including that of the Nasamones in Africa[12].

One of Domitian's most vehement critics is his contemporary the younger Pliny, who makes frequent mention of Domitian's finances. This is not surprising; he had first hand experience of financial management himself, having been praefectus aerari militaris in Domitian's later years, and afterwards praefectus aerari Saturni under Nerva and Trajan[13]. Most of the references to Domitian's finances appear in his Panegyric to Trajan, an expanded version of a speech delivered in the Senate by Pilny as consul in AD 100. Mention is made of Domitian's lavish court expenditure, gifts to the public, entertainments, and again the expensive peace treaty with the Dacians[14]. There are also frequent references to confiscations, although Pliny does not suggest that these were necessarily prompted by a shortage of funds. On the contrary, he refers to Domitian as "..that emperor who possessed far more than he needed, but always wanted more"[15]. Unfortunately the Panegyric is concerned primarily with eulogising Trajan, often at the expense of Domitian, so it presents a somewhat obsessive character assassination of the latter. This obviously reduces its value as an independent source.

A small, but not insignificant piece of evidence for Domitian's attitude to financial management is provided by another contemporary, Frontinus, who was appointed curator aquarum by Nerva in 97. On the subject of the maintenance of aqueducts in Rome he writes that two gangs of slaves were employed[16]: a "State" gang, whose wages came *ex aerario* (*aerarium Saturni*, the State treasury, at least nominally controlled by the Senate), and "Caesar's" gang, whose wages were paid *ex fisco* (the "privy purse"). He adds that the income from rentals of water rights was received by the *aerarium*, but had in the recent past been taken *in Domitiani loculos* (*fiscus*)[17]. It seems not unreasonable that the *fiscus* should have received at least part of this revenue, because it was paying for the larger slave gang (460 men, as opposed to 240 men in the State (*Publica*) gang). This could therefore be interpreted as a relatively justifiable example of fund raising by Domitian. However, the importance of the passage is that it illustrates Domitian's high-handed attitude to the question of "State" treasury[18], and it also shows how the Senate resented his appropriation of funds over which it normally had control : "..but with a due sense of right the deified Nerva restored it to the people"[19].

The remaining literary evidence provided by Domitian's contemporaries on the subject of the Emperor's finances is largely indirect. The poems of Statius (the *Silvae*) and the epigrams of Martial provide numerous references to actions of Domitian which would have incurred large-scale expenditure, such as the construction of public and private buildings, the erection of statues and the provision of public entertainments, but they include no direct information on financial history. Apart from the latest epigrams of Martial these works were all published while Domitian was still alive and in general their tone is grossly sycophantic. Therefore the overall impression of Domitian which they convey is one of a remarkably generous emperor, but this could be construed as little more than empty flattery.

The second century writer Plutarch provides a vivid illustration of Domitian's extravagance in the field of public building with his description of Domitian's restored Temple of Capitoline Jupiter[20]:-

> "..the greatest wealth now attributed to any private citizen of Rome would not pay the cost of the gilding alone of the present temple, which was more than twelve thousand talents."

It is clear that by Plutarch's time Domitian's reputation as a prolific and extravagant builder had become legendary[21]. A more unpleasant part of the Domitian legend was his reputation for avarice. Yet another contemporary of Domitian, the philosopher Dio Chrysostom, noted a recent act of imperial persecution motivated by a desire for financial gain :- "..they say he was put to death by the emperor for his wealth"[22]; but there is no certainty that the emperor involved in this instance was Domitian. However, in a similar scene recorded by the later Christian historian Eusebius the emperor is identified as Domitian. This is the interrogation of the "grandsons of Judas"[23]. Although Domitian's principal objection to these people is supposed to have been their religion, it is noticeable that he lost interest in pursuing the charge once he had established that they had little wealth or property.

The literary evidence for Domitian's finances, either direct or indirect, is thus by no means insignificant. However, this evidence is open to question. The main problem is the hostility of the tradition generated by those contemporaries of Domitian who belonged to the senatorial aristocracy. They cannot be looked on as impartial witnesses because Domitian's policies in general were not designed to conciliate this class. On the contrary, in steering an unconcealed course towards absolutism he came into direct conflict with the Senate. As a result a number of important and influential men were condemned and had their properties confiscated. Unfortunately for Domitian's reputation the principal literary figures writing soon after his death had personal connections with some of the senatorial victims[24]. It is easy to see how these writers could explain Domitian's attack on members of the propertied classes simply as a means of replacing funds which he had squandered. This interpretation would discredit Domitian and at the same time distract attention from the possibility that the victims may have been justly prosecuted. The charge levelled against most of Domitian's victims was treason, and it has in fact been argued that his persecutions were essentially political[25].

The hostility of Domitian's senatorial contemporaries was to a large extent passed on to their followers, including the equestrian Suetonius who, in addition, was a personal friend of Pliny, and the legend of Domitian being a "bad" emperor soon took firm root. The prejudices of the literary authorities were liable to make them impose a dubious explanation on even quite reasonable actions of Domitian, and after the tradition was established he was open to widespread misrepresentation and to having attached to his memory additional atrocities for which contemporary evidence is lacking[26]. This prevailing attitude of ancient writers was in many ways conditioned by faulty Roman assumptions on psychology, which prevented them from seeing any real "good" in a "bad" man[27].

It is unfortunate that almost all the literary evidence for Domitian's finances derives from members of the senatorial circle and their associates, whereas virtually nothing is heard from the other classes of Roman society. It must be noted that even the usually hostile sources concede that Domitian's efforts in other branches of administration were often worthy of praise. Suetonius was particularly impressed by some aspects. He writes that Domitian "administered justice scrupulously and conscientiously" and "took such care to exercise restraint over the city officials and the governors of the provinces, that at no time were they more honest or just, whereas after his time we have seen many of them charged with all manner of offences"[28]. Domitian's passion for rigid control of provincial administration may be seen as just another symptom of his authoritarian attitude, but his opposition to corruption must have provided greater protection for at least some of his provincial subjects[29]. However, these people are virtually without a spokesman, unlike the offended governing classes.

Any interpretation of the evidence for Domitian's finances provided by the ancient literary authorities should therefore be qualified by three major considerations:-

1) The contemporary literature is largely provided by a single class of Roman society whose opinion of Domitian was compromised by various factors. It dates from the period shortly after Domitian's death when a new regime was being established, and it was largely written by men who had served under Domitian, but who wished to make it clear that their association with him was neither close nor friendly[30].

2) The later ancient literature is affected by the existence of a hostile tradition.

3) The evidence for Domitian's management of finances seems to contrast sharply with the same writers' assessment of his abilities in other comparable fields of administration.

Numismatic evidence for financial history

The literary sources for Domitian's reign provide enough information to suggest that finances were a major issue, and archaeological evidence provides confirmation of intense activity in the expensive field of public and private building, as also does the epigraphic evidence that survived the "abolition of memory" decreed by the Senate after Domitian's assassination[31]; but a much more readily available source of information is the surviving coinage. However, to what extent can numismatic evidence be used for unravelling problems in financial history ?

It is first necessary to confirm that a definite connection exists between the imperial coinage and financial administration. In the first century AD there was a gradual centralisation of administrative responsibility for finances, and indeed for other aspects of government, under the personal control of the emperor. By the Flavian period the two treasuries, aerarium and fiscus, although theoretically quite separate, were in practical terms hardly distinguishable[32], and one example of Domitian's disregard for the distinction, on the subject of water rentals, has already been noted. Domitian was undoubtedly in a position to exercise overall control over financial administration and, because his government depended on coined money for conducting its finances, it is only natural that he should have had a similar control over the production and issue of coinage in all metals. Production of gold and silver coinage had always been under the direct control of the emperor, and although the bronze coinage bore on its reverse the "S C" mark of authority of the Senate (Senatus Consultum), by the time of Domitian this "S C" would have represented little more than the survival of a traditional formula. It was possibly regarded as a mark of genuineness by the people, but it otherwise signified only a formal administrative concession[33].

Domitian's financial secretary (a rationibus) had ultimate responsibility for coinage production. The evidence for this is provided by the poet Statius. In praising the abilities of the father of a certain Claudius Etruscus he assigns to this man a daunting list of responsibilities, including the production of coinage and supervision of, amongst others, the mines, corn-supply, State budget, taxes and trade[34]. Statius is offering here a poetic illustration of that part of the imperial administrative machine which he believed to have once been the concern of his subject. We might question how much he really knew about the true duties of the a rationibus, but what this passage clearly spells out is the essential link between the provision of coinage and the management of finances.

One noteworthy element in the duties of this a rationibus is his supervision of the mines because the availability of bullion is obviously a factor that might have influenced coinage production. It has been claimed that major disruptions of mining activity could have affected the fineness and the volume of production of silver coin[35]. Similarly, new discoveries of silver bearing ore could have led to injections of quantities of new bullion that would have been sufficiently large to affect coinage production. There is evidence of greatly increased exploitation of Spanish silver mines in the Flavian period but, without more specific information on the dates of arrival of any "windfalls" at the mint, it is unfortunately not yet possible to measure the effects of any increased availabilty of bullion on coinage output under Domitian[36].

If there were available for Domitian's reign detailed expenses and incomes accounts and mint records it would be possible to calculate exactly how coinage production was organised to meet financial requirements. Such records, of course, do not exist. For imperial expenses and incomes we have to rely on scattered pieces of usually quite vague information from various sources, mainly literary. It has been noted that for Domitian's reign there are references to a financial crisis and there is ample evidence for occasions which would have caused considerable expenditure, but few detailed figures for costs are provided and firm dates for many expenses are lacking. The survivng coinage can provide information on the quality and output of new money from the mint, so that it is possible to calculate approximately how much bullion was being turned into coin. However, we can only speculate on how the relationship between government expenses and coinage output really worked in practice. If the treasury contained no old coins new issues would have to be produced; but if old coins were available would these be re-struck as new pieces, or would they simply be re-issued as they were ? There is no evidence for a general rule on whether or not State payments in ancient Rome were normally made in new or old coin. It is probably best to assume that this would have been dictated by circumstances, such as the need to adhere to standards, the requirements of propaganda, the prevention of fraud, and, surely most of all, economic considerations. However, the sheer quantity of "old" coinage in hoards confirms that most State payments must have included plenty of recirculated money, otherwise hoards would have in general contained a much greater proportion of recently-issued coins[37].

The question of denominations has also to be considered. Obviously, if coinage output is to be linked to payments it is necessary to have some idea of which particular coins would have been needed. However, to avoid entering into a lengthy discussion of the possible mechanics of payment for various State expenses, it would be simplest to assume that any expenses which, in themselves, might have been sufficiently large to create increased mint output, would surely have been reflected primarily in production of precious metal issues. Although bronze coinage was certainly an essential part of the imperial monetary system its principal purpose was to provide a practical means of exchange, that is, as a back-up for the higher value currency. Even though bronze coins are the commonest finds in military camps, army pay (always the emperor's most essential expense[38]) had to be provided in the main in precious metal currency[39]. Also, the only Empire-wide currency was the precious metal coinage from the mint of Rome. The aurei and, even more so, the denarii were the coins with which people paid their taxes and usually stored their wealth; and the only means available to the State for putting this money into circulation was in using it to make payments for goods and services.

One final point to consider is the nature of State expenses, and especially the distinction between "regular" and "irregular" payments. For instance, the most obvious "regular" expense of the State was military pay. In the reign of Domitian there were 29 or 30 legions in service at any given time, each comprising some 5,500 men who were paid, at the beginning of the reign, at the rate of 225 denarii _per annum_ for each man. This would have cost Domitian in theory a total of 36 million denarii each year. When the cost of legionary officers' pay, plus the pay of auxiliaries and various specialised military units are added to this the total cost would have amounted to well over double this figure. However, it is difficult to judge how this and other "regular" expenses could be seen reflected in coinage output. On the other hand, notable changes to army pay, such as the pay rise of 33⅓% awarded by Domitian in 83-84 [40], and the additional military expenses which must have been incurred in times of war, should be expected to have had an effect on output; as also might the many "irregular" payments, such as donatives to the army, special subsidies paid to frontier allies, _congiaria_ paid to the Roman people, special games, festivals or triumphs, and of course payments for buildings.

Coinage output and finances, AD 81-96

Although modern historians have suggested that Domitian could not have inherited a healthy treasury both the generous actions of his early years (listed by Suetonius) and the rate of coinage output suggest otherwise. It would be very hard to explain Domitian's early liberality if Titus's claim that he was being ruined by the disasters with which he had to cope is to be believed. Titus, we are told, spared no expense in his efforts to relieve the suffering of the victims of the Vesuvius eruption (in 79), the great fire in Rome (80) and of plague. In anticipating the cost of repairing the fire damage in Rome Titus is alleged to have made the public pronouncement: "I am ruined"[41]. This claim seems hard to believe, or at least was an exaggeration, when we know that at the same time Titus was spending freely on lavish games and spectacles and on an expensive building programme[42], which Domitian was subsequently able to complete at the same time as he was so generously forfeiting revenue. Perhaps Titus's reputation for self-sacrificing liberality was being unreasonably exaggerated by these accounts of financial hardship. It suited Suetonius's purpose to inflate the reputation of Titus so that the contrast in personality with Domitian (in his later years) could be all the more dramatic. In fact Titus might have been well able to afford the money needed to compensate the disaster victims. This view of course pre-supposes that Titus himself had inherited a well-stocked treasury. His father Vespasian certainly had not, but his careful, indeed miserly, management of finances must have largely repaired the appalling situation which had faced him in 69.

The pattern of coinage output in the first year of Domitian's reign does not suggest a shortage of reserves. In the Figures illustrating output we have seen that one of the most eyecatching features is the commonness, at least in certain denominations, of the earliest issues. It is understandable that Domitian would have made every effort to advertise his elevation on the coinage, but the very large quantities of new coin issued quite soon after the accession suggest that there could not have been a serious shortage of metals for coining at that time. In particular there was a large output of denarii concentrated into the last few weeks of 81. A possible reason for this might have been Domitian's payment of the accession donative to his troops. This is exactly the sort of expense which we might expect to see provided in new coinage, and principally in denarii. The exact date of the donative is unknown, but it can be suggested that the large denarius issue, 81.3b, was produced to meet this payment. It is noticeable that the rate of output of asses was also high in 81, but then increased even more in 82. It is difficult to account for this; the evidence in the survey is mainly from a frontier region so perhaps there was an increasing need for this particular denomination for cash purposes in the camps, where the troops wished to exchange larger than usual numbers of denarii now circulating as a result of the donative. Later in 82 production of aes coinage ceased. The large output of 81-82 seems to have been sufficient for the time being because production did not resume until 84. The supply of aes to the western provinces seems to have been adequate, since there was no large scale outbreak of aes-imitations, such as had occurred, for instance, during times of supply shortage in the Julio-Claudian period.

Another aspect of Domitian's overhaul of the coinage in 82, his reform of standards, seems to have made a distinct impression on the output of gold and silver coins. During the Second Period, between issues 82.2 and 85.3, denarii were issued more sparingly than at any other time in the reign, whereas aurei were apparently issued in larger numbers than usual. It is fundamental for our understanding of the organisation of coinage and finances to know how to interpret this phenomenon, especially considering that it was during this very Period that Domitian introduced his famous pay increase for the soldiers.

The rise in quality of Domitian's gold and silver coinage in 82 represented an immediate loss of revenue to the treasury because fewer aurei and denarii than before could now be produced from the same amount of bullion. It also meant that older coins currently in circulation were immediately over-valued. D.R. Walker's explanation for the reform, namely that it was a part of Domitian's more general policy of restoring ancient standards has already been mentioned. Walker rejects other possible "economic" explanations, such as that it was part of a "deflationary" policy (an impossible concept for the period) or that the earlier, poorer, coins were being rejected by the people. Perhaps it is possible that the reform, as planned, may have included an adjustment of exchange rates between old and new coins, so that the loss of revenue would not be so great (if the government could still use old money). However, we should not, without firm evidence, attempt to attach complex or over-subtle economic accessories to the reform, simply because we presume there must have been a more devious reason behind it. Walker also points out that the reform was not simply a propaganda stunt :[43]

> "..if Domitian's improvement of the denarius had been intended to increase the prestige of his currency then he would surely have improved the weight of the coin rather than the fineness, since this would have been a far more obvious change from the point of view of the general public."

Finally, the increased standard of silver cannot simply be explained as the result of a re-coining of earlier (eg. Augustan) denarii of high fineness, because the consistency of fineness revealed by all pieces clearly denotes a coining of refined bullion.

Walker's explanation for the reform is certainly attractive. Domitian was determined to restore traditional standards and values;

and he may genuinely have believed that there was a need to re-stabilize the monetary system which his father and brother had failed to restore following the former's necessary devaluation of the currency at the end of the crisis of 68-69. Domitian's restoration of the Augustan coinage standards accords well with many other actions[44], and he seems to have had such rigid ideas on morals and order that it is unlikely he would have allowed economic considerations to stand in his way. It is possible, however, that the a rationibus did attempt to oppose the reform (perhaps on economic grounds), because the unfortunate father of Claudius Etruscus, who had surely gained considerable foresight on economic matters during his long tenure (70/71-82) of the post was, as has already been noted, dismissed at this time[45].

This currency reform was bound to have drastic repercussions for the government's finances. The subsequent pattern of coinage emission, together with the later currency devaluation, in 85, might be seen, at least to some extent, as a reflection of the efforts of a government attempting to come to terms with the financial realities of the new policy.

The years 82 to 85 were costly for Domitian. In 83 he fought a war in Germany against the Chatti, and this campaign possibly prompted the foundation of the new legion, I Minervia. The success of the German war resulted in celebrations, including a triumph and the distribution of a congiarium[46], and presumably a donative; and all this following the recent (82) dedication (presumably with costly celebrations) of the sumptuous new Temple of Capitoline Jupiter[47]. Finally, and most important of all, Domitian also at this time awarded the troops their aforementioned pay rise. Each legionary now received 300 denarii, instead of 225, per year. It is worth stressing that if the improvement in coinage standards in 82 is a measure of financial stability in Domitian's early years, then so also are these expenses, particularly the generous army pay rise.

The pay of the army was unquestionably the most important single item of "regular" expenditure on the imperial budget. A rise of 33⅓% should therefore have had a dramatic effect on the government's finances. It is not to be assumed that the rise should necessarily be mirrored by an enormous increase in coinage output, because the method of army payment involved the holding back of a great deal of the soldiers' gross pay for deductions and compulsory savings[48]. It is likely that the government, in effect, would not have to meet the full commitments involved in the pay rise until the following years, when the soldiers serving at the time of the increase began to retire. However, much of the cash was sent to the camps for storage in camp savings, and the best way for the government to capitalise on the obvious propaganda value of the rise would have been to make at least some payments of the increased rates in newly struck coins[49]. We might therefore expect to see the increase reflected in some way in coinage output.

But what do the Figures reveal ? The rate of emission of denarii appears to have remained very low throughout the Second Period. This, incidentally, surely confirms that the increase in silver fineness had nothing to do with a sudden "windfall" of bullion (eg. from new silver mine workings). On the other hand, the high level of aureus output which began in late 82 continued through 83, and although it then apparently fell away in 84-85 it can be said that the rate of emission of aurei in the Second Period was in general high compared with the rest of the reign. This would suggest that for these years the State's important payments, including military expenses, which otherwise might usually have been made in denarii, were now being met with issues of both aurei and denarii (note that every aureus was worth twenty-five denarii). It is possible that the initial increase in army pay was advertised with a distribution of new gold to the soldiers[50]. Domitian obviously had plentiful reserves of gold at this time. His cautious issuing of the new improved silver may indicate that the authorities wished to see how the new coinage would be received, and to observe the effects it might have on the coinage already in circulation.

Then in 85 Domitian debased the coinage. There can be no doubt that this was an economic necessity, because only the most pressing reasons could have compelled Domitian to turn back from his policy of improving standards.

In the years 85 to 87 there were further military campaigns, against the Dacians, and in Africa against the Nasamones. It is worth remembering that according to Dio the Nasamones went into revolt at this time (85/86) because of the violent nature of tribute exactions. If we can believe this comment it is possible that Domitian's tribute collectors were acting harshly because of a need to improve the Emperor's finances. In this period there was, according to the Figures illustrating coinage output, only a slight increase in emission of denarii, and output of aurei was also quite low. Then in 88-89 we saw a sudden rise in output of denarii, accompanied by a fall in production of aes. This suggests a concentration of resources at the mint towards the manufacture of silver coin. Gold production remained steady, but it seems there had been a definite shift back towards greater reliance on denarii for meeting State expenses (compared with in the Second Period).

88 and 89 were very expensive years for Domitian. The Secular Games, the revolt of Saturninus in Germany, further military campaigns in the Danube against the Dacians (resulting in an allegedly costly peace treaty) and other tribes, and finally the great double triumph (with associated congiarium and donative) would all have cost a great deal. The intense military activity on the northern frontier at this time is particularly significant, because it has been suggested that the output of denarii in 88-89 illustrated by the hoard survey might to some extent reflect the supply of coinage to the armies and / or the allies of the Romans beyond this frontier.

Although there were no new military campaigns in 90-91, nor any other obvious events that might have prompted increased output, it is noticeable that the rate of coinage production did not fall. In fact, according to the surveys, denarius output either continued to rise (Figure 3) or dropped only slightly from the high level of production in 89 (Figure 4), while aureus and aes emission both rose significantly. The very high rate of aureus output suggests that once again aurei may have been used more extensively for State expenses.

In 92 Domitian embarked on his final military campaign, against the Suebi and Sarmatians. No triumph was celebrated as a result of this war[51], but it is believed that a congiarium and presumably another donative would have been given. The Suebo-Sarmatian war, which cost Domitian a legion[52], would obviously have been an expensive operation. Also, by now the cumulative effects of the army pay rise would presumably have been biting harder than ever into the State's reserves. We have seen that, according to Figures 3 and 4 the year 92 witnessed the highest rate of output of denarii in the entire reign, while at the same time emission of gold and aes seems to have fallen dramatically[53]. Indeed, from now until the end of the reign it appears that the mint concentrated largely on maintaining the supply of new denarii. Much less attention was paid to the other denominations. It seems that, whatever might have been behind the earlier fluctuations in output, the denarius was now firmly re-established as the principal denomination produced by the State for its financial requirements.

After 92-93 there are no recorded events or actions which should have caused Domitian any extraordinarily heavy expense, although he would obviously have continued to meet his regular financial commitments, including the costs of his active programme of public works both in Rome and the Provinces[54]. Correspondingly, there appears to have been a definite fall in output of denarii, although the rate of emission seems still to have been much higher than was usual in the first half of the reign. Another rise in denarius output was detected for 96, but this may be slightly misleading because only part of a year was involved.

The pattern of coinage output for the last few years of Domitian's reign is of particular interest because this is the period which has often been referred to as the "Terror", following the accounts of persecutions and the descriptions of the atmosphere in Rome provided by such writers as Suetonius, Pliny and Tacitus[55]. According to some sources the principal motivation behind this Terror, which involved the trials for _lèse majesté_ (and subsequent confiscations of property) of many members of the aristocracy, was the Emperor's _inopia_. It is now time to conclude with a consideration of Domitian's _inopia rapax_.

Inopia Rapax

The most provocative reference to Domitian's financial situation in the ancient sources is the _inopia rapax_ noted by Suetonius[56]. The reasons given by the various literary sources for Domitian's alleged _inopia_ have already been outlined. Another, possibly crucial reason was the reform of the coinage in 82.

One of Vespasian's first economy measures when he came to power amid the financial ruins at the end of the civil wars of 68-69 was his debasement of the currency. Neither Vespasian himself nor Titus later made any effort to restore the coinage to pre-69 standards. However, this should not be construed as confirmation that the State finances had still not recovered. Improvements in standards of Roman imperial coinage were a rare phenomenon, and they can apparently never be explained entirely in economic terms[57]. Domitian's monetary reform of 82 can be seen as part of a much wider policy to restore former standards of morals and order. We cannot know if Domitian was aware of the likely financial consequences of his reform, although it has been hinted that his _a rationibus_ probably was, and he might have suffered his banishment because of his opposition to the reform. That Domitian believed the government could (or must) tolerate the loss of revenue entailed by the reform cannot be doubted. Although there seems to have followed a shift in volume of output from silver to gold, suggesting a possible saving of silver reserves, no real economies were made to compensate the loss. On the contrary, as we have seen, in 83 Domitian went to war and upon his return he awarded the troops a generous pay increase. This course of action can only mean that despite all the expenses he had already incurred by his early liberality and vigorous building, Domitian was still in a sufficiently stable financial state to contemplate further large-scale expenditure.

When, therefore, did Domitian become rapax? Suetonius says that he "turned to cruelty somewhat more speedily than to avarice"[58]. It is not possible to ascertain with certainty the exact chronology of Domitian's alleged character deterioration. Some examples of his cruelty, for instance the murder of the actor, Paris, and the trials of three Vestals, the sisters Oculata and Varonilla, can be dated early (by 83)[59]. There is also evidence that Domitian exiled some senators, possibly following a conspiracy hatched during the Emperor's absence in Germany in 83 [60]. Another conspiracy was put down in 87 [61], and Suetonius notes that Domitian's cruelty increased following the rebellion of Saturninus (88-89)[62]. In passing it might be noted that none of these examples of Domitian's "cruelty" seem to have been motivated in any way by considerations of financial gain.

The worst period for treason trials and confiscations is normally thought to have been the years 93 to 96 (the "Terror")[63]. However, the tradition that confines the Terror to these particular years may stem largely from the fact that seven well known dissidents, forming a close-knit group, were tried in 93 [64]. Pliny was friendly with this group[65], and the anti-Domitianic tradition generated by such as he may have amplified these trials and, adding to them certain other, later trials, including those of the religious non-conformists Flavius Clemens, Flavia Domitilla and Acilius Glabrio (in 95)[66], built up a picture of a general persecution, perhaps unjustifiably attributed to the Emperor's financial embarrassment.

From this brief outline of the history of Domitian's "cruelty" it can be seen that various subjects (including senators) were coming into conflict with the Emperor throughout the period 83 to 96. In fact, as soon as Domitian began to assert his own particular style of government there seems to have followed a steady stream of victims. Domitian's moral and religious reforms, together with the philosophical and political opposition these reforms provoked, seem to have been the basic cause behind the long list of banishments and executions. Financial gain, however, did become a noticeable feature of the persecutions, not necessarily as a prime motive, but certainly as a not unwelcome by-product. To ignore this aspect would be to reject entirely the testimony of some sources, who may have exaggerated the tradition of Domitian's rapacity, but whose claims must have had some basis on fact. We have already seen that the revolt of the Nasamones in 85 or 86 was explained by Dio as a reaction against over-vigorous tribute collection. We know from Suetonius that, albeit as part of a wider, religious, reaction, Domitian was collecting the Jewish tax with undue harshness probably by the late 80s[67]. Also, subjects who, as a result of trials, were condemned to relegatio now forfeited their property to the treasury[68]. It is understandable that, with rich pickings to be gained, the *delatores*, whom Domitian had originally suppressed[69], were now given a *free hand* to bring subjects to trial.

The date of Domitian's second coinage reform, the debasement of 85, may be crucial for the chronology of the Emperor's alleged decline into rapacity. This debasement is seen by Walker as proof that Domitian had overestimated the capacity of the treasury to withstand the combined assault of a restoration of coinage standards and a programme of heavy expenditure[70]. The debasement may have heralded a general hardening of the Emperor's attitude to finances. Possibly because of a growing awareness of impending financial difficulties he perhaps now began the rigorous enforcement and collection of taxes, including the Jewish tax. At the same time Domitian's growing austerity in moral and religious matters would have yielded an increased revenue from trials under such laws as the *Lex Voconia*, *Lex Iulia de adulteriis* and *Lex Scantinia*[71]. It is worth noting that it was also in 85 that Domitian became first *Censor* and later *Censor Perpetuus*.

In the years after 85 frequent heavy expenditure on buildings, on shows and on wars (which would not have have had their expenses off-set by large returns of booty), added to the gradually increasing burden of the army pay rise, would have continued to stretch Domitian's financial resources. Other emperors in a similar position might have opted for the usual expedient of further debasing the currency. Nero and Vespasian had recently set precedents, and in the second century, following the lead of Trajan in 107, debasements were to occur with steadily increasing frequency. But Domitian would not take such a step. We have seen that for the denarius a "Neronian" standard was strictly maintained until the end of the reign. For the same period the quantitative analyses have shown that, at least from 88, there was a regular and plentiful emission of denarii, perhaps amounting to an average of between 20 and 23 million denarii each year if Tables K and L can be believed. This proves that plenty of bullion was available to the Emperor. Whether he acquired this silver largely by confiscations or by careful (perhaps severe) management of revenue, or indeed by some other means, cannot be proved. All we can say is that Domitian was well established in his policy of moral and religious reform before any hint of financial gain appears to have entered the picture. His awareness of financial realities began as early as 85; from then his general attitude hardened, and perhaps a contributory factor to this was a realisation that financial gains would accrue from convictions. However, the persecutions of the subsequent period should still be viewed in the context of a systematic attack on corruption, moral and religious non-conformity, and on the political and philosophical opposition which his uncompromising and autocratic attitude and policies provoked[72].

In conclusion, the view that Domitian's financial history represents a failure to restore a difficult situation inherited from the reign of Titus should be rejected. The financial situation early in the reign was sufficiently secure for Domitian to attempt a new, reforming style of government, which included a dramatic restoration of coinage standards. In continuing the programme of expenditure that was necessary in pursuance of his ideas, which included a refusal to take the "easy option" of corrupting the coinage further than a limited reduction of standards in 85, Domitian was probably driven towards the financial difficulties claimed by the literary tradition. However, the steadily accelerating currency debasements of the second and third centuries AD suggest that the Empire was in any case essentially built on an inadequate economic foundation, with income perhaps rarely covering expenditure. Therefore, the eventual outcome of Domitian's initially bold and reforming actions was probably inevitable.

NOTES

1. S. Gsell, *Essai*.., 333-4.

2. R. Syme, *JRS* 1930, 55-70. As well as discussing the expenses of Nerva and Trajan, Syme also endeavoured to show that during the later years of Domitian's reign insufficient amounts were spent to have left an embarrassed treasury (a view challenged by D. Robathan, *TAPA* 1942, 130-144). He later modified his position, admitting that there were doubts about the well-being of the *fiscus* at the end of the reign: *Tacitus*, 630.

3. C.H.V. Sutherland, *JRS* 1935, 150-162.

4. A. Garzetti, *From Tiberius*.., 281-4.

5. *Dom* 9.

6. *Dom* 3,2.

7. *Dom* 4,5. His three *congiaria* amounted to a total of 225 denarii - by no means an excessive sum (see R. Syme, *JRS* 1930, 59).

8. *Dom* 5 (buildings); 6 (wars); 7,3 (army pay).

9. *Dom* 12,1.

10. *Dom* 12,1.

11. 67,4,4; 67,8,1-5 (entertainments); 67,8,1 (statues); 67,3,5 (army pay); 67,7,4 (peace treaty with Dacians).

12. 67,4,5 (persecutions); 67,4,6 (Nasamones: this revolt took place in 85 or 86).

13. See A.N. Sherwin-White, *The Letters of Pliny* (Oxford 1966), 75-7.

14. *Pan* 20,4-5 (court expenses); 27,2-4; 28,1-3 (gifts); 33,4 (entertainments); 12,2 (peace treaty with Dacians).

15. *Pan* 50,5.

16. *De aquis* 2,116-8.

17. Frontinus uses the term "coffers" rather than *fiscus*, but they were no doubt synonymous.

18. cf. Pliny, *Pan* 50,2, where he states that Trajan restored many confiscated properties "*ex patrimonio*.....*in imperium*", implying that Domitian had taken personal control of funds which should have gone to the State.

19. *De aquis* 2,118.

20. *Parallel Lives*: *Publicola* 15,3.

21. cf. *Publicola* 15,5: "...you desire that every thing becomes gold and stone at your touch."

22. *Discourses* 7,12.

23. *Ecclesiastical History* 3,20. Another reference to confiscations appears in 3,17.

24. This was especially true of Pliny: see S. Gsell, *Essai*.., 320.

25. See R.S. Rogers, *CP* 1960, 19-23; H. Pleket, *Mnemosyne* 1961, 297-301, 309-313. The senatorial opposition to earlier emperors (see D. McAlindon, "Senatorial opposition to Claudius and Nero", *AJP* 77 (1956), 113-132) continued with equal venom into the Flavian period. This ideological opposition was often likely to provoke a harsh reaction from the emperor (see J.M.C. Toynbee, "Dictators and Philosophers in the First Century AD", *Greece and Rome* 13 (1944), 43-58.

26. For example, there is no direct, first hand, evidence for Domitian's alleged persecution of Christians (for which extensive discussion and bibliography is provided in W. Pöhlmann, *Die heidnische, jüdische und christliche Opposition gegen Domitian* (Nürnberg 1966) but he was an obvious candidate for the later Christian writers to select as a persecutor:

> "When Domitian had given many proofs of his great cruelty and had put to death without any reasonable trial no small number of men...and had punished without a cause myriads of other notable men by banishment and confiscation of their property, he finally showed himself the successor of Nero's campaign of hostility to God." (Eusebius, *Ecclesiastical History* 3,17).

27. The Romans believed that a man's *ingenium* was a fixed entity from birth to death; if he ended up "bad" he must have been "bad" from the start, and his apparently good acts were either a cover or could be attributed to the influence of others: cf. Syme, *Tacitus*, 421; B.H. Warmington, *Nero: Legend and Reality* (London 1969), 27. For the hostility of the literary tradition specifically relating to the character of Domitian, see K.H. Waters, *Phoenix* 1964, 49-77.

28. *Dom* 8,2.

29. For Domitian's interest in, and concern for, the welfare of his provincial subjects, see H. Pleket, *Mnemosyne* 1961, 301-8. However, for a more critical assessment of Domitian's provincial activities see B. Levick, "Domitian and the Provinces", *Latomus* 41.1 (1982), 50-73.

30. Under Domitian in the 90s Pliny's official career progressed from the quaestorship (90?) to the tribunate, praetorship (93?), and the *praefectura aerari militaris* (94-96?). This rapid rise, following a delayed start, has been attributed to the continuous *suffragatio* ("support") of Domitian (A.N. Sherwin-White, *The Letters of Pliny*, 74). Tacitus was praetor in 88, and in the

same year he had a special involvement with the ceremonials of the Secular Games as quindecemvir sacris faciundis (Annals, 11, 11,1).

31. Suetonius, Dom 23,1.

32. The question of imperial financial responsibility, and especially the relationship between the two treasuries, has been dealt with in great detail by modern scholars; eg: H. Last, "The Fiscus: A Note", JRS 34 (1944), 51-9; C.H.V. Sutherland, " Aerarium and Fiscus during the Early Empire", AJP 66 (1945), 151-70; A.H.M. Jones, The Aerarium and the Fiscus", JRS 40 (1950), 22-9; F. Millar, "The Fiscus in the First Two Centuries", JRS 53 (1963), 29-42; "The Aerarium and its Officials under the Roman Empire", JRS 54 (1964), 33-40; The Emperor in the Roman World (London 1977) 148-53, 189-201, 623-5; P.A. Brunt, "The Fiscus and its Development", JRS 56 (1966), 75-91.

33. For various theories on S C see: T. Mommsen, (Römisches Staatsrecht (3rd ed., Leipzig 1887), III, 1146; K. Kraft, "Senatus Consulto", JNG 12 (1962), 7-49; A. Bay, "The Letters S C on Augustan Aes Coinage", JRS 62 (1972), 111-22; C.H.V. Sutherland, The Emperor and the Coinage (London 1976), 12-22; A. Burnett, "The Authority to Coin in the Late Republic and Early Empire", NC 7.17 (1977), 45-63.

34. Silvae 3,3,86-105. Claudius Etruscus's father was an imperial freedman who became a rationibus in 70/71 and kept this position until 82, when Domitian removed and banished him: see I. Carradice, LCM 1979, 101-3.

35. G.D.B. Jones, "The Roman Mines at Riotinto", JRS 70 (1980), 162-3.

36. On Flavian mining in Spain, see G.D.B. Jones, op. cit., 163.

37. For hoard evidence for the use of old coin in official payments, see the Lay hoard: P. Fustier, Revue Archeologique de l'Est et du Centre-Est 1 (1950), 175-80.

38. Note Septimius Severus's dying advice to his sons: "...enrich the soldiers, and scorn all other men". (Dio 77,15,2).

39. The bulk of the money stored in a camp headquarters must have been in the form of denarii (and aurei). Suetonius records that Domitian prohibited the deposition of more than 1,000 sestertii in the camp treasury by any one soldier. If the saving of such large sums could be contemplated, practical considerations would demand that they be stored in the form of large denomination coin. Also, it is surely significant that in times of civil wars (eg. 1st century BC and AD 68-9), when regular army pay was most essential to secure the loyalty of troops, aes production frequently lapsed, whereas gold and (especially) silver production was always maintained.

40. See S. Gsell, Essai.., 156; C.M. Kraay, ANS Museum Notes 1960, 115-6.

41. Suetonius, Divus Titus 8.

42. A. Garzetti, From Tiberius.., 261-2

43. Metrology III, 118. The public was certainly aware of some improvement in the coinage (nova moneta: Martial, 12,55,7-8); the new aurei were nick-named domini (Martial 4,28,5) or flavi ("yellow-boys") (Martial 12,65,6). However, it is interesting that the contemporary poets ignored the potential of the "restoration of the coinage" for flattering the Emperor.

44. His revival of ancient laws and customs and his reactionary attitude in general can clearly be seen in his moral and religious reforms: see S. Gsell, Essai.., 80-87.

45. See I. Carradice, LCM 1979, 102-3.

46. Domitian's three congiaria are believed to have been given in 83, 89 and 93. See D. van Berchem, Les Distributions de Blé et d'Argent a la Plèbe Romaine sous l'Empire (Geneva 1939), 150-1.

47. The task of completing the other major works carried over from the reigns of Vespasian and Titus, and the rebuilding following the fire of 80, would presumably have been concentrated into the early years of Domitian's reign. For the dates of Domitian's buildings see F.C. Bourne, The Public Works.., 64-9; M.E. Blake, Roman Construction in Italy from Tiberius through the Flavians (Washington 1959), 99-157.

48. See R.O. Fink, Roman Military Records on Papyrus (American Phil. Assoc. Monograph no. 26, New York 1971), nos. 68-73; P.A. Brunt, "Pay and superannuation in the Roman army", PBSR 18 (1950), 60-1.

49. Note the sestertius of 84 with reverse type alluding to the pay increase (C.M. Kraay, ANS Museum Notes 1960, 114-6).

50. The arm-purse discovered at Birdoswald confirms that gold was available to soldiers at camp; see I.A. Richmond, "The Birdoswald hoard and its composition", TCWAAS n.s.55 (1955), 56-60; G.R. Watson, "The Birdoswald hoard: the pay and the purse", TCWAAS n.s. 55 (1955), 61-5.

51. Suetonius, Dom 6,1; Statius, Silvae 3,3,170-1.

52. Suetonius, Dom 6,1; Tacitus, Agricola 41.

53. Although it has to be remembered that the emission of post-92 aurei indicated by the survey may be suspect.

54. See D. Robathan, TAPA 1942, 130-44.

55. eg. Tacitus, Histories I,ii; Pliny, Letters III,xi,3. See S. Gsell, Essai.., 262-74 (= Chapter 8: "Periode de Terreur")

56. Dom 3,2.

57. See D.R. Walker, Metrology III, 117-8 (Domitian's reform); 128-9 (Pertinax's reform); 132-3 (Macrinus's reform). On the other hand, debasements were invariably motivated by financial needs (Metrology III, 138).

58. Dom 10,1.

59. Dio 67,3,3-4. These events are placed before the Chatti campaign.

60. See S. Gsell, Essai.., p.247 n.7. Domitian's cousin T. Flavius Sabinus was also executed in this period.

61. On 22 September the Arval Brethren recorded the discovery of the conspiracy (CIL VI, 2065 = M. McCrum and A.G. Woodhead, Select Documents.., 27).

62. Dom 10,5. The trial and brutal sentence of the chief Vestal, Cornelia, has also been attributed to 89 (S. Gsell, Essai.., 80-1).

63. Tacitus, Agricola 44-5. Tacitus says that Agricola, who died on August 23, 93, was fortunate not to witness the persecutions of the subsequent period.

64. See A.N. Sherwin-White, The Letters of Pliny (Oxford 1966), 242. The seven were: Helvidius Priscus (the Younger), Junius Arulenus Rusticus, Herennius Senecio, Fannia (wife of Senecio), Arria (Fannia's mother), Verulana Gratilla and Junius Mauricus (brother of Rusticus).

65. Letters 3,11.

66. Dio 67,14.

67. Dom 12,2. See S. Gsell, Essai.., 290-1.

68. Digest 48,22,1.

69. Suetonius, Dom 9,3.

70. D.R. Walker, Metrology III, 119. Walker also notes the coincidence of this debasement and the abandonment of plans for the total conquest of northern Britain. In fact the reasons for Agricola's recall and the change in policy in Britain were essentially strategic; they marked a shift of emphasis towards the more important northern European frontiers. Nevertheless, the termination of Rome's expansion in Britain at this time is perhaps symbolic of the mood of economy that was becoming increasingly necessary as Domitian's reign progressed.

71. Suetonius, Dom 8,3; Pliny, Pan 42,1.

72. Also, this attack was intensified because of the steadily increasing (and justified) paranoia about assassination (Suetonius, Dom 14,4; 15,3; 16,1) of an Emperor who probably by nature felt isolated, insecure and suspicious (cf. the picture of the lonely, brooding tyrant painted by Pliny, Pan 48).

APPENDIX 1

INVENTORY OF DENARIUS COIN HOARDS

The following hoards were included in the survey of denarii*:

1. ACARNANIA, Greece, 1976/7.
   Details of discovery uncertain, but the hoard was thought to be complete when recorded. 42 denarii, Nero to Nerva (AD 97).
   Domitian 81-96 : 15 (14 accurately identified); pre-81 : 5.
   Ref. *Coin Hoards* 4 (1978), 33 (no.108). This reference records a total of 39 denarii, a further 3 coins subsequently came to light.

2. LAVENHAM, England, 1874.
   Discovered during ploughing; 184 coins noted from a total of 197. 179 denarii published in detail, M.Antony to Trajan (AD 103-111).
   Domitian 81-96 : 35 (34 accurately identified); pre-81 : 3.
   Ref. C. Babington, "Account of Roman silver coins found at Lavenham, Suffolk, in June, 1874", *NC* 2.15 (1875), 140-3 (reprinted from *Proceedings of the Suffolk Institute of Archaeology and Natural History* 4(1874), 414-6.

3. VERULAMIUM, England, 1958.
   Discovered during archaeological excavations; hoard complete. 50 denarii, Republic to Trajan (AD 112-117).
   Domitian 81-96 : 7; pre-81 : 2.
   Ref. C.M. Kraay, "A hoard of denarii from Verulamium", *NC* 6.20 (1960), 271-3.

4. EGYPT, Nile Delta (?), before 1932.
   Details of discovery uncertain, but the hoard was thought to be complete when published. 262 denarii, Nero to Trajan (AD 112-117); 5 eastern imperial AR (Caesarea in Cappadocia); 33 Greek AR (2nd - 1st centuries BC).
   Domitian 81-96 : 60 denarii (59 accurately id.); pre-81 : 6 denarii.
   Ref. S.H. Weber, *An Egyptian hoard of the second century AD*. *A.N.S. Numismatic Notes and Monographs* 54 (New York 1932).

5. MALLERSTANG, England, 1926.
   Complete hoard. 138 denarii, Galba to Hadrian (AD 134-138).
   Domitian 81-96 : 11; pre-81 : 4.
   Ref. H. Mattingly and R.G. Collingwood, "The Mallerstang Hoard", *Transactions of the Cumberland and Westmorland Antiquarian and Archaeological Society* n.s. 27 (1927), 205-17.

6. SWABY, England, 1934.
Discovered during ploughing; hoard complete. 178 denarii, M. Antony to Hadrian (AD 137).
Domitian 81-96 : 27, plus 1 plated hybrid; pre-81 : 4.
Ref. H. Mattingly, "The Swaby Hoard", NC 5.14 (1934), 216-9.

7. CASTAGNARO, Italy, 1903.
Discovered during ditch working. 20 aurei and 1109 denarii, Nero to Hadrian (AD 126), recorded from a total of 20 aurei and 1207 denarii.
Domitian 81-96 : 1 aureus, 128 denarii; pre-81 : 1 aureus, 19 denarii.
Ref. L. Rizzoli, "Castagnaro (Verona) Tesoretto Monetale", Riv.It. 27 (1914), 349-64.

8. ERLA, Austria, 1966.
Discovered during ditch working. 103 aurei and 666 denarii, M. Antony to Hadrian (AD 134-138), plus 5 eastern imperial AR (Lycia).
Domitian 81-96 : 1 aureus, 68 denarii, 1 Lycian AR; pre-81 : 5 aurei, 19 denarii.
Ref. H. Jungwirth, "Der Münzschatsfund von Erla", NZ 82 (1967), 26-48.

9. TISZANAGYREV, Hungary, 1925.
Discovered during work in a vineyard. 63 denarii, Nero to Hadrian (AD 134-138).
Domitian 81-96 : 16.
Ref. E. Jónás, "A tiszanagyrévi római éremlelet", NK 23-24 (1924-5), 38-40

10. MURABBA 'AT, Israel, 1952.
Details of discovery unknown; hoard incomplete. 51 denarii, Republic to Hadrian (AD 119-122); 57 eastern imperial AR (14 Antioch, 43 Caesarea in Cappadocia?); 119 Nabataean AR.
Domitian 81-96 : 6 denarii.
Ref. J.T. Milik and H. Seyrig, "Trésor monétaire de Murabba 'Ât", RN 6.1 (1958), 11-26.

11. VOLUBILIS, Morocco, 1930.
Discovered within a bracelet uncovered during archaeological excavations. 105 denarii recorded, M. Antony to Hadrian (AD 119-122), from a total of 115 coins.
Domitian 81-96 : 18; pre-81 : 3.
Ref. A. Ruhlmann, "Le Bracelet-Bourse Romain de Volubilis (Maroc)", RN 4.36 (1933), 51-9; J. Marion, "Les Trésors Monétaires de Volubilis et de Banasa", Antiquités africaines 12 (1978), 179-215

12. ELEUTHEROPOLIS, Israel, before 1907.
Discovered in a tomb; hoard incomplete. 177 denarii, Republic to Hadrian (AD 134-138); 108 eastern AR.
Domitian 81-96 : 17 denarii; pre-81 : 4 denarii.
Ref. I.N. Svoronos, "Perigrafikos katalogos ton prosktematon ton ethnikou nomismatikou mouseiou", Journale Internationale d'Archeologie numismatique 10 (1907), 230-48.

13. MIDDELS OSTERLOOG, West Germany, 1892.
Details of discovery uncertain. 177 denarii, Republic to Antoninus Pius (AD 140-144); 1 eastern imperial AR (Lycia).

Domitia 81-96 : 10 denarii, 1 Lycian AR.
Ref. K. Regling, "Beschreibung des Denare des Schatzes von Middels Osterloog", ZfN 29 (1912), 207-12.

14. LONDONTHORPE, England, 1976.
Complete hoard. 420 denarii, M. Antony to Antoninus Pius (AD 153-4).
Domitian 81-96 : 46; pre-81 : 8.
Ref. R.A.G. Carson and A.M. Burnett, Recent Coin Hoards from Roman Britain (British Museum Occasional Paper no. 5, London 1979), 9-24.

15. DIMBAU, Romania, 1921.
Hoard incomplete. 135 denarii, Nero to Antoninus Pius (AD 143)
Domitian 81-96 : 10; pre-81 : 4.
Ref. C. Preda, "Tezaurul monetar de la Dîmbău, reg. Stalin, și tulburările pricinuite de Daci în anul 143, sub Antonin Piul", SCN 1 (1957), 113-131.

16. VYSKOVCE, Czechoslovakia, 1930.
Complete hoard. 1,063 denarii, Nero to Antoninus Pius (AD 152-153); 4 eastern imperial AR (Lycia); (plus 1 later denarius apparently not belonging to the hoard).
Domitian 81-96 : 108 denarii, 1 Lycian AR; pre-81 : 33 denarii.
Ref. V. Ondrouch, Der römische Denarfund von Vyskovce aus der Frühkaiserzeit, Bratislava 1934.

17. VISA, Romania, before 1908.
Details of discovery unknown. 85 denarii, Nero to Antoninus Pius (AD 155-156).
Domitian 81-96 : 7.
Ref. P. Harsányi, "Eremleletek", NK 7-8 (1908-9), 120.

18. SALASURI, Romania, 1959.
Complete hoard. 3,197 denarii, Republic to Antoninus Pius (AD 158); 2 barbarous imitations; 3 eastern imperial AR (Lycia).
Domitian 81-96 : 202 denarii (201 accurately identified), 1 Lycian AR; pre-81 : 66 denarii.
Ref. I. Molnar and I. Winkler, "Tezaurul de monede Romane de la Salașuri", Acta Musei Napocensis 2 (1965), 269-293; I. Carradice, "The Domitianic denarii in the Salasuri hoard", Coin Hoards 3 (1977), 70-72 (no. 149).

19. TIPASA, Algeria, 1948.
Discovered during archaeological excavations. 83 denarii, M. Antony to Antoninus Pius; 1 as (Vespasian).
Domitian 81-96 : 6.
Ref. J. Baradez, "Le Trésor de Tipasa", Libyca, Archéologie-Epigraphie 2 (1954), 91-3.

20. ALLERTON BYWATER, England, 1923.
Discovered by a grave digger; hoard complete. 296 denarii, M. Antony to Marcus Aurelius (AD 164-169).
Domitian 81-96 : 6; pre-81 : 8.
Ref. H. Mattingly, "Allerton Bywater", NC 5.5 (1925), 400-401.

21. STOCKSTADT-AM-MAIN, West Germany, 1926.
Discovered during building foundation work; hoard complete.
7 aurei; 1,346 denarii, Nero to Marcus Aurelius (AD 167-168);

4 eastern imperial AR (Lycia).
Domitian 81-96 : 1 aureus, 69 denarii, 1 Lycian AR; pre-81 : 18 denarii.
Ref. FMRD 1.6, 67-95.

22. EDWINSTOWE, England, 1910.
Discovered during ploughing; hoard complete. 369 denarii (incl. 1 forgery), Nero to Marcus Aurelius (AD 179-180); 1 eastern imperial AR (Lycia).
Domitian 81-96 : 19 denarii; pre-81 : 7 denarii.
Ref. G.C. Brooke, "The Edwinstowe find of Roman coins", NC 4.12 (1912), 149-178.

23. OSIEK, Yugoslavia, 1921.
1,290 coins noted from a total of more than 2,500, following the sale of "badly preserved" specimens. 1,247 denarii recorded, Republic to Marcus Aurelius (AD 164-165); 4 eastern imperial AR (3 Lycia, 1 Caesarea in Cappadocia).
Domitian 81-96 : 63 denarii, 2 Lycian AR; pre-81 : 15 denarii.
Ref. W. Wruck, "Der Denarfund von Osiek (Mursa)", Berliner (Deutsche) Münzblätter 12 (1938), 289-95, 311-6.

24. MOCSOLAD, Hungary, before 1905.
Details of discovery uncertain. 1,235 denarii, Republic to Marcus Aurelius (AD 164-165); 1 AE ? (Cohen ed. I, Domitian 422); 2 eastern imperial AR (Caesarea in Cappadocia).
Domitian 81-96 : 77 denarii; pre-81 : 25 denarii, 1 AE ?
Ref. O. Gohl, "A mocsoladi éremlelet", NK 4-5 (1905-6), 75-9.

25. KURD-GYULAJI, Hungary, 1931.
Complete hoard. 1,136 denarii identified, M. Antony to Marcus Aurelius (AD 164-165), from a total of 1,143 coins noted.
Domitian 81-96 : 78; pre-81 : 16; unidentified : 2.
Ref. A. Mérey, "Kurd-gyulaji római éremlelet", NK 34-5 (1935-6), 77-8.

26. LENGOWO, Poland, 1906.
Discovered during peat cutting. 215 denarii identified, Nero to Marcus Aurelius (AD 165-166), from a total of 236 coins noted.
Domitian 81-96 : 18; pre-81 : 3.
Ref. K. Regling, "Römische Denarfund von Lengowo", ZfN 26 (1908), 304-16; A. Kunisz, Katalog Skarbów Monet Rzymskich Odkrytych na Ziemiach Polskich (Materialy do Prahistorii Ziem Polskich V,5, Warsaw 1973), 61-2.

27. SOTIN, Yugoslavia, 1909.
Discovered during ploughing. 1,940 coins recorded from a total of 2,050. 1,935 denarii, Republic to Marcus Aurelius (AD 165-166); 5 eastern imperial AR (3 Lycia, 2 Caesarea in Cappadocia).
Domitian 81-96 : 69 denarii; pre-81 : 21 denarii.
Ref. J. Brunšmid, "Nahodaj rimskih denara I i II stoljeća Sotinu (kotar Vukovar)", Vjesnik hrvatskoga arkheološkoga društva 2 (1910-11), 241-277.

28. APETLON II, Austria, 1961.
Discovered in a marsh. 177 denarii, M. Antony to Marcus Aurelius (AD 166-167).
Domitian 81-96 : 8.

Ref. R. Göbl, Zwei römische Münzhorte aus dem Burgenland : Illmutz (1960) und Apetlon II (1961) (Wissenschaftliche Arbeiten aus dem Burgenland, 37, Eisenstadt 1967).

29. SZOMBATHELY, Hungary, 1959.
Discovered in a brickyard. 1,000 denarii, Vitellius to Marcus Aurelius (AD 176-177), identified from a total of 1,006 recorded coins.
Domitian 81-96 : 47, plus 1 plated hybrid; pre-81 : 1.
Ref. K.B.-Sey, "A Szombathelyi Koracsászárkori Denárlelet", Folia Archaeologica 12 (1960), 75-88; NK 64-5 (1965-6), 69-70.

30. SIMIONESTI, Romania, 1966.
Details of discovery unknown. 101 denarii identified, Vitellius to Marcus Aurelius (AD 177-178), from a total of 102.
Domitian 81-96 : 7; pre-81 : 2.
Ref. M. Chitescu and M. Ursache, "Tezaurul de Denari Romani Imperiali Descoperit la Simionesti (jud. Neamt)", SCN 4 (1968), 385-91.

31. BIRGAOANI, Romania, 1965.
Discovered during agricultural work. 735 denarii, Nero to Marcus Aurelius (AD 177-180).
Domitian 81-96 : 27; pre-81 : 10.
Ref. V. Mihăilescu-Bîrliba, "Noi descoperiri de tezaure imperiale romane la Piatra Neamt", Carpica 1 (1968), 209-31; 2 (1969), 157-78; C. Petolescu, Muzeul National 3 (1976), 143-51.

32. BARWAY, England, 1958-.
Discovered during ploughing; a total of 395 coins have so far come to light. 4 aurei; 389 denarii, M. Antony to Commodus (after AD 180); 1 as (Nero); 1 eastern imperial AR (Lycia).
Domitian 81-96 : 11 denarii; pre-81 : 3 denarii.
Ref. R.A.G. Carson, "The Barway, Cambs., treasure trove of Roman coins", NC 6.20 (1960), 237-9. (Notes on further finds on file in British Museum).

33. BLETCHLEY, England, 1967.
Unearthed by a mechanical digger. 296 denarii, M. Antony to Commodus (AD 183).
Domitian 81-96 : 14; pre-81 : 4.
Ref. M.H. Crawford, "Bletchley Treasure Trove of Roman Imperial Denarii", NC 7.9 (1969), 113-122.

34. BRIGLANDS, Scotland, 1948-.
Coins gradually appearing in a river bank. 179 denarii, Nero to Commodus (AD 186-187).
Domitian 81-96 : 7; pre-81 : 2.
Ref. A.S. Robertson, "A Hoard of Roman Silver Coins from Briglands, Rumbling Bridge, Kinross-shire", PSAS 90 (1956-7), 241-6.

35. BARGERCOMPASCUUM, Holland, 1952.
Discovered in a peat marsh. 317 denarii, Nero to Commodus (AD 187-188); 1 eastern imperial AR (Pontus).
Domitian 81-96 : 7 denarii.
Ref. W.A. van Es, De Romeinse muntvondsten uit de drie noordelijke provincies, (Groningen 1960), 106-112.

36. PARAVA, Romania, 1937.
Hoard thought to be almost complete when recorded (one denarius of Domitian had been made into a ring). 270 denarii, Nero to Commodus (AD 183-184).
Domitian 81-96 : 9; pre-81 : 6.
Ref. O. Iliescu et al., "Tezaurel de dinari imperiali de la Parava", Caiet Selectiv de informare Asupra Creşterii Colecţiilor Bibliotecii Academei R.P.R. 12 (1965), 308-342.

37. PRZEWODOWA, Poland, 1937.
Hoard incomplete. 149 denarii, Republic to Commodus (AD 186-187), recorded from a total of several hundred coins.
Domitian 81-96 : 28, plus 1 hybrid; pre-81 : 6.
Ref. S. Skowronek, "Znalezisko Denarów Rzymskich z Przewodowa", WN 9 (1965), 203-8.

38. SASCUT, Romania, 1932.
Details of discovery uncertain. 901 denarii, Nero to Commodus (AD 187).
Domitian 81-96 : 29, plus 1 barbarous imitation; pre-81 : 14.
Ref. G. Severeanu, "Tezaurul monetar din Sascut din epoca imperiului roman", Bucurestii 1 (1935), 218-232.

39. HANDLEY, England, 1877.
Discovered in an allotment garden; 571 coins recorded from a total of 639 (440 published). 440 denarii, M. Antony to Septimius Severus (AD 194-195).
Domitian 81-96 : 19; pre-81 : 7.
Ref. A.S. Robertson, "A hoard of denarii from Handley, Dorset", NC 6.10 (1950), 311-5.

40. CHMIELOW PIASKOWY, Poland, 1927.
Discovered by a farmer. 322 denarii recorded, Nero to Septimius Severus (AD 193), from a total of about 400 coins.
Domitian 81-96 : 9 (7 accurately identified); pre-81 : 6.
Ref. M. Haisig and H.Hołubowiczowa, "Skarb rzymskich denarów z Chmielowa Piaskowego pow Opatów", Wiadomosci Archeologiczne 18 (1951-2), 291-322; T. Opozda, WN 13 (1969), 19-23.

41. PURICENI, Romania, 1961.
Hoard thought to have comprised 1,170 coins originally, of which 1,159 were recorded in the published list. 1,158 denarii, Nero to Septimius Severus (AD 194); 1 eastern imperial AR (Caesarea in Cappadocia).
Domitian 81-96 : 39 denarii (37 accurately identified); pre-81 : 18 denarii.
Ref. V. Mihăilescu-Bîrliba, "Tezaurul de denari romani imperiali de la Puriceni (com. Borleşti, jud. Neamt), Memoria Antiquitatis 4-5 (1972-3), 125-130.

42. MAGURA, Romania, 1976.
Complete hoard. 2,828 denarii, Augustus to Septimius Severus (AD 196); 2 eastern imperial AR (1 Amisus, 1 Caesarea in Cappadocia).
Domitian 81-96 : 90 denarii (89 accurately identified); pre-81 : 51 denarii.
Ref. V. Mihăilescu-Bîrliba and I. Mitrea, Tezaurul de Magura, Bacau 1977.

43. VIDIN, Bulgaria, 1930/1.
Two separate parcels discovered. 339 denarii, Nero to Septimius Severus (AD 201-207); 1 eastern imperial AR (Lycia).
Domitian 81-96 : 12 denarii, 1 Lycian AR; pre-81 : 5 denarii.
Ref. Z. Jiroudkova, "Dva Poklady římských denáru z Balkanu", Numismaticky Sbornik 4 (1957), 49-72.

44. ABERGELE, Wales, about 1842.
Discovered during drainage work. 350 denarii recorded, M. Antony to Septimius Severus (AD 201-206), from a total of about 800 coins.
Domitian 81-96 : 6; pre-81 : 9.
Ref. A.S. Robertson, "A hoard of Roman silver from Abergele, Denbighshire", Bulletin of the Board of Celtic Studies 8 (1935-7), 188-201.

45. MUSWELL HILL, England, 1928.
Discovered in a garden. 654 denarii, M. Antony to Septimius Severus (AD 209); 1 eastern imperial AR (Caesarea in Cappadocia).
Domitian 81-96 : 20 denarii, plus 1 plated forgery; pre-81 : 10 denarii.
Ref. H. Mattingly, "Cranley Gardens, Muswell Hill", NC 5.9 (1929), 315-8.

46. DARFIELD, England, 1948.
Discovered during building foundation work. 497 denarii, M. Antony to Caracalla (AD 213), recorded from a total of 500 coins.
Domitian 81-96 : 6; pre-81 : 11.
Ref. R.A.G. Carson, "A second hoard of Roman denarii from Darfield", NC 6.8 (1948), 78-81.

47. TELL KALAK, Jordan, before 1956.
1,985 denarii, Nero to Elagabalus (AD 222); 365 eastern imperial AR (329 "Caesarea in Cappadocia"+, 32 Antioch, 2 Lycia, 2 Amisus).
Domitian 81-96 : 21 denarii, 1 "Caesarean" AR; pre-81 : 29 denarii.
Ref. W.E. Metcalf, "The Tell Kalak Hoard and Trajan's Arabian Mint", A.N.S. Museum Notes 20 (1975), 39-108.

48. FALKIRK, Scotland, 1933.
Discovered during building foundation work; hoard thought to be almost complete. 1,931 denarii, Republic to Alexander Severus (AD 230).
Domitian 81-96 : 39; pre-81 : 46.
Ref. G. Macdonald, "A hoard of Roman denarii from Scotland", NC 5.14 (1934), 1-30; PSAS 68 (1933-4), 32 ff.; PSAS 73 (1938-9), 244-5; A.S. Robertson, PSAS 103 (1971-2), 129-30.

49. EAST ENGLAND, before 1898.
Details of discovery unknown. 3,169 denarii and antoniniani, Nero to Alexander Severus (AD 231-235).
Domitian 81-96 : 12 denarii; pre-81 : 6 denarii.
Ref. J. Evans, "A hoard of Roman coins", NC 3.18 (1898), 126-184.

50. TURKEY, before 1966.
Details of discovery unknown; hoard incomplete, 2,711 coins noted (1,911 identified in report). 1,906 denarii and antoniniani, Republic to Trajan Decius (AD 249-251); 5 eastern imperial AR (3 Lycia, 2 Caesarea in Cappadocia).

Domitian 81-96 : 17 denarii; pre-81 : 4 denarii.
Ref. S. Bendall, "An eastern hoard of Roman imperial silver", NC 7.6 (1966), 165-70.

51. REKA DEVNIA, Bulgaria, 1929.
Discovered in the cellar of an ancient building. 81,044 coins recorded from a total of over 100,000. 81,014 denarii and antoniniani, M. Antony to Trajan Decius (AD 249-251); 30 eastern imperial AR (includes Lycia, Amisus, Caesarea in Cappadocia, etc.)
Domitian 632 coins (621 identified). 81-96 : 296 denarii (plus 1 hybrid); pre-81 : 323 denarii, 1 AR of Caesarea in Cappadocia.
Ref. N.A. Mouchmov, Le Trésor Numismatique de Réka Devnia (Marcianopolis), Sofia 1934.

Notes : * The phrase "eastern imperial AR" is used in this inventory to denote all issues of silver coinage produced in the eastern half of the Empire with the emperor's head on the obverse and with legends usually in Greek (eg. didrachms and drachms of Caesarea in Cappadocia and Lycia). This category does not include eastern-produced denarii with Latin legends (eg. some issues of Septimius Severus); these are included under "denarii".

+ The attribution of certain groups of eastern imperial silver coins to Caesarea in Cappadocia has been shown to be wrong in the publication of this hoard. As a result, attributions to "Caesarea" in all the above hoards must be treated with caution.

APPENDIX 2

INVENTORY OF AUREUS COIN HOARDS

The following hoards were included in the survey of aurei; information on the circumstances of discovery is not included for these hoards :

1. ZIRKOWITZ, Austria, 1850.
   79 aurei recorded, Tiberius to Domitian (AD 92-94).
   Domitian 81-96 : 10; pre-81 : 8.
   Ref. R. Knabl, "Fund römischer Goldmünzen zu Cirkowic", *Mittheilungen des historischen Vereines für Steiermark* 2 (1851), 173-81; F. Pichler, *Die Münzen der römischen und byzantinischen Kaiser* (Repertorium der Steierischen Münzkunde II, Graz 1867), 6-31.

2. CLUNIA, Spain, 1973.
   20 aurei, Nero to Nerva (AD 98).
   Domitian 81-96 : 3; pre-81 : 1.
   Ref. P. de Palol, *El tesoro de Aureos Imperiales de Clunia*, Barcelona 1974.

3. ZEMUN, Yugoslavia, 1875.
   230 aurei, Nero to Trajan (AD 98-99).
   Domitian 81-96 : 187; pre-81 : 10.
   Ref. S. Ljubić, *Der Fund römischer Goldmünzen aus dem ersten Jahrhunderte der Kaiserzeit gemacht in Semlin*, Zagreb 1876

4. FINS D'ANNECY, France, 1893.
   36 aurei recorded, Vespasian to Trajan (AD 104-110).
   Domitian 81-96 : 12; pre-81 : 3.
   Ref. Raymond Serrure sale, Paris, 25 May, 1894 , *Le Trésor des Fins d'Annecy*.

5. EMONA, Yugoslavia, 1963.
   16 aurei, Vespasian to Trajan (AD 107-111).
   Domitian 81-96 : 4.
   Ref. A. Jelocnik, "Najdba Rimskih Zlatnikov iz Emone", *Situla* 8 (1965), 125-140.

6. CASTAGNARO, Italy, 1903. (See Appendix 1, no. 7).
   Domitian 81-96 : 1; pre-81 : 1.

7. ERLA, Austria, 1966. (See Appendix 1, no. 8).
   Domitian 81-96 : 1; pre-81 : 5.

8. VIDY, Switzerland, 1936.
   72 aurei, Vespasian to Antoninus Pius (AD 140-144).
   Domitian 81-96 : 2.

Ref. C. Martin, "Le Trésor monétaire de Vidy", Revue historique vaudoise 49 (1941), 15-36; 73 (1965), 157-171.

9. CORBRIDGE, England, 1911.
160 aurei, Nero to Antoninus Pius (AD 159-160).
Domitian 81-96 : - ; pre-81 : 5.
Ref. H.H.E. Craster and F. Haverfield, "Hoards of Roman Gold Coins found in Britain (i) Corbridge Second Century Hoard", NC 4.12. (1912), 265-312.

10. LIBERCHIES, Belgium, 1970.
368 aurei, Nero to Marcus Aurelius (AD 166).
Domitian 81-96 : 2; pre-81 : 15.
Ref. M. Thirion, Le Trésor de Liberchies, Brussels 1972.

11. BRAGA (?), Portugal, 1954.
170 aurei recorded, Nero to Marcus Aurelius (AD 167-168).
Domitian 81-96 : - ; pre-81 : 9.
Ref. R.M.S. Centeno, "Um Tesouro de Aurei do Norte de Portugal", Nummus 2.1 (1978), 5-66.

12. DIARBEKIR (MARDIN), Turkey, before 1931.
302 aurei recorded, Nero to Marcus Aurelius (AD 177-178).
Domitian 81-96 : 2; pre-81 : 8.
Ref. K. Regling, "Der Schatz römischer Goldmünzen von Diarbekir (Mardin)", Blätter für Münzfreunde 621 (Nov. 1931), 353-365; 622 (Dec. 1931), 369-381.

13. VILLACH, Austria, 1955.
100 aurei recorded, Nero to Septimius Severus (AD 194-197).
Domitian 81-96 : 1; pre-81 : 8.
Ref. W. Görlich, "Der Münzfund von Villach", Carinthia 1 (1957), 140-145.

14. SZONY, Hungary, 1959.
114 aurei recorded, Nero to Septimius Severus (AD 196-211), from a total of 118 pieces.
Domitian 81-96 : - ; pre-81 : 4.
Ref. L. Barkóczi and K.B.-Sey, "Brigetioi aranylelet", NK 62-3 (1963-4), 3-8.

15. CANNET, France, 1938
129 aurei recorded, Vespasian to Geta (AD 211).
Domitian 81-96 : - ; pre-81 : 3.
Ref. H. Rolland, "Un Trésor de Monnaies Romaines découvert au Cannet (Var.)", RN 5.7 (1943), 149-159.

APPENDIX 3

MUSEUM COLLECTIONS

The following Collections provided casts, photographs, or information for the surveys of Domitian's coinage :

Bacau, Muzeul Judetean
Basel, Historisches Museum
Belfast, Ulster Museum
Berlin, Staatliche Museen
Brussels, Bibliothèque Royale Albert Ier
Bucharest, Institutul de Arheologie
Cambridge, Fitzwilliam Museum
Copenhagen, Nationalmuseet
Edinburgh, National Museum of Antiquities
Edinburgh, Royal Scottish Museum
Glasgow, Hunterian Museum
The Hague, Koninklijk Kabinet
Krakow, Muzeum Narodowe
Liverpool, City Museum
Livorno, Museo Civico
London, British Museum
Milan, Castello Sforzesco
Munich, Staatliche Münzsammlung
New York, American Numismatic Society
Oslo, University
Oxford, Ashmolean Museum
Paris, Bibliothèque Nationale
Rome, Biblioteca Apostolica Vaticana
Rome, Musei Capitolini
Rome, Museo Nazionale
Stockholm, Kungelige Myntkabinett
Varna, Regional Museum of History
Vienna, Institut für Antike Numismatik
Vienna, Kunsthistorisches Museum
Winterthur, Stadtbibliothek
Zurich, Schweizerisches Landesmuseum

BIBLIOGRAPHY

(1) Sale catalogues

In the catalogues of coinage issues coins noted from "trade" are usually referenced with the name of the vendors. However, the following sales of collections have also been noted:

Magnaguti sale 2	=	P. & P. Santamaria, Rome, 14 Oct. 1949 (A. Magnaguti collection II).
Martinetti sale	=	C. & E. Canessa, Naples, 18 Nov. 1907 (F. Martinetti collection).
Montagu sale	=	Rollin and Feuardent, Paris, 20-28 April 1896 (H. Montagu collection).
Nordheim sale	=	Glendinning, London, 3 Dec. 1929 (E. Nordheim collection).
Vierordt sale	=	J. Schulman, Amsterdam, 5 March 1923 (L. Vierordt collection).

(2) Primary sources for Domitian (finances)

Translations from the Loeb editions have been used for all passages quoted from literary sources.

Cassius Dio, *Dio's Roman History*.

Dio Chrysostom, *Discourses*

Eusebius, *Ecclesiastical History*

Frontinus, *De aquis urbis Romae*

Martial, *Epigrams*

Oracula Sibyllina (Book 12)

Pliny the Younger, *Epistulae curatus scriptae (Letters)*
Panegyricus (Pan)

Plutarch, *Parallel Lives*

Select Papyri = A.S. Hunt and C.C. Edgar, Select Papyri, 2 vols., (London 1932-1934).

Statius, Silvae

Suetonius, De vita Caesarum. The life of Domitian (Dom) is in Book VIII.

Tacitus, De vita Iulii Agricolae
Annals
Histories

(3) Secondary sources (including bibliographical abbreviations)

AE = L'Annee Epigraphique

Alfoldi, M.R., "Silberspiegel mit Domitianporträt in Karlsruhe", in Overdruk uit Festoen (Festschrift for A.N. Zadoks-Josephus Jitta), Groningen - Bussum, 1976, 15-22.

AJA = American Journal of Archaeology

AJP = American Journal of Philology

ANS = American Numismatic Society

ASFN = Annuaire de la Société Française de Numismatique et d'Archéologie

BMC Galatia, etc. = W. Wroth, A Catalogue of Greek Coins in the British Museum, vol. 23, Galatia, Cappadocia and Syria (London 1899).

BMCRE II = H. Mattingly, Coins of the Roman Empire in the British Museum, vol. II, Vespasian to Domitian, 2nd. ed. London 1976 (abbreviation shortened to BMC for catalogue numbers).

BNS = Bulletino di Numismatica e Sfragista

Bolin, S., State and Currency in the Roman Empire, Stockholm, 1958

Bourne, F.C., The Public Works of the Julio-Claudians and Flavians, Princeton, 1946

Buttrey, T.V., "Domitian's Perpetual Censorship and the Numismatic Evidence", The Classical Journal, 71 (1975), 26-34.

Buttrey, T.V., Documentary Evidence for the Chronology of the Flavian Titulature (Beiträge zur klassischen Philologie, H. 112, Meisenheim, 1980).(= Chronology)

Carradice, I., "A Denarius of AD 92", Zeitschrift für Papyrologie und Epigraphik, 28 (1978), 159-60.

Carradice, I., "The banishment of the father of Claudius Etruscus : numismatic evidence", LCM 4.5 (May, 1979). 101-3.

Carradice, I., "Coins, monuments and literature : some important sestertii of Domitian", Proceedings of the 9th International Congress on Numismatics (I.A.P.N. publications no. 7, Louvain and Luxembourg, 1982), 373-383.

Carradice, I. and Cowell, M., "An analysis of Roman silver coins of the Flavian family from the period 80-85" in Metallurgy in Numismatics 1 (R.N.S., London 1980), 168-173.

Chantraine, A., Novaesium III. Die Antiken Fundmünzen der Ausgrabungen in Neuss (Limesforschungen 8, Berlin 1968).

CIL = Corpus Inscriptionum Latinarum, Berlin, 1863-

Cohen = H. Cohen, Description historique des Monnaies frappées sous l'Empire Romain, vol. 1. 2nd ed., Paris, 1880.

Crawford, M.H., "Money and Exchange in the Roman World", JRS 60 (1970), 40-8.

Crawford, M.H., Roman Republican Coinage, Cambridge 1974. (RRC).

Duncan-Jones, R., The Economy of the Roman Empire, Cambridge, 1974.

ERCHM = R.A.G. Carson and C.H.V. Sutherland (ed.), Essays in Roman Coinage presented to Harold Mattingly, Oxford, 1956.

FMRD = H. Gebhart and K. Kraft, Die Fundmünzen der römischen Zeit in Deutschland, Berlin, 1960-.

FMRL = R. Weiller, Monnaies Antiques découvertes au Grand-Duché de Luxembourg, Berlin, 1972-.

FMRO = W. Hahn, Die Fundmünzen der römischen Zeit in Österreich (III,1, Carnuntum), Vienna, 1976.

Frier, B.W. and Parker, A., "Roman Coins from the River Liri", NC 7.10 (1970), 89-107.

Garzetti, A., From Tiberius to the Antonines, London, 1974.

Grierson, P., "The Interpretation of Coin Finds". Presidential address in NC 7.5 (1965), i-xii, and NC 7.6 (1966), i-xv.

Gsell, S., Essai sur le Règne de l'Empereur Domitien, Paris, 1893.

HCC I = A.S. Robertson, Roman Imperial Coins in the Hunter Coin Cabinet, vol. I, Augustus to Nerva, Glasgow, 1962.

Heesch, J. van, Studie over de Semis en de Quadrans van Domitianus tot en met Antoninus Pius (unpublished Ph.D., Ghent 1979).

Hill, G.F., Becker the Counterfeiter, part II, London, 1925.

Hopkins, K., "Taxes and Trade in the Roman Empire (200 BC - AD 400)", *JRS* 70 (1980), 101-125.

Jones, B.W., "Senatorial influence in the revolt of Saturninus", *Latomus* 33 (1974), 529-35.

JNG = *Jahrbuch für Numismatik und Geldgeschichte*.

JRS = *Journal of Roman Studies*

Kraay, C.M., *The aes coinage of Rome and its subsidiary mints in the West, AD 68-81* (unpublished D.Phil., Oxford, 1953).

Kraay, C.M., "Two new sestertii of Domitian", *ANS Museum Notes* 9 (1960), 109-116.

Kraay, C.M., *Die Münzfunde von Vindonissa,(bis Trajan)*, (Veröff. der Gesellschaft Pro Vindonissa, 5, Basel 1962).

Kunisz, A., "Le Monnayage de Domitien (81-96)", *WN* 23.1 (1979), 1-19.

LCM = *Liverpool Classical Monthly*.

B. Levick, "Domitian and the Provinces", *Latomus* 41.1 (1982), 50-73.

Ljubic, S., *Der Fund römischer Goldmünzen aus dem ersten Jahrhunderte der Kaiserzeit gemacht in Semlin*, Zagreb, 1876.

Lyon, C.S.S., "The estimation of the number of dies employed in a coinage", *Numismatic Circular* 73.9 (Sept. 1965), 180-181.

M. McCrum and A.G. Woodhead, *Select Documents of the Principates of the Flavian Emperors*, Cambridge, 1961.

Mazzini = G. Mazzini, *Monete Imperiali Romane*,(I, Pompey to Domitian), Turin, 1963.

Metcalf, W.E., "Roman Coins from the River Liri II", *NC* 7.14 (1974), 42-52.

Morawiecki, L., "The symbolism of Minerva on the coins of Domitianus", *Klio* 59.1 (1977), 185-93.

NC = *Numismatic Chronicle*

NK = *Numizmatikai Közlöny*

NNÅ = *Nordisk Numismatisk Årsskrift*

NZ = *Numismatische Zeitschrift*

Pleket, H., "Domitian, the Senate and the Provinces", *Mnemosyne* 14 (1961), 296-315.

PSAS = *Proceedings of the Society of Antiquaries of Scotland*

RIC II = H. Mattingly and E.A. Sydenham, *The Roman Imperial Coinage*, vol. II, Vespasian to Hadrian, London, 1926.

Riv.It. = *Rivista Italiana di Numismatica*

Robathan, D., "Domitian's Midas Touch", *Transactions of the American Philological Association* 73 (1942), 130-144.

Robertson, A.S., "Romano-British Coin Hoards : Their Numismatic, Archaeological and Historical Significance", in J. Casey and R. Reece (ed.), *Coins and the Archaeologist* (B.A.R. 4, Oxford, 1974), 12-35.

Rogers, R.S., "A Group of Domitianic Treason-Trials", *Classical Philology* 55 (1960), 19-23.

SCN = *Studii şi Circetări de Numismatică*

Sutherland, C.H.V., "The State of the Imperial Treasury at the Death of Domitian", *JRS* 25 (1935), 150-162.

Syme, R., "The Imperial Finances under Domitian, Nerva and Trajan", *JRS* 20 (1930), 55-70.

Syme, R., *Tacitus*, Oxford, 1958

Thordeman, "The Lohe Hoard - a contribution to the methodology of Numismatics", *NC* 6.8 (1948), 188-204.

Toynbee, J.M.C., *Roman Medallions*, ANS Numismatic Studies 5, New York, 1944.

TCWAAS = *Transactions of the Cumberland and Westmorland Antiquarian and Archaeological Society*.

Vietinghoff, A. von, "Die Fundmünzen aus Avenches, 2, von Domitian bis Trajan", *Schweizerische Numismatische Rundschau* 54 (1975), 97-163.

Walker, D.R., *The Metrology of the Roman Silver Coinage* : Part I, Augustus to Domitian (= *Metrology I*), B.A.R. s.s. 5, Oxford 1976; Part III, Pertinax to Uranius Antoninus (= *Metrology* III), B.A.R. s.s. 40, Oxford 1978.

Waters, K.H., "The Character of Domitian", *Phoenix* 18 (1964), 49-77.

WN = *Wiadomosći Numizmatyczne*

ZfN = *Zeitschrift für Numismatik*

ILLUSTRATIONS

Plate I

1	AR	BMC 1	81.1	Table, thunderbolt
2	AR	BMC 5	81.1	Tripod
3	AR	BMC 6	81.2a	Table, corn ears
4	AR	BMC 7	81.2a	Table, crescents
5	AR	BMC 11	81.3b	Minerva 1
6	AR	BMC 16	81.3b	Table, thunderbolt
7	AU	BMC 12	81.3b	Minerva holding Victory
8	AR	BMC 19	81.3b	Curule chairs
9	AR	BMC 21	81.3b	Dolphin and anchor
10	AR	Milan	81.3b	Tripod
11	AU	BMC 31	82.1	Altar
12	ARQ	BMC 56	81-82	Victory
13	AU	BMC 33	82.2	Minerva bust
14	AR	BMC 34	82.2	Fortuna
15	AU	BMC 51	82-83(a)	Eagle
16	AR	BMC 54	(b)	Salus
17	AU	BMC 68	(c)	Domitilla
18	AU	BMC 69	(d)	Julia
19	AU	BMC 58	(e)	Domitia
20	AU	BMC 60	(f)	Peacock
21	AU	BMC 62	(g)	Baby Caesar
22	AR	BMC 65	(h)	Pietas
23	AR	BMC Titus 137	(i)	Fortuna
24	AR	BMC 37	83.1	Minerva 4
25	ARQ	BMC 38	83.1	Caduceus

Plate II

1	AU	BMC 39	83.2	Minerva 1
2	AR	BMC 40	83.2	Minerva 2
3	AU	BMC 42	83.2	Minerva 3
4	AU	BMC 44	83.2	Minerva 4
5	AU	BMC 46	84.1	Minerva 2
6	AR	BMC 48	84.2a	Minerva 3
7	AU	BMC 49	84.2a	Eagle
8	AR	Paris	84.2a	Eagle
9	AU	BMC 45	84.2a	Minerva bust
10	ARQ	BMC 50A	84.2b	Victory
11	AU	Santamaria sale, 25 May 1926, lot 281	84.3(a)	Germania
12	AR	BMC 71	85.1a	Minerva 1
13	AU	BMC 73	85.1a	Minerva 4
14	ARQ	BMC 77	85.1b	Victory
15	AU	BMC 81	85.2	Germania
16	AR	BMC 82	85.3	Germania
17	AR	BMC 79	85.4	Minerva 3
18	ARMed	BMC 83	85.5a	Minerva seated
19	ARMed	BMC 85	85.5a	Germania
20	AR	BMC 84	85.5b	Minerva 4
21	AR	BMC 86	85.6	Minerva 1

Plate III

1	AU	BMC 89	86.1	Minerva 2
2	AU	BMC 91	86.1	Germania
3	AR	BMC 90	86.1	Minerva 3
4	ARQ	BMC 92	86.1	Victory
5	AU	BMC 94	86.2	Germania
6	ARQ	BMC 95	86.2	Victory
7	AR	BMC 96	86.3	Minerva 2
8	AR	BMC 98	86.5	Minerva 2
9	AR	BMC 101	87.1	Minerva 1
10	AR	BMC 102	87.1	Minerva 1
11	ARQ	BMC 109	87.1	Victory
12	AR	BMC 114	87.2	Minerva 4
13	AR	BMC 100	87	Minerva 4
14	AR	BMC 119	88.1	Minerva 3
15	AU	BMC 125	88.1	Germania
16	AUMed	-	88.1	Minerva 2
17	AUQ	BMC 126	88.1	Victory
18	AR	BMC 129A	88.2	Minerva 3
19	AR	Oxford	88	Minerva 2
20	AR	BMC 133	88.3(a)	Herald
21	ARQ	BMC 134	88.3(a)	Herald
22	AR	BMC 135	88.3(c)	Herald and column
23	AR	BMC 137	88.3(b)	Column

Plate IV

1	AU	BMC 142	88-89A	Minerva 3
2	AU	BMC 144	88-89A	Quadriga
3	AR	BMC 139	88-89A	Minerva 3
4	AR	BM 1956-1-7-1	88-89A	Minerva 1
5	AR	BMC 141	88-89A	Minerva 1
6	AR	BMC 146	88-89B1	Minerva 2
7	AR	BMC 147	88-89B2	Minerva 1
8	AR	BMC 150A	88-89B3	Minerva 2
9	AR	BMC 154A	88-89B4	Minerva 4
10	AR	BMC 156	88-89B4	Victory
11	AR	BMC 157	88-89B5	Minerva 1
12	AU	BMC 249	88-89?(a)	Peacock
13	AU	BMC 250	88-89?(b)	Peacock facing
14	AR	BMC 159	89	Minerva 2
15	AR	BMC 161	89	Minerva 3
16	AR	BMC 169	90	Minerva 4
17	ARQ	BMC 170	90	Victory
18	AU	BMC 171	90-91A	Minerva 3
19	AU	BMC 173	90-91A	Minerva 4
20	AU	BMC 174	90-91A	Germania
21	AR	BMC 178	90-91B	Minerva 1
22	AU	Zagreb	90-91?	Diva Julia
23	AR	BMC 185	91	Minerva 3
24	AR	BMC 186	91	Minerva 4
25	AR	BMC 188	92.1	Minerva 1

Plate V

1	ARMed	BMC 191	92.1	Minerva 2
2	AR	BM 1977-7-1-1	92.2	Minerva 3
3	AR	BMC 202	92-93	Minerva 2
4	AU	BMC 209	92-94	Minerva 3
5	AU	BMC 213	92-94	Quadriga
6	AR	BMC 214	93-94	Minerva 1
7	AR	BMC 220	93-94	Minerva 4
8	AR	BMC 220A	94	Minerva 2
9	AR	BMC 223	95	Minerva 2
10	AR	BMC 224	95	Minerva 3
11	AU	BM 1937-12-10-26	95-96A	Minerva 2
12	AU	BMC 228	95-96A	Germania
13	AR	BMC 232	95-96B	Minerva 2
14	AR	BMC 235	95-96B	Minerva 4
15	AR	BMC 237	95-96B	Minerva winged
16	AR	BMC 237A	95-96B	Pax?
17	AR	BMC 237B	95-96B	Altar
18	AR	BMC 238	95-96?	Temple
19	AR	BMC 239	95-96?	Temple
20	AR	BMC 241	95-96?	Temple
21	AR	BMC 242	95-96?	Temple
22	AR	BMC 243	95-96?	Temple
23	AR	BMC 237C	96	Minerva 3

Plate VI

1	sestertius	BMC 260	81	Minerva 1
2	dupondius	BMC 267	81	Pax
3	sestertius	BMC 513	81	"Lugdunum" Mars
4	sestertius	BMC 265	81	Domitian, palladium
5	sestertius	BMC 273	82	
6	sestertius	BMC 275	82	Minerva 4
7	dupondius	BMC 279	82	Minerva 3
8	as	BMC 281	82	Minerva 1
9	sestertius	BMC 516	82	"Lugdunum" Pax
10	dupondius	BMC 518	82	"Lugdunum" Roma
11	as	BMC 520	82	"Lugdunum" Ceres

Plate VII

1	sestertius	BMC 284	81-82	Divus Titus
2	sestertius	BMC 501	81-82	Domitia
3	dupondius	BMC 503	81-82	Domitia
4	as	BMC 506	81-82	Restoration Augustus
5	as	BMC 509	81-82	Restoration Tiberius
6	as	BMC 510	81-82	Restoration Agrippa
7	semis	BMC 481	81-82	Cornucopiae
8	quadrans	BMC 485	81-82	Minerva bust/wreath SC
9	as	BMC 286A	84.1	Altar
10	dupondius	BMC 287	84.2	Mars
11	as	BMC 288	84.2	Moneta

Plate VIII

1	sestertius	BMC 294	85.1	Germania Capta
2	sestertius	BMC 295	85.1	Pax burning arms
3	sestertius	BMC 296	85.1	Domitian sacrificing
4	sestertius	BMC 301	85.1	Domitian with soldiers
5	semis	BMC 318	85.1	Apollo/lyre
6	semis	BMC 319	85.1	Apollo/tripod
7	quadrans	BMC 321	85.1	Ceres/modius
8	dupondius	BMC 304	85.1	Annona
9	as	BMC 316	85.1	Altar
10	sestertius	BMC 339	85.2	Domitian riding down German
11	as	BMC 354	85.2	Jupiter Conservator
12	as	BMC 355	85.2	Victory l.
13	dupondius	BMC 352	85.2	German shields crossed

Plate IX

1	dupondius	BMC 363	85.3	Fides
2	as	BMC 367	85.3	Victoriae Augusti
3	as	BM 1980-10-24-3	85.3	Aeternitas
4	sestertius	BMC 371	86	Annona August
5	sestertius	BMC 374	86	Victory inscribing shield
6	sestertius	BMC 379	86	Domitian and German
7	sestertius	BMC 396	87	Domitian and Rhenus
8	as	BMC 403	87	Moneta
9	as	BMC 404	87	Virtus
10	sestertius	BMC 428	88	Secular Games

Plate X

1	sestertius	BMC 424	88	Secular Games
2	sestertius	BMC 422	88	Secular Games
3	dupondius	BMC 430	88	Secular Games
4	sestertius	BMC 410	88-89	Domitian crowned by Victory
5	semis	BMC 418	88-89	Minerva bust/owl
6	semis	BMC 454	90-91	Apollo bust/raven
7	quadrans	BMC 457	90-91	Apollo bust l./raven
8	sestertius	BMC 440	90-91	Iovi Victori
9	dupondius	BMC 444	90-91	Fortuna
10	sestertius	BMC 458	90-91	Diva Julia,Carpentum
11	dupondius	BMC 468	92-94	Virtus
12	sestertius	BMC 475	95-96	Iovi Victori

Plate XI

1	sestertius	BM 1978-10-21-5	95-96	Equestrian statue
2	sestertius	Paris	95-96	Triumphal arch
3	sestertius	Niggeler sale (Basel 1965-7), lot 1190 (ex Walters coll.)	95-96	Three-storey building
4	dupondius	BMC 478	95-96	Helmet and shield
5	as	BM 1936-10-13-30	95-96	Fortuna
6	as	Paris	95-96	Eagle
7	as	BMC 479C	95-96	Owl
8	quadrans	BMC 483	undated	
9	quadrans	BMC 490	undated	
10	quadrans	BMC 492	undated	
11	quadrans	BMC 494	undated	
12	quadrans	BMC 496	undated	
13	quadrans	BMC 499	undated	

Plate XII : Portraits

1	AR	BMC Titus 98	AD 80	Domitian Caesar
2	AR	BMC 15	81.3b	
3	AU	BMC 12	81.3b	
4	AR	BMC Titus 25	AD 79	Titus
5	AR	Vienna	81.3b	
6	sestertius	BMC 260	81	
7	sestertius	BMC 516	82	"Lugdunum"
8	AU	BMC 46	84.1	
9	AU	BMC 49	84.2a	
10	AR	BMC 79	85.4	
11	ARMed	BMC 83	85.5a	
12	sestertius	BMC 340	85.2	
13	dupondius	BMC 363	85.3	
14	as	BMC 365A	85.3	
15	AR	BMC 84	85.6	
16	AR	BMC 214	93-94	
17	AU	BMC 213	92-94	
18	sestertius	Paris	95-96	
19	AU	BMC 69	82-83	Julia
20	AU	BMC 250	88-89?	Julia
21	AR	BMC 65	82-83	Domitia
22	dupondius	BMC 503	81-82	Domitia
23	sestertius	BMC 501	81-82	Domitia
24	AU	BMC 249	88-89?	Domitia

Photographs of British Museum coins are reproduced by permission of the Trustees of the British Museum

Plate I

Plate II

Plate III

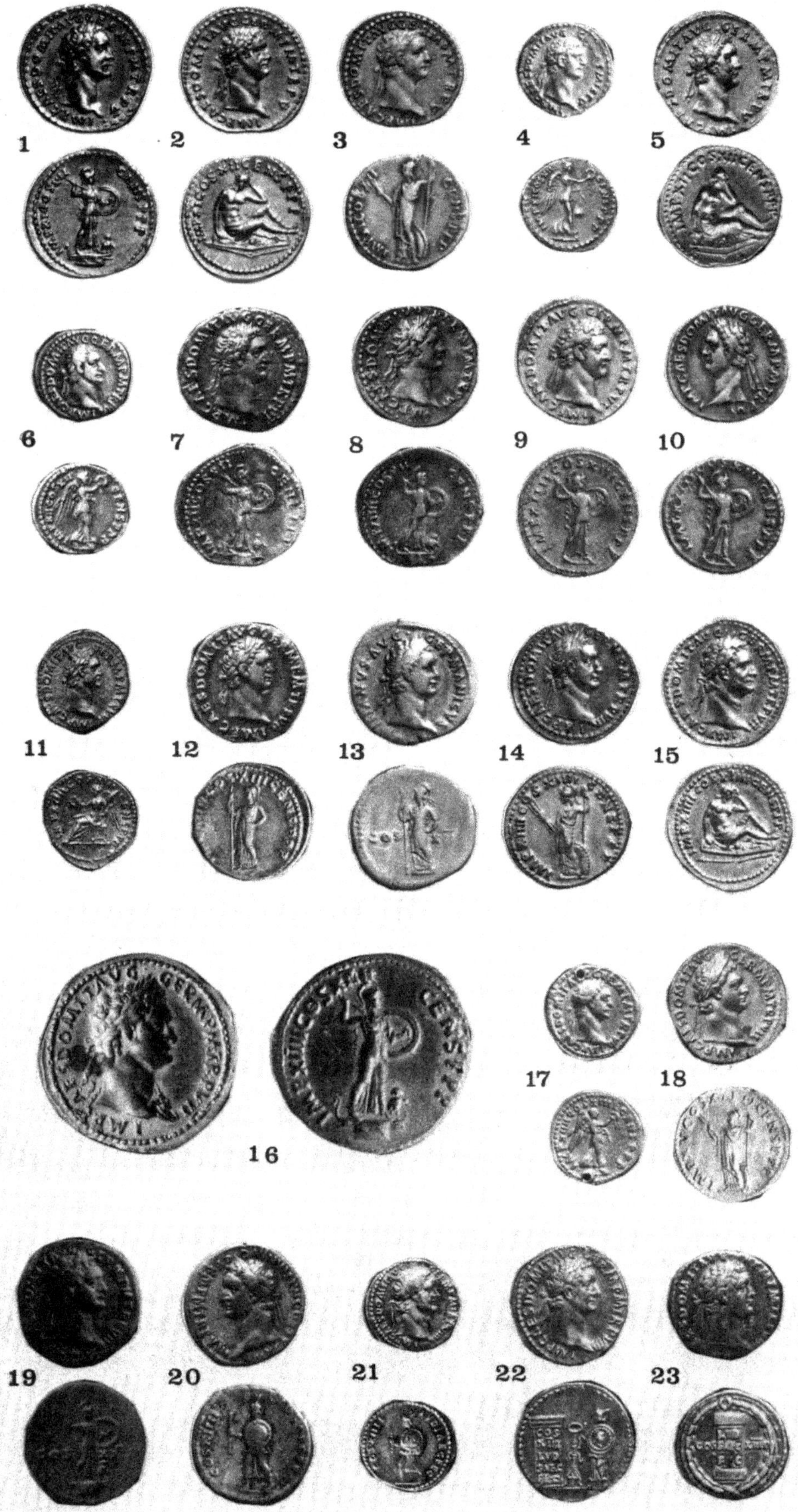

Plate IV

Plate V

Plate VI

Plate VII

Plate VIII

Plate IX

1 2 3 4 5 6 7 8 9 10

Plate X

Plate XI

Plate XII : Portraits

www.ingramcontent.com/pod-product-compliance
Lightning Source LLC
LaVergne TN
LVHW071207210926
848482LV00015B/743